The Documentarian

The Way to a Successful and
Creative Professional Life in
the Documentary Business

Roger Nygard

APPLAUSE
THEATRE & CINEMA BOOKS

Essex, Connecticut

APPLAUSE
THEATRE & CINEMA BOOKS

An imprint of Globe Pequot, the trade division of
The Rowman & Littlefield Publishing Group, Inc.
4501 Forbes Blvd., Ste. 200
Lanham, MD 20706
www.rowman.com

Distributed by NATIONAL BOOK NETWORK

www.TheDocumentarianBook.com

Unless otherwise noted, all images are from the author's collection.

Filming Trekkies (1999). Sound mixer Larry Scharf, actor/producer Denise Crosby, director Roger Nygard, director of photography Harris Done.

British Library Cataloguing in Publication Information available

Library of Congress Cataloging-in-Publication Data available
ISBN 978-1-4930-8622-1 (paperback)
ISBN 978-1-4930-8623-8 (electronic)

∞™ The paper used in this publication meets the minimum requirements of American National Standard for Information Sciences—Permanence of Paper for Printed Library Materials, ANSI/NISO Z39.48-1992

Contents

Acknowledgements

I would like to thank all who contributed and helped me edit this book, and an especially gigantic thanks to those who gave generously of their time to be interviewed: Ken Burns, Sylvia Desrochers, Davis Guggenheim, Liz Garbus, Rachel Grady, Freida Lee Mock, Errol Morris, Sam Pollard, Mike Rabehl, Glen Reynolds, Michael Tollin, Jonathan Vogler, Frederick Wiseman, and Marina Zenovich.

Foreword

I wish this book existed when we were filming *Trekkies*! It's invaluable, with step-by-step instructions covering every aspect of the filmmaking process, from gathering information, securing licenses, the equipment needed, striking the right tone, editing, scoring, festival submissions, and how to get your film seen. Roger has laid out everything you need to know to make and sell a documentary, and he's done it from practical experience.

I am still laughing, thinking about our first *Trekkies* shoot at a convention at the LAX Hilton. We commandeered an empty room, grabbed a fancy chair and a potted plant from the hall, borrowed a couple of paintings from the lobby, and changed the lighting with colored gels to make the room look different for each *Star Trek* actor. Magic! A big part of making a film is being able to think on your feet.

It was such a pleasure to revisit the time when we made a film together, the excitements and the frustrations, and the sense of accomplishment from pursuing an idea we hatched over lunch. I remember sitting in my car on my way to our first screening at Paramount and saying to myself, *Wow!* Our journey was more than the making of a movie; it was about friendship and trust. We laughed and cried, and sometimes wanted to pull our hair out, but I wouldn't change a thing. Making *Trekkies* was one of the greatest joys I've had in this business. Now, with this book, lucky reader, you have a road map for finding your own *Trekkies*. I hope you have as much fun as we did!

—Denise Crosby

Introduction

Hitting a million-dollar home run with a documentary is rare, but I made a profitable documentary, and you can too; regardless, anybody dedicated to success can build a solid profession as a documentarian. Now, about your million dollars . . . it's not going to be easy. And when you do sell that lucrative docu-sensation, you will probably spend it on your next passion projects, averaging out your docu-income to minimum wage. Amazingly, an epic payday happened right out of the gate with my first documentary, *Trekkies* (1997); after twenty-five years, that film is still generating royalties. Even more important, the creative process was supremely satisfying.

I have often been asked, "How did you get started making documentaries?" It's like asking an addict how they got hooked. Be forewarned, if you make a documentary, the process is so rewarding you will likely become obsessed with making more. In this book, I relate the knowledge I've gained from my obsession, along with the experiences of other documentarians I've interviewed.

Documentaries were not something I sought when I was young. Aside from educational films, my first exposure was when I learned to use video equipment at University Community Video, an extension school loosely affiliated with the University of Minnesota. The organization was ensconced in a former church, with editing booths in repurposed chapels. Most of the video-making coterie were artists spotlighting serious issues, but I wanted to make funny short films.

One day, I saw a poster there, advertising a screening of a film called *D.O.A.* (1981), about the first and only Sex Pistols tour of the United States. The movie was filmed in grainy, hand-held 16mm. The filmmakers captured the music and behind-the-scenes mayhem of the punk scene. I loved it and wanted more. However, documentary films were scarce outside

Johnny Rotten singing the Sex Pistols song "Bodies" in the documentary D.O.A. *(1981).*

of PBS and rarely showing at local movie theaters. Streaming services were not yet even an idea. But once consumer Betamax and VHS video players proliferated, documentaries were readily available, from unsettling niche films like *Faces of Death* (1978) to hugely successful Academy-Award-winning films like *Woodstock* (1970).

One documentary that greatly affected me was a twenty-eight-minute short called "Mondo Elvis" (1984). Filmmaker Tom Corboy interviewed obsessed—arguably delusional—Elvis Presley fans, such as Jerry and Judy Carroll, identical twins who insisted they were Elvis Presley's daughters and that Elvis was still alive. The film is funny and jaw-dropping. A decade later, the feeling that saturated my psyche while watching "Mondo Elvis" was what I pursued while making *Trekkies* (1997).

It's notoriously difficult to make a living as an artist. So, should you gamble precious time and resources making a documentary? Yes! Why? First, there has never been a better time to get into the business. There are more buyers, outlets, and opportunities than ever before. Second, those who express themselves creatively live a better, more stimulating life than others immersed only in noncreative endeavors. Do you want to spend your life moving papers from one tray to another, chasing numbers on a grid, or loading boxes into a truck? (On second thought, you'll do all those things while making your film.) A documentary is a creative statement designed to be shared, like a sculpture, a painting, a poem, a book, or an architect's plan. Human beings are imbued with a need to express themselves. Read on for ideas about how to express that creativity bursting to get out of the documentarian inside you—and get paid for it.

—Roger Nygard

CHAPTER ONE

The Documentary

A documentary is a story written with a camera featuring real people and events.

While editing my first documentary, *Trekkies* (1997), I discovered that my film's biggest strength—its downright belly laughs—was also its weakness. It was difficult for viewers to navigate between funny segments and serious moments. After screening the latest cut for Denise Crosby, one of my partners in the project, she was afraid she wouldn't be able to stop laughing after watching *Star Trek* fan Richard Kronfeld driving his Captain Pike chair down a snowy Minneapolis sidewalk. I had placed this scene near the front of the film with other fan introductions, but it was almost impossible to become somber enough afterward for a James Doohan suicide-letter story. I had to move the Pike-chair segment as far toward the end as possible because nothing could follow it. And that wasn't the only controversy surrounding this part.

The Documentary Reality

Audiences sometimes have the perception that everything in documentaries is real. While we were making *Trekkies*, Richard Kronfeld was filming Minneapolis-based comedy sketches featuring a twitchy, sweaty character named Dr. Sphincter. *Trekkies* executive producer Michael Leahy was afraid people would recognize Kronfeld as a comedic performer. He took me aside and said, "Come on, you can tell me; the Pike chair guy, it's a gag, isn't it?"

1

I replied, "He owns that chair. And his Enterprise telephone. I swear, he owns all that stuff."

Leahy wasn't convinced. "Come on. That hair is a gag. The crumpled-up drawings. It has to be."

Does everything in a documentary have to be 100 percent true? How real does reality have to be? How much can you re-enact or fake something? As Leahy and I debated boundaries,

Richard Kronfeld in Trekkies *(1999), riding in his Captain Pike chair.*

I argued that everything in a documentary is "managed reality" to some degree. I cited examples: David Greenstein doesn't go shopping in his *Star Trek* uniform every day, but he did for our camera. When we discovered that coworkers called Barbara Adams "Commander," we set up a situation to capture it on camera. Gabriel Koerner waited for our camera to arrive before he picked up his new *Star Trek* uniform so we could film his reaction.

A few days later, Leahy read a dictionary definition of the word "documentary" to me: "a film, TV program, etc. that dramatically shows or analyzes news events, social conditions, etc., with little or no fictionalization."[1] He was greatly relieved that a "little" fictionalization was allowed.

When I asked Denise Crosby about the Kronfeld segment, she said, "Of course documentaries manipulate. It's the nature of the form. In *Brother's Keeper*, they controlled all the aspects of their interviews; they took them back to the locations of the original events and asked them questions."

Kronfeld is a funny performer, but he's also a bona fide *Star Trek* fan. I felt we were justified in keeping his segment. But I predicted other documentarians would finger us for shaping scenes for maximum effect. Nature films, such as *Microcosmos* (1996), staged their insects for the best possible lighting and angles. It can be argued that hidden camera shows are the only true documentary approach, when subjects have no idea they are on camera. People change their behavior when they know they are being watched. Sociologists call it the Hawthorne effect or the observer effect.[2] This also appears to occur in physics. How a particle is being observed can alter its behavior and affect experimental findings.[3] Sometimes, this is a problem to be managed. Other times, an interviewee is chosen precisely because they amp up their charisma for the camera. When we filmed *Star Trek* theme bands in *Trekkies 2* (2004), they emphasized their fandom to such an extreme fashion that they could have possibly played up *Star Trek* geekdom more. A member of the Klingon band called Stovokor says in the film, "When reality stops being so lame, we'll stop doing this." The lesson for documentarians is to be aware of the observer effect and to edit in such a way that truth is maintained, not diminished.

Klingon band Stovokor interviewed for Trekkies 2 (2004); director of photography David Doyle, sound mixer Bill Martel, and director Roger Nygard.

Subjective Truth

This debate about documentary ethics feels quaint today when re-enactments are common, reality shows routinely stage events, and graphics and animation are used to stand in for people and ideas.

Robert Flaherty was the first to make a feature-length documentary called *Nanook of the North* (1922). Flaherty cast the film with Inuit locals and staged the hunting scenes, building igloos, and how they lived traditional lives. The film was hugely successful and became a prototype for documentaries that followed.[4,5,6]

Davis Guggenheim is a documentarian who made *An Inconvenient Truth* (2006) and *Waiting for Superman* (2010). I asked about his standard for deciding what is appropriate, and he said, "If something is inaccurate, I'm not putting it in my movie. But there are a lot of dishonest documentaries where every fact in that movie is true, but your experience or the conclusion

The first feature-length documentary, Robert Flaherty's Nanook of the North *(1922).*

you take away feels dishonest. I insist all the facts in my movie be true, but I'm more interested in whether the movie is authentic. Does it feel honest?"

Guggenheim related a story about when he was on the border between Jordan and Syria at sunrise with Malala Yousafzai during a refugee crisis, filming what would become *He Named Me Malala* (2015). He had heard a group was

Photograph courtesy of Paramount Pictures Corporation, © Global Warming Documentary, LLC.

Davis Guggenheim interviews Vice President Al Gore for An Inconvenient Truth *(2006).*

on the way to the border, escaping the Syrian regime. He saw two hundred figures approaching in the distance: mothers, fathers, and children. "It was heartbreaking," he said. "I was crying. Malala was crying. Her father was crying. The refugees arrived and got food, got cleaned up, and climbed onto trucks to take them to temporary homes. I was devastated."

Afterward, Guggenheim got in the car with his sixteen-year-old son and asked, "What do you think of that, Miles?"

He said, "You're a fraud."

"What?! What do you mean?"

"You told Malala where to stand."

Guggenheim laughed as he recalled the story. He admitted to his son, "I do that all the time."

Guggenheim had asked Malala to move because she was standing outside the frame, and the camera needed to see her in the shot. He didn't tell Malala what to do, say, or how to act. However, his son thought he might be breaking the "Documentary Rules." Guggenheim elaborated, "It's impossible to make a documentary without making choices. Even with the purest forms, as in the films of the great master Frederick Wiseman, he decides when to turn off the camera. He decides whether to shoot down this hallway and not that hallway. There's always an element of subjectivity."

Frederick Wiseman is one of the pioneers of fly-on-the-wall documentaries, or cinéma vérité. His films *Titicut Follies* (1967), *High School* (1968), and *Welfare* (1975) follow a realistic, observational approach presented without commentary. Wiseman terms his style "reality fictions." He admits his own perspective comes into play: "All the material is manipulated so that the final film is totally fictional in form, although it's based on real events."[7,8]

Photograph by Adrien Toubiana, courtesy of Zipporah Films.
Frederick Wiseman at Zipporah Films.

When I asked Wiseman if there are boundaries to what's allowable in his approach with respect to re-enactments or restaging, he said, "I've never done that whatsoever." He attempts to be 100 percent, to the limits of human ability, unobtrusive in capturing whatever he is filming. I asked why that is so important. "I don't think most people are good enough actors," he said, "so if you ask them to repeat something, they're not going to do it in the same way with the same intensity. The expression will be false. I will feel it's false, and the viewer will feel it's false."

An inmate addressing everyone and no one in Frederick Wiseman's Titicut Follies *(1967).*

Wiseman makes the argument that his documentaries are "fiction films" because they are experienced differently from the way the eye, and therefore the mind, experience the same event:

> Structurally, I may start the film with a sequence we shot the last day and end with a sequence shot the first day. And I'm reducing each sequence to make it usable. For example, in *At Berkeley*, there are many administrative meetings that went on for an hour and a half. I might use six or seven minutes of it in the film, but it is made to appear as if it took place the way you're watching it. I would describe that as fictional. I'll never add something to a sequence that didn't take place within the original sequence. And I usually don't change the order of events; I don't change the temporal aspect of it. Because the themes that I'm extracting from the footage find

expression in different places, I'm editing them together to impose a coherent form.

Filmmaker Errol Morris has made the documentaries *The Thin Blue Line* (1988), *A Brief History of Time* (1991), and *The Fog of War: Eleven Lessons from the Life of Robert S. McNamara* (2003). Morris rejected the notion that documentarians should not control and stylize their films: "Cinéma vérité set back documentary filmmaking twenty or thirty years. It sees documentary as a sub-species of journalism. . . . Truth isn't guaranteed by style or expression. It isn't guaranteed by anything."[9]

Photograph by Nafis Azad

Errol Morris, comfortable in a noire background.

Morris said that he became a documentary filmmaker almost by accident. While pursuing an undergraduate degree in history at the University of Wisconsin at Madison, he took advantage of the 35mm film library at The Wisconsin Historical Society Library. "They also had 16-millimeter reduction prints. You could go to the library and thread them up yourself on a Kodak Pageant Projector and project them against the wall." Morris was most attracted to drama, particularly film noir.

While working toward a doctoral degree in philosophy at Berkeley in 1972, he became interested in murderers, the insanity plea, and criminal responsibility. Preparing to write a thesis on the topic, Morris interviewed serial killers on audio tape. That experience later influenced his approach to his first film, *Gates of Heaven* (1978), which Morris calls "a bizarre interview film." When it was shown at the New York Film Festival, a newspaper strike occurred, resulting in no papers and no reviews. As a result, Morris thought the whole endeavor was going to be a disaster. "Then out of nowhere," he recalled, "these two reviewers in Chicago, Roger Ebert and Gene Siskel, started reviewing *Gates of Heaven* in the papers and on television, probably four separate times. And they loved it." Ebert called it, "one of the greatest films ever made."[10]

Over the years, when Morris discussed *Gates of Heaven* with Ebert, he would argue, "*Gates of Heaven* is not as good as you think it is."

Ebert said, "Yes, it is."

Morris, "No, it isn't."

Ebert, "Yes, it is."

Morris acknowledged it was a weird position to be in with one of the most famous reviewers in the United States. I asked Morris why he was adamant about taking that position.

> Because I wondered about the movie. Is it even really a movie? By my own admission, it breaks all of the documentary rules. You're supposed to observe and not be observed. I would set up shots. I'd have people looking directly into the camera. I'd art direct the shots rather than have some kind of cinéma vérité where you would just capture what was there. I would endlessly modify and design things. Often the camera was fixed in place. Not always, but often. It was a kind of a fuck you to vérité. The interviews were spontaneous, they weren't written out, but they didn't look like anything else I had seen in documentary films.

Errol Morris art directed the frame, and instructed subjects to look directly into the camera in Gates of Heaven *(1978).*

Morris said he loves Wiseman's cinéma vérité movies, but he has always had an enthusiasm for breaking the rules. Morris's goal is to create something different and new, to create art, to create something that defines itself in its own way and creates meaning. He said, "*Gates of Heaven* was a lonely film, isolating the people by individual shots, as if you would put each of them in their own prison. And whether it's all conscious when one lays something like that out, it becomes an element of style and an element of the meaning in the film."

There is a spectrum of styles in the documentary world, from strictly staying out of the way like Wiseman to bending and shaping like Morris. They can all work successfully in getting at their kind of truth. From Guggenheim's perspective, "A filmmaker is absolutely a participant in the movie. The problem arises when a filmmaker is not clear with the audience, when they are not upfront about their intention."

Sam Pollard produced and edited the documentaries *4 Little Girls* (1997) and *Sammy Davis, Jr.: I've Gotta Be Me* (2017). Pollard said he does not work within one singular approach. "Style is informed by the subject. Each of my films requires a different approach, cinematically or directorially." In directing *Slavery by Another Name* (2012), Pollard utilized re-enactments because there weren't any characters alive who could tell the story. He said, "You're recreating a real event as you try to heighten it into a cinematic experience. You're not trying to fake things that didn't happen." However, he used no re-enactments in *MLK/FBI* (2020). He felt he could tell that story without recreations because many of the subjects, who knew Martin Luther King, Jr., were still alive and able to fill in the contextual perspective.

Pollard acknowledges there is no such thing as objective truth. "I'm creating subjective truth from my perspective. Even when *The New York Times* or *The Boston Globe* presents facts, a writer brings his or her approach to that material."

Photograph by Henry Adebonojo

Sam Pollard shooting Lowndes County and The Road to Black Power *(2022; co-directed with Geeta Ghandbhir).*

8

Pollard cited the multitude of articles, books, and films about Abraham Lincoln and how each author brings a different perspective. If a filmmaker were to simply present the facts about Lincoln, they'd put an audience to sleep. "That's what makes Lincoln such a compelling character, because there are so many facets to his personality, to where he stands in the history of America. Was he the great emancipator? What was his motive behind wanting to free the slaves? Where did he really stand on the notion of slavery in America? Life is not black or white. Life is shades of gray. And a good documentary filmmaker brings variation in shading to the story." Pollard made a documentary called *Maynard* (2017) about Atlanta's first black mayor. He said, "There are people to this day who probably feel like I didn't get the story right, or I didn't deal with the character in enough of a positive way. All I can say is, if you feel like I did a disservice to somebody, you should make your own film about that character."

Intent is a crucial part of a documentary's level of truth. A documentarian is a writer using a filmmaker's tools to create a product that represents reality. But there is a limit to the amount of dramatization a documentarian can employ. A documentary is related to journalism, but it's different; it's more cinematic, not a straight reporting of facts. No matter how much the reality is shaped, the salient question becomes: is the presentation an accurate portrait? Before you can answer that question, it helps to understand exactly what kind of documentary you are making. The definitional stuff might seem a bit academic, but bear with me; it will coalesce in the end.

Types of Documentaries

In the book *Introduction to Documentary* (2001), Bill Nichols breaks down documentaries into six "modes" that can be mixed and matched:

1. **Expository**: Advocacy for a particular argument, point of view, ideology, or grievance is supported by presenting footage, re-enactments, and evidence that supports a conclusion or solution. Strong narration often guides a logical argument. This is a style that most associate with documentaries. Examples are Guggenheim's *Waiting for Superman* (2010), Ken Burns's *The Vietnam War* (2017), and Jeff Orlowski's *The Social Dilemma* (2020).

2. **Poetic:** Visuals are emphasized over dialogue. It might be experimental or avant-garde. Impactful, related images are combined to give a sense of a place, construct a metaphor, or create a mood. There can be story and message, but it is implied. Leni Riefenstahl's *Olympia* (1938), Godfrey Reggio's *Koyaanisqatsi* (1982), and Kevin Macdonald, Loressa Clisby, and Tegan Bukowski's *Life in a Day* (2011) are examples.

3. **Observational:** Also known as cinéma vérité, where the unobtrusive camera observes "real life" to try to capture an accurate portrait. *Vérité* is French for truth. There is minimal intrusion into what is being documented. Nature documentaries, Wiseman's *Titicut Follies* (1967), D.A. Pennebaker's *Bob Dylan: Don't Look Back* (1967), Albert and David Maysles and Charlotte Zwerin's *Salesman* (1969) are examples.

4. **Participatory:** The filmmaker interacts with the subject(s) on camera, interviewing or provoking, drawing emotional responses, usually with a goal or point to prove. Agnès Varda's *The Gleaners and I* (2000), Michael Moore's *Bowling for Columbine* (2002), and Werner Herzog's *Grizzly Man* (2005) are examples.

5. **Performative:** The filmmaker is the focus of the documentary, subjectively exploring or investigating a subject (something they may be directly immersed in), and they are personally affected by the outcome. Tony Montana and Mark Brian Smith's *Overnight* (2003), Morgan Spurlock's *Super Size Me* (2004), and Banksy's *Exit Through the Gift Shop* (2010) are examples.

6. **Reflexive:** This is a meta-approach, calling attention to the behind-the-scenes process of making a documentary and the relationship between the filmmaker and the audience. Documentaries including aspects about filmmaking itself naturally reflect the filmmaking process. Dziga Vertov's *Man with a Movie Camera* (1929), Louis Theroux's *Weird Weekends* (1998), and Jeff Orlowski's *Chasing Coral* (2017) are examples.[11]

We can add a seventh category that has emerged.

7. **Mockumentary:** Comedy filmmakers appropriated the documentary style to satirize or parody ideas, people, and bona fide documentaries. Actor L.M. Kit Carson and writer-director James McBride are credited with making the first mockumentary: *David Holzman's Diary* (1967) is a send-up of the cinéma vérité films. Christopher Guest (*Waiting for*

L.M. Kit Carson stars in director James McBride's David Holzman's Diary (1967).

Christopher Guest and Rob Reiner inprovise in Billy Crystal's HBO special Don't Get Me Started (1986), a parody of the mockumentary This is Spinal Tap (1984).

Director-writer-actor Dean Fleischer Camp pretends to be interviewed by Leslie Stahl for Marcel the Shell with Shoes On (2021).

Guffman, 1996) and Sacha Baron Cohen (*Borat*, 2006) have worked extensively in this genre. *Documentary Now!* (2015–TBD) is a series devoted to satirizing the form. *Marcel the Shell with Shoes On* (2021) is a narrative pretending to use a documentary style—also with a reflexive aspect.

Nichols's categories might feel abstract, so I'll simplify documentaries to two main categories: narrative and concept. They can be combined, but your film is probably firmly in one camp or the other. How do you know which type you are making? Ask yourself the following: Are you making a documentary about a *person* or a *thing*? Narrative documentaries follow persons and tell human stories, and they may or may not take a position. Concept documentaries examine ideas, things, or places, and they usually advocate for a particular conclusion.

Narrative Documentary

After a screening of *The Great Buster* (2018), a documentary about silent-film star Buster Keaton, during the question-and-answer session, director Peter Bogdanovich said, "With a narrative, you write it, then shoot it. With a documentary, you shoot it, then write it." Finding the plot in your documentary is job one. Anybody can shoot interviews and string them together. However, most successful documentaries are plotted as carefully as narrative films, whether pre-planned or found in editing. Documentarians don't simply show their footage like a PowerPoint presentation. Great documentarians are master storytellers.

Documentaries are often structured in three acts (or four, or five), the same as screenplays. That simply means there is a beginning (a main character, the goal, and an obstacle are introduced), a middle (conflict builds in pursuit of the goal against bigger and bigger obstacles), and an end (after a crisis point or climax, a resolution is reached). The story arc might be the following: rise to greatness, fall from grace, and then a comeback. If an act is missing, you may have to consider whether the idea is fully formed. A documentary does not always have to be in a three-act structure. Building a robust structure is just one way to improve a film's chance for success. Davis Guggenheim always has a story, a structure, or a scene in mind before he begins shooting. He's also paying attention to tone and character development. Because you can't design real life, he stays flexible when reality shifts and sends things in a more exciting direction.

Some documentaries are presented as a series. Ken Burns is especially known for this approach, such as *Jazz* (2001), which has ten episodes running nineteen hours. Burns explained, "Our attention spans are often quite small, but all meaning accrues in duration. That which we are proudest of has benefited from our attention. And so what do we do with this tsunami of stuff? We binge. We are after consistent, sustained experience of content. . . . And now with streaming they can do it on their own time."[12] A documentary series may have a larger structure extending over the run of episodes. But each episode needs to resolve in its own way. When I was working on the docuseries *The Comedy Store* (2020), Mike Binder wrote outlines, and I would revise and rewrite them as I edited. We bounced ideas off each other, and Binder would keep rewriting. We looked for stories buried in the hundreds of hours of footage he had been gathering from interviewing scores of comedians. You begin with a plan, but it changes while shooting, and then it changes again during editing. Or, to use a musical analogy, a screenplay is like a concerto, and a documentary is like jazz, which has a basic harmonic framework that allows space for improvisation. These story-telling rules for documentaries can apply just as strongly to narrative podcasts if not more so because podcasters often have to get their ideas across without the help of visual information.

Who Is the Protagonist?

To figure out your story, you must identify a protagonist. Who is experiencing the most significant journey, and what are their goals? You can start by searching for a subject's surface motivations: success, money, fame, being chosen. But then go deeper. Maybe a need for belonging, self-esteem, freedom, affection, connection, approval, love? Who is changing the most by learning the lesson of the film? Is it your primary interviewee (*Man on Wire*, 2008)? Is it the filmmaker, who is one of the protagonists (*Grizzly Man*, 2005)? Is it a *group* of protagonists (*Some Kind of Heaven*, 2021)? Are multiple people telling the story (*The King of Kong: A Fistful of Quarters*, 2007)? Is the filmmaker on a mission to solve a mystery (*Paradise Lost: The Child Murders at Robin Hood Hills*, 1996)? The investigation angle is common in true crime documentaries, one of the genres in greatest demand. Once you identify the protagonist(s), you can ensure each scene is connected to that person's journey. If a scene is unrelated to the protagonist(s), it may be hard to justify its inclusion in the movie.

Find the Conflict

Next, identify the antagonist. Who or what is standing in the protagonist's way? Conflict flows from the clash of opposing forces. An engaging protagonist needs a purpose or a goal, with solid obstacles, often created by an antagonist—a person or entity that appears stronger than the protagonist and wants to stop the protagonist from getting what they want. If you're not sure where the conflict is, look for fights, disagreements, arguing, and conflicting points of view. When Sam Pollard examines a new project, he looks for conflict and how to make it come alive: "If somebody approaches you with a film idea, or you have an idea, you have to think: *Is there any drama? Is this story going to feel compelling?* If it's just a history lesson, maybe you shouldn't do it. But if you can find the moments where there's tension and conflict, that'll give you a reason to dive in." Obstacles create conflict, which builds rising action, leading to a climax and a resolution.

When I was editing *Trekkies*, I realized there was no single protagonist with a goal and obstacles heading toward a surprising ending. I was in the process of making all the biggest mistakes. I had to figure out how to hold the audience's attention for ninety minutes without that all-important narrative through line. The solution I attempted to employ was to lean into the mistake and craft the film as a series of short chapters while constructing an overall portrait of a subculture of obsessed fans. I hoped that if a viewer was not captivated by one character, there would be another quirky person soon; each segment would be more colorful, funnier, and more engaging than the last. To create a twist at the end, I showcased some of the oddest characters in the film's first half, giving viewers the eccentricity they expected. Then I shifted to more positive portrayals and altruistic activities, which led to an audience realization: *Hey, these people aren't so bad. There are worse things to be obsessed with than a television show with a message of a positive future.* The film changes perceptions about a much-maligned group. Some of the best documentaries are catalysts for change. Curiously, because *Trekkies* became successful, its structural flaws and lack of story arc have sometimes been copied by other documentaries, often to their structural disadvantage.

How closely must you follow a structural blueprint when making a documentary? You don't have to follow *any* of these guidelines if you can figure out a better way. And if you do, let me know so I can add it to the list. Some films succeed in violation of narrative conventions—but without the support of a good storyline, a documentary will have to excel greatly in other ways to make up for this flaw. It will have to be exceptionally funny, have a built-in core audience, have an amazingly charismatic subject, ask a captivating question, or just get lucky and be incredibly timely. Your best strategy, though, is using story structure to build in some insurance that your film will be engaging.

Biography

Biography is a subcategory of narrative documentary. When telling the story of somebody's life, this structure is limited by what actually happened. If they didn't live an extraordinary three-act structure, it will be harder to build an engaging film. Not everybody's life deserves two hours of precious viewing time. But if you choose someone who became the best at something, there is probably a powerful story underneath, such as *Pelé* (2021), which is about a man who went from shining shoes to three-time soccer world champion.

Music documentary is a subset of the biography subcategory. *This Is Elvis* (1981) has a built-in structure: rise, fall, comeback, and death. Sometimes the strength of the music is enough to overcome a thin story. Music documentaries sometimes feel familiar or repetitive because all musicians seem to be fighting the same demons: drugs, money, insanity, other band members, record labels, struggling for success, and creative dry spells. Because bands have those types of built-in conflicts, it provides good material for a story arc. The documentarian can't simply show that a band wrote this one song, and then they wrote that other song, and this third song is pretty good too. Ideally, there needs to be some kind of a fight with lots of struggles.

Band documentaries without a strong narrative arc often only appeal to fans. *The Beatles: Get Back* (2021) has little story and conflict. Beatles fans love the inside look at the songwriting process, but there's not much to hang onto for non-fans. *Lemmy* (2010) is about the leader of the famous heavy-metal band Motorhead, whose fans may consider it a masterpiece, but probably few beyond the fan demographic have seen the film. *Anvil* (2008) is about a band nobody had heard of, yet the engaging story crossed over to non-fans. Cinequest Film Festival programmer Michael Rabehl explained, "I see documentaries every year about independent music bands. What makes that kind of documentary special is when they go deeper into their lives, not just focus on the music."

Liz Garbus made the acclaimed documentaries *The Farm: Angola, USA* (1998), *Ghosts of Abu Ghraib* (2007),

Photograph courtesy of Story Syndicate

Liz Garbus interviewing Meghan Markle and Prince Harry for Harry & Meghan *(2022).*

and *Bobby Fischer Against the World* (2011). Garbus suggested that documentaries that allude to universal journeys appeal to audiences beyond the fans. In her film *What Happened, Miss Simone?* (2016), the story is about a woman who was misunderstood, had a liberation from an abusive husband, and went through a civil rights movement that disappointed her. "It was a journey about strength and resilience. When you make sure people understand they'll find something to relate to, that's how you bring everyone in."

Concept Documentary

In another category are concept-based documentaries. They are generally more challenging to create, finance, and sell. For some masochistic reason, those are the documentaries I tend to make. Concept documentaries can be about any topic: anthropology (*Guns, Germs and Steel*, 1997), comedy (*Jackass: The Movie*, 2002), music (*The Last Waltz*, 1978), politics (*The War on Democracy*, 2007), nature (*March of the Penguins*, 2005), science (*Hubble*, 2010), travel (*The Endless Summer*, 1965), history (*Wild Wild Country*, 2018), institutions (*Hospital*, 1970), and so on.

A concept documentary often relies upon a core question that a filmmaker poses and sets out to answer. This is the mystery that will be solved, a theme that will be explored, a premise that will be proven, and that's what

16

holds the viewer to the end waiting for the big answer. Michael Moore investigates and builds cases in his films. *Sicko* (2007) is an indictment of the United States health insurance industry. Moore said, "I am confronting the American audience with a question: Who are we, and what has happened to our soul? To me, that's maybe more confrontation than going after the CEO of Aetna or the CEO of Pfizer."[13] Lee Fulkerson said the conclusion he builds to in *Forks Over Knives* (2011) is: "Fight disease by changing what you eat, and you can avoid going under a surgeon's knife."[14]

The best way to present a concept is to find a character, hero, or investigator immersed in the idea search. The argument that climate change is real had already been presented in many documentaries, but the thing that made *An Inconvenient Truth* (2006) unique was the narrative structure and character development. Al Gore is the protagonist with a goal. He says at the beginning, "I've been trying to tell the story for a long time. And I feel like I have failed." Jay Cassidy, who edited the movie, approached the film as a redemption story. He and Davis Guggenheim show Gore's journey trying to get his message out, first as a student at Harvard University, then trying to warn Congress, later losing the 2000 election, and then taking his message on the road.

Theme

When Guggenheim was making *Still: A Michael J. Fox Movie* (2023), he said, "The big idea was: how do you strip away the expectations of a celebrity biopic and really figure out, at the core, who a person is, which is usually not what people present as themselves." When Guggenheim was working with editor Michael Harte, as they pulled clips from Michael J. Fox's movies and television episodes, they noticed that Fox was constantly running. "That became a big theme in this documentary. He's running toward Hollywood, and then he's running away from Parkinson's disease."

Frederick Wiseman said a film must work on two levels: literal and abstract. The literal level is the story, the dialogue, and the problems or needs being addressed. The abstract level comprises the general ideas suggested by the literal encounters viewers are observing or, to some extent, participating in as an observer. This abstract level is also called the theme, which is an idea that pervades and drives a film. A theme, or thesis statement, is a filmmaker's point of view about the world, society, human nature, or some kind of revelation. It is related to the moral reached at the end of the story. Examples of themes include: love conquers all; corporations are destructive; justice is not available to the poor; courage is needed to defeat evil; absolute power corrupts absolutely. When I began editing *The Comedy Store* (2020), I realized that simply going sequentially through the building's history was not a strong through line. I suggested to Mike Binder that each episode needed its own unique theme. When we focused in on a thematic idea for each episode, that helped us improve storylines.

A film's story begins when a core question is posed: Will the hero defeat the evil threat? Will the protagonist win over the love interest? Will the investigator solve the crime? Will the family get to safety? This question is answered at the end, after a climax. When a documentary is not engaging, it's often because there was no clear theme, or a core question was not clearly asked at the start. Every scene should relate to the core question in some way.

A mystery often begins with the question: "Why?" Robert Kenner's *Food, Inc.* (2008) asks: Why is food from corporate farming unhealthy? We watch to learn the answer. Pose an engaging question at the start to hook the audience. What mystery will you solve by the end? What lesson will you teach? What secret will be revealed? It turns out I was born annoying. I annoyed my parents with endless questions. I drove my teachers crazy with questions. Now my insatiable curiosity is an asset.

Rachel Grady has made documentaries such as *Jesus Camp* (2006), *Freakonomics* (2010), and *One of Us* (2017). She suggested, "Come up with a hypothesis. And then be totally open to being completely wrong. You are flexible, but you aren't floating along like a jellyfish. You do have to direct the action, but you're not controlling the story too much; follow paths you think are going somewhere." Sam Pollard agreed, "If I'm doing a

Photograph by Charlie Gross

Rachel Grady.

story about Dr. King, slavery, or post-slavery after Reconstruction, I have a theme in mind. But sometimes the theme evolves and changes as I interact with people and different ideas. You've got to be malleable. You can't be rigid about what you think the theme or the structure is."

In *The Thin Blue Line* (1988), Errol Morris asks: Is convicted murderer Randall Dale Adams innocent? Morris's fundamental theme is that the judicial process is flawed. In *Bowling for Columbine* (2002), Michael Moore sets out to answer the question: Why does the United States have more deaths due to guns than any other Western democracy? Moore's thematic premise is that violence is not a proper way to bring change in modern society.

Film agent Glen Reynolds at Circus Road Films has been representing filmmakers for fifteen years, having sold over seven hundred films. Reynolds has found that theme, or a filmmaker's point of view, works best when it is narrowed and sharpened: "If you're making a film about politics, you're less likely to find an audience if you are taking an even-handed, journalistic bird's-eye-view of the subject, presenting all sides, rather than having a strong point of view."

There is an inherent perspective at work when taking a pile of footage and pulling a story out of it. Reynolds said when he watches documentaries, he often wonders what was left on the cutting room floor that would have opposed the filmmaker's point of view or told a different story. Reynolds cited the documentary *Fire of Love* (2022), about two French volcano experts who became the world's most famous volcanologists. The movie was primarily constructed from found footage. Documentarian

Two dedicated-yet-reckless scientists in Werner Herzog's The Fire Within, *presented in 1.78 aspect ratio (2022).*

A story of two lovebirds in Sara Dosa's Fire of Love, *presented in 1.33 aspect ratio (2022).*

Sara Dosa created a narrative about two people who fell in love and died together while studying volcanos. A love theme was there in the footage, but Dosa had to unearth it. Filmmaker Werner Herzog utilized the exact same library-source footage about these two volcano experts, and yet his film is entirely different, even in aspect ratio. The theme of *The Fire Within: A Requiem for Katia and Maurice Krafft* (2022) is in the title; it is a visual requiem for two extraordinary, perhaps reckless, scientists. Make a film that only you can make, that nobody else would make, even when it is about the same subject, with exactly the same information.

Theme is so important that I want you to take a moment right now and write down a theme that is bursting to get out of your head. What message must you get out to the world? What question are you dying to answer? What is your point of view about a core idea, topic, or mystery? Make a note. Then look at it tomorrow. See if you feel the same. If not, revise it, add to it, and refine it until you have a solid theme. Then you will have your mission.

Good Stories Change Minds

Advocacy films begin by identifying a problem, investigating the issue, and, finally, making a case for solving the problem—still three parts. Many are issue-driven works that serve as a tool for social change. The key is to ask a question intriguing enough to hold an audience to the end. It also has to be compelling enough to keep you, the filmmaker, engaged for the span of time and amount of money it will take to complete the film.

If a documentary makes an impact, it is natural that it will advocate for a particular idea. Frederick Wiseman said his goal has been to make films that reflect the ambiguity and complexity of the material, while resisting any effort to simplify it in service of an ideology. However, he doesn't feel responsible for viewers' reactions. If his films have an impact on society, causing change, he feels it is inherent in the material, a function of the choices he made in the selection of the sequences, their order, and the resulting form of the film.

Rachel Grady avoids overt advocacy. She personally believes there should be a separation between church and state, but she didn't approach

Jesus Camp (2006) as an activist. "I try to stay open-minded, so I can find people's humanity and tell a better story. If your mind is made up from the beginning, it's boring. You should be open to being wrong. There's nothing more exciting than being totally wrong."

Photograph by Daniel J. White, courtesy of Florentine Films.

Ken Burns, conducting an interview for The Roosevelts *(2014).*

The name Ken Burns is synonymous with documentaries. Burns has made dozens of acclaimed works, such as *The Civil War* (1990), *Baseball* (1994), and *Jazz* (2001). Burns acknowledged that "there is an honorable tradition in documentary, in which advocacy is the central *raison d'être* for the film. And that's absolutely fine. But I just want to tell stories. I was lucky that by age twenty-two, I knew I was going to be making documentaries about American history. Not with a focus on advocacy but about story and the complexities of narrative. I was steeped in Aristotle's *Poetics*, which governs all storytelling." Burns referenced a quote by novelist Richard Powers, who wrote, "The best arguments in the world won't change a person's mind. The only thing that can do that is a good story."[15] Burns added, "There aren't just good guys and bad guys. It's not completely binary. There's complexity. I'm not trying to consciously change a point of view. I'm trying to rearrange viewers' molecules by telling a complex story that has undertones that assault preconceptions, misconceptions, and deceptions that people operate under."

Filmmaker Freida Lee Mock has directed the documentaries *Anita: Speaking Truth to Power* (2013), *RUTH: Justice Ginsburg in Her Own Words* (2021), and *The Choir and the Conductor* (2022). Mock went to graduate school thinking she would become a lawyer. "I woke up one day and decided I wanted to make documentaries. It was like a light bulb turned on." She graduated with a major in American history, focusing on the 1920s and the muckraking era. She said that books influenced her more than films. When she read *The Octopus* (1901) by Frank Norris and *The Jungle* (1906) by Upton Sinclair, about corrupt corporate monopolies and the suffering they caused during the early part of the twentieth century, she thought she would become a documentary filmmaker in the spirit of those muckrakers exposing corruption and mendacity. "I soon realized that agitprop-style filmmaking and lecturing people about what's good for them didn't feel right. I thought a better way to approach the audience was with respect and to simply share stories about ideas and characters. The film projects I develop independently (instead of for hire or on commission) typically have a political and social underpinning. If I'm lucky, there's self-discovery on the part of the audience who are immersed in the journey of the film and who come out at the end feeling that the film had a positive and surprising impact."

Mock related how a young Asian-American filmmaker wrote to her, describing how his Asian-American identity was shaped by three films, one of which was *Maya Lin: A Strong Clear Vision* (1995). Mock said, "I did not intend to talk about *Maya Lin* as an expression of, or advocacy for, understanding Asian-American identity. You never know what will come across to your audience, but you hope it is multifaceted. You put your film out there and hope they don't fall asleep, and that they laugh, they cry, they're astonished, and have a good time."

Propaganda

An approach to beware of is when a filmmaker begins with a fervent belief in an agenda, selectively presenting a preferred position, despite contrary evidence. The result can edge into propaganda. A biased approach can mislead, based on an appeal to emotion rather than logic. Political partisans, religious organizations, corporations, and countries at war, trying to persuade or cover up, have funded films promoting preferred ideologies. Among the most famous is Leni Riefenstahl's *Triumph of the Will* (1935), which glorified Adolph Hitler and the Nazi Party. Frank Capra's response for the United States was the documentary series *Why We Fight* (1942–1945). More recent examples include *Expelled: No Intelligence Allowed* (2008), which promotes a belief in intelligent design; *Cowspiracy: The Sustainability Secret* (2014), which posits that animal agriculture is a more significant contributor to global warming than burning fossil fuels; and *2000 Mules* (2022), which speculates without verifiable evidence about voting irregularities.

Strong advocacy can be financially successful, especially if the group of true believers is large. Michael Moore's polemic *Fahrenheit 9/11* (2004) is one of the highest-grossing documentaries of all time at $221 million worldwide. Absolute neutrality is impossible and to be avoided in a documentary with a point of view. But how can you differentiate an expository documentary from propaganda? It's probably propaganda if all four of the following aspects are present: a filmmaker elevates the theme from subtext to front-and-center, the ideology is presented as irrefutable truth, there is no effort to stay in the realm of what is verifiable, and the project is funded by those desiring to promote the ideology.

The Outsider's Perspective

An outsider often has a more objective view of a subject than those immersed in it. Many of history's greatest filmmakers were foreigners who came to Hollywood and made films about America, such as Frank Capra (*Mr. Smith Goes to Washington*, 1939), William Wyler (*The Best Years of Our Lives*, 1946), Elia Kazan (*East of Eden*, 1955), Billy Wilder (*The Apartment*, 1960), and Ang Lee (*The Ice Storm*, 1997).

A trap some documentary filmmakers fall into is to make a glossy valentine about a world they love; they end up evangelizing. It doesn't mean you can't be objective if you are a part of the subject you are presenting; it just takes awareness and discipline.

In my documentaries, I have mostly been an outsider entering new worlds and learning about them, and then the audience observes that world through my experience. In *Trekkies*, I didn't have a stake in how *Star Trek* aficionados were portrayed. If my goal had been to show that *Star Trek* fans are "normal," I would have made a vastly different film. *Six Days in Roswell* (1999) is another anthropological portrait, this time of Americana, of a small town gripped with alien mania. I took no position on whether aliens are here on Earth. I wanted to find the quirky side of this colorful world. When I made this film, I corrected my *Trekkies* error and made sure the main character had a story arc, with a mission he stated early: "There are people who can show me how to meet the aliens and get abducted because nobody from Minnesota gets abducted. . . . I myself would like to get abducted." And

23

then we sent him on his journey to pursue his goal. We also played with the level of reality. Edging into mockumentary at times, we created a docu-hybrid by fabricating scenes for his home life in Minnesota to introduce his character and provide a basis for his journey. Our protagonist is playing a character obsessed with UFOs, but all the people he meets in Roswell are real. He improvises with them, much as Sacha Baron Cohen did in *Da Ali G Show* (2000–2004) and *Who is America?* (2018).

Following Up

If you begin shooting a documentary but it stalls out and you put it on the shelf for a while, this could turn into a terrific opportunity to follow up in the future to find out how your subjects' lives have changed. During the hiatus, a story might have blossomed. Michael Apted's brilliant *Up* series (1964–TBD) utilized this technique to perfection, checking in with fourteen individuals every seven years, beginning when they were seven years old.

For *The Truth About Marriage* (2020), I shot my first interview in 2012 with a rapper I met while traveling through Brazil. Don Blanquito was charismatic, funny, and the most unabashedly single person I had ever met. Calling himself "the Indiana Jones of the golden booty," he said, "We're not designed to be with the same person for six years. If you turn on the Discovery Channel, you'll see female spiders trying to kill the males if they stick around too long." He struck me as a prime documentary subject. After interviewing him about his relationship doctrines, I put the footage aside as I tried to figure out the rest of the film. Seven years later, this man, who had been living the epitome of bachelorhood, was married and had a daughter, so I interviewed him again. I also did a follow-up years later with a polyamorous couple and with a Hollywood screenwriter and his foreign bride from the Czech Republic. This gave my film part of the missing ending it needed.

Reality Shows

Reality television is a cousin of documentaries, and they break down into news or human-interest features (concept), game shows (competition), and docu-sitcoms (narrative). *Frontline* (1983–TBD) and *Vice* (2013–TBD) are concept-documentary series telling human-interest or news-feature stories. When somebody gets a rose on *The Bachelorette* (2003–TBD), is voted off the island on *Survivor* (2000–TBD), or wins the singing contest on *American Idol* (2002–TBD), it is a competition. Waiting to see who wins the game show keeps the audience tuned in. Biographical docu-sitcoms follow a person, family, or group and present a slice of their lives. Much of it is semi-scripted, loosely based on their lives, and punched up with drama and jokes. *An American Family* (1973), *The Real World* (1992–TBD), *The Farmer's Wife* (1998), and *The Osbournes* (2002–2005) were progenitors of this now-pervasive style.

Write an Outline

You've chosen a theme and know what type of documentary you will make; now, write an outline. To figure out your story, put each idea or scene on a notecard and revise the order until there is a flow. Making a documentary (and writing an outline) is not dissimilar to writing a term paper or a dissertation. Rachel Grady said her outlines change hundreds of times. But you need to start somewhere, even if it's pie in the sky. "Once we start collecting footage, we move stuff around based on: 'Well, that didn't read, so that's not true.' Or, 'That's actually not a scene, that's only a shot.' Or, 'There was more to that scene than I remembered. There was this other little exchange that now has more significance because this other thing happened.' It's not linear; it's a live process."

Marina Zenovich's documentaries include *Roman Polanski: Wanted and Desired* (2008), *Robin Williams: Come Inside My Mind* (2018), and *LANCE* (2020). Zenovich said she started working with writer/producer P.G. Morgan (who happens to be her husband), who helps her create a framework. "I'm not good at structure at all, and I know it. So he can map it out, and I go into the field and get it. I deliver. We really complement each other because I'm in the moment. I'm all heart. He's all brain." Zenovich's process resonated with me because with *Trekkies*, Denise Crosby was the heart, and I was the technocrat.

The writer of the documentary is primarily the one who writes the story outline and then decides which clips to use in which order (and writes the narrative voiceover, if any). Freida Lee Mock considers it writing when she conceptualizes a storyline and creates the narrative arc. "It's not writing in the way you write a script in the fiction space, but in nonfiction, I'm developing and creating the story, the choice of characters, ideas, and themes in a documentary. Typically this is expressed in a written form for pitching, marketing, and initial meetings with the key creatives on the team."

Once you have the basics of a story outline figured out, divide it into three (or more) acts written as concisely as possible. This will be your blueprint. You might follow it closely or deviate wildly as the journey continues. Without a map, you may wander lost within a forest of choices.

Courtesy of HBO Max.

Marina Zenovich with director of photography Nick Higgins, on the set of The Way Down *(2021).*

Before beginning with the editor, some producers and directors transcribe every interview. Then they copy and paste sound bites into what becomes the script. Some utilize an editor who will not be making creative decisions and who is just "a pair of hands." The editor starts once a paper edit is completed. In the opposite case, an editor watches everything, makes all the decisions, and forms the story. There's a middle ground where both watch everything and pull pieces to match an outline. Mock said, "I never hand over footage to an editor without mediating what it means or what the core ideas and characters are. I look at every frame, all the dailies, with the editor before we make pulls. It's a total collaboration with creative input from the editor whose specialty in the art and craft of editing I rely upon."

For *The Comedy Store*, when we wanted to do a segment about a particular comedian or topic, we asked an assistant editor to word-search all the transcripts for every time someone mentioned that person or idea and then make a string-out, collecting all those clips into one timeline. And then I took that collection, moved things around, whittled it down, and molded it until it flowed as a segment or chapter.

It's All About People

Tell human stories—especially when making concept films. For example, if the concept is about "greed," contrast people living greedily with people living selflessly. We need to see why the people profiled are so incredibly fascinating. What crises are they facing? What are the risks in their lives? The higher the stakes, the better. The docuseries *Cheer* (2020–2022) and *Last Chance U* (2016–2020) present huge stakes for the people involved. Director Sue Kim made *The Speed Cubers* (2020) captivating by focusing on the friendship and rivalry between two young men. Winning is just as important to them as it would be to a Super Bowl quarterback.

The films that first inspired Liz Garbus, and showed her the potential in documentaries, were *Sherman's March* (1986), *Titicut Follies* (1967), and *Hoop Dreams* (1994), the latter of which Garbus credits with presenting a layered, massively entertaining story with huge narrative stakes, making it as exciting as anything scripted. Garbus said, "At the heart, it's about race and class, mobility and possibility. I saw in it a crystallization of what I wanted to do:

High school student Arthur Agee dreams of playing professionally in Hoop Dreams *(1994).*

make films that captured a narrative excitement while being meaningful at their core about issues I was passionate about."

When I asked Ken Burns how to make a story about a *thing* captivating, he said you can't make a documentary about things. "Everything is about people. *Brooklyn Bridge* is the story of the Roebling family. When the father dies, his young son takes over but gets the bends working on the pneumatic caissons deep under the East River. His wife becomes his right arm, his eyes and his ears, as he recuperates while watching the construction progress with a spyglass from his bedroom in Brooklyn Heights. And then she gets to be the first person to ride over the bridge." Burns also referenced how, in *The Civil War* (1990), on a Good Friday, General Lee surrendered to General Grant at Appomattox Courthouse in southwestern Virginia. "And the following Tuesday, the President feels like he's got enough time now to take the evening off and go to the theater. You cannot make this up. And so you have to get out of the way sometimes of what actually happens."

Focus on the people around the thing. Documentaries solely about collectibles, aquatic life, or a television show have difficulty sustaining for thirty minutes. But a documentary about an obsessed *collector* who amassed 100,000 owl figurines, or about the *person* who follows and befriends an octopus, or about the fervent *fans* of a television show has the potential to hold interest to the ninety-minute mark.

If you choose to make a personal story inspired by your own life, it can consume you. When I started making *The Nature of Existence* (2010), my core question was: *Why do we exist?* I didn't realize it would take me eighty sub-questions, four years, one hundred seventy interviews, and four hundred fifty hours of footage to get my answer. If I had known at the start of my film career what I was in for, I would have probably become a doctor. Sure, medical school is hard, but you don't have to constantly create new ideas.

CHAPTER TWO

The Next Great Idea

Choice of subject is the most important factor for the success of a documentary.

Where will you get that next great idea? You might conceive of an incredible concept but do a mediocre job and yet still have a popular documentary. However, if you choose a topic that nobody is interested in, it won't matter how slick and polished the film looks.

People often say to me, "I have a great idea for a documentary."

My first thought is *Yeah, but is it worth two years of your life?*

They usually disappear when I reply, "That *is* a good idea. Can you put up two hundred thousand dollars?" They are quick to spend *your* time and money, not so much their own.

When to Start

If you are wondering if you should jump into the pool, the answer is yes! Start now. If you have an idea, shoot a test. Edit a scene. Create a sample. That will give you a sense of whether the idea is working. Before you sit down with your big interviewees, do at least one practice interview to test the concept. Interview a friend. Have somebody interview you. Or interview a lesser priority from your list. You can cut a documentary-ette from that footage. It will give a taste and provide a proof of concept to show investors. It will also help you refine your questions and adjust your approach. Conversely, it may demonstrate that the project isn't as intriguing as you thought, and it's better to move on to something else.

Jonathan Vogler, producer of *The Comedy Store* (2020), started as a production assistant at Mandalay Sports Media on *Kareem: Minority of One* (2015). Vogler discovered he loved the documentary process so much that he started showing up at the office even when he wasn't on a project. "I volunteered to help with research or vacuum the floors; whatever they needed. I just wanted to be around it." He was earning the trust of the people making the films. They gradually gave him more responsibilities, and the credit caught up. Soon, he was pitching ideas, and the first to come to fruition was a short documentary for *Vice Sports:* "John and the Dons" (2016).

Photograph by Bo Billstrup.

Jonathan Vogler setting up for an interview.

Teenagers on the streets in director Martin Bell's documentary Streetwise *(1984).*

Filmmaker Rachel Grady's passion for documentaries was triggered at age ten by Martin Bell's film, *Streetwise* (1984), an observational documentary following a group of nine homeless runaways in downtown Seattle. Grady said, "It just blew me away. My mom took me to see it in the movie theater. I don't know why, maybe because she read 'it's about kids.' I saw it and I was obsessed. I made her take me back to see it again. I had never seen anything like that." Grady thought she wanted to be a journalist, but when she was in school, she had an epiphany. "Journalists can be great writers, but they should not be an artist. There's something about making artistic choices that takes away journalistic integrity. As a documentarian, it's the best of both worlds, being a journalist with the freedom to be an artist as well."

My own documentary career was sparked by Denise Crosby, who played the role of Lt. Natasha "Tasha" Yar on *Star Trek: The Next Generation* (1987–1994) and later was invited to science fiction conventions all over the world. I cast Denise in my first film in 1991, *High Strung*, and a couple of years later, when we met for lunch, as she related what it was like attending conventions, she said, "I can't believe no one has made a documentary about this, these Trekkies."

We were surprised nobody had done it. It seemed so obvious. The catalyst was when Denise was invited to appear at a convention called FantastiCon in 1996. We figured this shoot would be a good test. The event was organized and hosted by William Campbell, known for playing the charac-

Star Trek actor, DeForest Kelley, interviewed by Denise Crosby for Trekkies *(1997).*

ter Trelane in the original *Star Trek* (1966–1969) episode "The Squire of Gothos." Because Denise was a former cast member, we had *access*—one of the most important things needed for a documentary. Fans were much more willing to talk to her than an unknown person with a camera.

Neither of us had made a documentary, and Denise worried, "We have no idea what we're doing."

I said, "We'll figure it out." Blissfully unaware of how difficult the documentary process could be, I went to a video store in Santa Monica called Vidiots, which had all the good, weird stuff. I grabbed a pile of documentaries, including *Brother's Keeper* (1992), *Hoop Dreams* (1994), *Crumb* (1994), and various Les Blank films. Denise and I watched a mini-seminar in her living room. Next, Neo Motion Pictures producer W.K. (Keith) Border set up a meeting with Lisa Leeman, a documentarian with whom his partner, Joel Soisson, had gone to film school. Leeman's Sundance Filmmakers Trophy-winning documentary *Metamorphosis: Man Into Woman* (1990) had been licensed by PBS. We grilled her on every aspect of documentary production. Then I wrote interview questions, and we started shooting. The footage was so colorful that we never stopped.

Keep It Engaging

Consider the business aspect of your project. If you don't pick a subject with wide appeal, you probably won't get paid for the next year(s) of work.

You might be making a glorified home movie—which is fine if that's your goal. There are exceptions, such as *Sherman's March* (1986), a film that wildly exceeded its limitations. It begins as a Civil War documentary but subverts viewer expectations as it metamorphoses into a character study of the filmmaker's personal dating history and mental state. *Britney vs Spears* (2021) is an example of picking a topic with an obvious built-in core group. No matter what happens, with a famous subject, you know there is an interested audience.

First, choose a subject *you* like that will entertain and engage you. Your film will only inspire people if it inspires you first. Big laughs may not be what audiences expected when they selected a documentary about *Star Trek* fans, but audiences like being surprised. You can't show them what they've seen before. Even serious documentaries have funny moments because real life is like that.

Tone

Before shooting begins on a television episode, there is usually a "tone meeting" to ensure the new director is on the same page with writers and producers. Tone is the attitude of the writer(s) to the subject matter, and the director needs to bring out performances that are consistent with that intention. Is this scene meant to be slyly funny, while this other scene needs to be played deadly straight? Is this moment meant to be overly outrageous but not played so broadly it violates reality? While navigating disparate material, it is important to keep all the components consistent. When Marina Zenovich was directing *Robin Williams: Come Inside My Mind* (2018), she said it was difficult to hit the right tone. "It had to be funny but sad. We had to deal with the suicide, which was the elephant in the room."

The way a documentary subject is perceived by an audience is preceded by how the filmmaker feels. One reason the tone of *Trekkies* seems affectionate toward *Star Trek* fans is because I liked the people I met. I never wanted anybody in the film to feel bad about their participation. I wanted to be laughing *with* them. I wanted *Star Trek* fans, as well as non-fans, to enjoy the film. If your documentary is an exposé about a murderer, you may not like that person, and that could come across by how you present them. But even if you don't like them, if you strive to be as fair as possible, the resulting tone will reflect your attitude. Plus, you may not want to make a habit of angering a ton of murderers.

Seek the Exceptional

One of the biggest criticisms I've received about *Trekkies* from *Star Trek* fans is, "You didn't show enough normal fans." Hearing this, my first thought was: *Who gets to decide what's normal?* Second thought: *Normal is boring.* Even the people complaining wouldn't watch if I made a film about the "normal" people they claimed to want to see. I turned this criticism into a theme in *Trekkies 2.* The subtitle for that film is: *How much is too much?* I asked fans to explain what is "normal" for a *Star Trek* fan. Nobody agreed. Everybody felt whatever level of fandom they chose for themselves was the correct amount; anything beyond that was too much, regardless of where they were on the continuum.

I don't consider people in my films to be weird or strange; I see them as *exceptional.* As Brent Spiner put it in *Trekkies*, "There's this preconceived notion that they are a peculiar bunch of people. I don't think I ever met anyone, *Star Trek* fan or not, who wasn't peculiar. I mean, we're all peculiar, aren't we?"

A synonym for normal is average. Let's say you are going to make a documentary about *Baseball* (1994). Ken Burns didn't focus on average baseball players. He profiled many exceptional players, such as Ted Williams batting .400, or Joe DiMaggio achieving a fifty-six-game hitting streak. Find the most outstanding individuals who embody a subject. Colorful, engaging, dynamic, charismatic subjects make the final cut. Also, look for signs of obsession. Profilees who are extremely into something make good subjects.

Burns said he never asks what audiences want or pursues stories because the subjects are famous. "Most of the films we make are informed by bottom-up considerations. I want to know more about these people that we've never heard of that we discover while researching." Burns is looking for complexity in his characters, whether unknown or amazingly famous. "I have in my editing room, written in cursive, a small neon sign that says, 'It's complicated.' What's so interesting about those so-called amazing people is that, like Greek gods, they remind us that they're not perfect. They're heroes but in the classical sense. They are deeply flawed, and yet endure, like Ernest Hemingway, because who knew that a guy who advertised himself as a macho brawler, a man's man, had a gender fluidity that allowed him to put himself within the mindset of women."

Finding Ideas Is Like Falling in Love

I didn't see some topics coming until they hit me: *Star Trek* fans, aliens, existentialism, marriage. . . . Documentaries can blossom from questions and conversations you have with friends, through exorcising your own demons and obsessions, from reading the news, or wandering around the Internet.

I consider every lead seriously, no matter how ridiculous. One of the most memorable segments in *The Nature of Existence* was about the Ultimate Christian Wrestlers, and it came through a suggestion. Somebody sent me a link to the wrestlers' website as a joke, saying, "Hey, you should interview these guys."

I looked at the site and thought, *They're perfect!* I made arrangements with their leader, Rob Adonis. At the end of their wrestling show, the lights dimmed, Jesus appeared, and they presented a passion play in the wrestling ring. The wrestlers turned out to be super nice guys—when they weren't bashing heads.

Davis Guggenheim described how he finds ideas: "It's like falling in love. You don't know where or when it will happen. You put yourself out in the world, stay open, read and watch things until a great idea just appears." Guggenheim has a board on the wall where he writes words and phrases to inspire, describing what he wants in his next movie. When we spoke, the words he had up were: "surprising, adventurous, intimate audio, hybrid, not a cause film, not what you'd expect from me." He wrote the last one because he had been making a lot of issue-oriented films. Also on his board was "not with a famous person," but he ended up contradicting himself when he fell in love with Michael J. Fox's book, *No Time Like the Future: An Optimist Considers Mortality* (2020). He contacted Fox and developed the project, which became *Still: A Michael J. Fox Movie* (2023).

Marina Zenovich found a new project when she went to a retrospective screening of a French film called *Men, Women: A User's Manual* (1996), and the director, Claude Lelouch, said, "This film is dedicated to the star of the film, Bernard Tapie, who's in jail tonight." She thought, *Who is Bernard Tapie, and why is he in jail?* And from that moment, she became intrigued. "I had just finished my first film, and suddenly I had a lightbulb moment for the second. That was the beginning of my career as a documentarian, realizing you're always on the lookout for ideas. You have to be reading and seeking and trying to be inspired, looking for new characters and stories. That's the homework, but it's fun."

Maya Lin: A Strong Clear Vision (1995) originated when Freida Lee Mock read an article about Maya Lin, who was designing her second and final memorial, the Civil Rights Memorial (1989) in Montgomery, Alabama, commissioned by the Southern Poverty Law Center. Lin's first major project was the Vietnam Veterans Memorial (1982) in Washington, DC. As Mock was reading about Lin's Memorial design, she thought, "It would be interesting and dramatic to see in a film how an artist approached these big

Photograph by Adam Stoltman, courtesy of Sanders & Mock Productions.

Frieda Lee Mock, director of photography Eddie Marritz, associate producer and sound mixer Jessica Yu, Maya Lin, and Civil Rights Memorial granite fabrication foreman.

ideas about war and race in a three-dimensional form. Before filming and conceptualizing the aesthetic look of the film, I first researched as much as possible to understand the story and subject and to gain a big-picture idea of what the film might be."

When Mock wrote to Maya Lin about her interest in doing a film about her life and work, focusing on the intersection of art and politics, she was surprised how quickly Lin responded, "Yes. What do you have in mind?"

Mock didn't have a fully developed idea ready. "I knew I wanted to do the film, but I hadn't worked out the details."

She replied, "I need to do some reading and basic research."

Lightning struck again when Mock came across a blurb about a new book, *Tattoos of the Heart* (2011). "The words in the write-up were striking: gangs, unconditional love, Jesuit priest," Mock said. "Those five words were the spark for the film." The result was *G-Dog* (2012) about Father Greg Boyle, the charismatic founder of Homeboy Industries in Los Angeles, the world's largest gang intervention, rehab, and reentry program. "It's an amazing story about second chances for at-risk kids and young adults. I knew nothing about that place. It's unforgettable—you walk into Homeboy, and it's the most positive, beautiful, spirited place you have ever seen. I was lucky to stumble upon this story."

Ken Burns said, "Ideas choose me. An idea is just an idea. But when it drops down into your head, or your heart or gut, that's when you say, 'yes.'"

A friend of Burns once asked him, "Why don't you do something on country music?"

Burns replied, "Oh, what a good idea." He turned to his writing/producing partner Dayton Duncan and said, "Country music."

Duncan said simply, "Yes."

Burns said, "And like that, we were off and running on it a day later."

Burns recently finished *The American Buffalo* (2023), which he and his team had talked about for thirty years. "We had an extensive proposal from the mid-1990s that we came across in the files. Sometimes it takes that long to find where an idea will fit in. My interest in 'history' is the fact that the word is mostly made up of the word 'story.' I couldn't run out of topics in American history in a thousand years."

Do the Research

Once you are on the trail of an idea, the first step is research. It's more expensive to throw away a half-filmed documentary than an unfinished outline. Michael Tollin has produced dozens of documentaries, including *Hank Aaron: Chasing the Dream* (1995), *30 for 30* (2009–2010, 2012–2015), and *The Last Dance* (2020). Tollin still has two daily newspapers delivered to his door, *The New York Times* and *The Los Angeles Times*. He scours them every day for ideas. "I'm a big fan of research. If you're going to do ten episodes, ten hours on a subject, there's no excuse for leaving stones unturned." Every Monday morning, all fifteen Mandalay Sports Media employees meet. All are encouraged to pitch. "If you don't take advantage of your people as your greatest resource, you're missing the boat," Tollin said. "And I love when the great idea comes from the person in the first week of their internship. Our guy answering the phones, Henry, walked in two weeks ago with an idea and gave me a page full of notes. There's the research! And now we have a shopping agreement to push forward on the project." A shopping agreement is a contract giving the producer a period of time to exclusively pitch to buyers.

Michael Tollin at Mandalay Sports Media.

Tollin said he once went to a screening of Frederick Wiseman's film *Racetrack* (1985), and afterward, in the lobby, he approached the filmmaker and said, "Mr. Wiseman, I just wondered what went into this filmmaking because it felt like you went out to the racetrack and turned your camera on and shot wherever it happened to be pointed."

Wiseman laughed, looked around at his admirers, and said, "Son, let me tell you something about documentary filmmaking. You know how they say the three most important things in real estate are location, location, location? Well, in documentary filmmaking, the three most important things are research, research, research."

You need to have a thorough understanding of the topic before you sit across from interviewees. Before I start filming, I typically read a stack of books. I make a list of experts who could be potential interview subjects. As I learn more, I write questions, which form the backbone of interviews. The spine of the film is a progression of questions that are probed and answered within the context of the journey. In my outline, I summarize what I have learned from the reading as though I'm writing a dissertation—this becomes the first draft of a documentary script. The research process aims to find a new understanding toward answering a core question. The result is often unexpected, sometimes counterintuitive, and that's what makes the pursuit exciting.

The Three Rs

A process that evolved for me for finding interviewees is something I called "The Three Rs": research, referrals, and random chance. After I do the research and begin interviewing people, I ask them to refer others they think would be interesting. They often know people involved in their field. If you make the interview enjoyable, they are often ready to offer up their contacts. And then it helps to be able to drop their name when contacting subsequent referrals. Julia Sweeney is a brilliant comedian/monologist of works such as *God Said, 'Ha!'* (1998). When I interviewed her for *The Nature of Existence*, she said, "In my search for God I kept doing what everyone does, which is to have a very narrow definition of God. And then as they look for evidence and don't find it, they keep broadening the definition of God until it becomes 'God is air,' or 'God is a life force.'"

As I was packing up my gear, I asked who else she might recommend. Sweeney said, "I was recently at a convention in Iceland with Richard Dawkins. You must talk to him. He would be perfect."

Richard Dawkins is an evolutionary biologist, famous for his criticism of creationism and intelligent design. I read Dawkins's book *The Selfish Gene* (1976) and noticed that the inner cover read, "Richard Dawkins is the Charles Simonyi Professor for the Public Understanding of Science at Oxford University."

I called the school's main phone number and a woman answered: "Oxford University."

I said, "Richard Dawkins, please."

"One moment."

The phone rang and then a man answered, "Hello?"

I stammered, "Uh, hi, I'm looking for Richard Dawkins."

"This is he."

Oh crap, I've got Richard Dawkins on the line! I thought, at best, I would get an assistant's voicemail. I launched into my pitch. I didn't sense overwhelming interest until I said, "I just interviewed Julia Sweeney, and she said I absolutely must talk to you."

Mentioning Sweeney brightened him up. "Well, what day were you thinking?"

I randomly picked a date three weeks hence, and he agreed. Then I had to plan a trip to England.

The third R is random chance. While shooting *Trekkies*, we would often show up at conventions and see who we bumped into. I never turn down an opportunity to interview somebody. You never know what you will get. Prejudging people or rejecting opportunities deprives you of wonderful surprises. Of course, many interviews don't gel, or they fail to provide anything useful, but any interview could even lead to an idea for a whole new project.

The documentary script is a living, changing document. As you collect test interviews and scenes, you will know if you are onto something. You will feel the energy during an interview or an event when it clicks. Freida Lee Mock said, "Be open and ready for happenstance, unexpected moments while filming. You have to enjoy the unknown if you do vérité filmmaking. It's like an emergency medical doctor trained and ready for what happens in the ER on a Saturday night."

Sometimes a project will not pan out, and you have to abandon it. There is always risk in putting a lot of time, effort, and heart into something you realize you're not going to be able to bring to fruition. Rachel Grady lamented, "Sometimes that means no one will ever know about this important story. A light will be dimmed and go out and die. That's very upsetting and frustrating." But when a documentary works, it takes you on a journey where a story continually evolves until you arrive. The process is exhilarating.

CHAPTER THREE

Production

The production process is brutal, but that's part of the attraction.

W hy do you need to make a documentary? What's inside that drives you? Do you have a grievance that you want to express? An inspired concept with an unassailable conclusion? An injustice to investigate? Filmmaker Rachel Grady described making documentaries as "the least efficient way to make a living. Even things you think will be easy, they're never easy. Thousands of hours go into a two-hour film. It's a major commitment." A documentary gets made because you have a story that *must* be told. That's the engine that gets you to the finish line when a production takes two or five or ten years or longer.

You may have to brave difficult circumstances: rain, cold, heat, dust, bugs. It seems like practically all of India is a holy site where shoes must be removed. Bring flip-flops. When I filmed one of Sri Sri Ravi Shankar's massive outdoor events, I was shoeless because the dirt field they set up in became a holy site. His meditation seminars are like a U2 concert, huge and exciting. To get the footage, I ran all over the field in my socks, breathing dust and stepping on rocks in the dark. Even when you stub your toe on hallowed ground, it doesn't hurt any less. In the raw footage, you hear me cursing in the background at this spiritual event.

Triple-Check Everything

When you start making your own films, you will probably have to do most every job. And that's good because you need to learn to write, shoot, light, edit, make props, manage people, and do whatever it takes. The deepest learning experiences happen when everything goes wrong. That's why you should make that short film before taking on the big project, or you'll be making first-time mistakes on the bigger-budget film.

Double- and triple-check everything. I made a mistake on *Trekkies* when I didn't double-confirm a van rental. I had everybody waiting for me to figure out where to get another van. Another time I assumed I had packed my camera batteries after charging. When I landed in Missouri, I realized the batteries were still home on the floor. I called every store within fifty miles on a Sunday looking for replacements.

Making it to post-production is the goal. You think, *I'm safe now!* But disasters happen there as well. Marina Zenovich's documentary *Roman Polanski: Odd Man Out* (2012) was an international production. Roman Polanski lived in France, but he was filming in Germany, and he was arrested in Switzerland. She was at the film's premiere at the Zurich Film Festival. Early in the film, there's a shot of a city that says, "Berlin, Germany." The audience burst out laughing.

Zenovich turned to her Swiss friend and asked, "Why are they laughing?"

He said, "That's not Berlin. That's Zurich." Zenovich was mortified.

Jim Abrams and the Zucker Brothers made this same mistake on purpose in *The Kentucky Fried Movie* (1977); the opening shot of their kung-fu parody "A Fistful of Yen" is of Manhattan, but the subtitle says Hong Kong. Once back home, Zenovich realized there was nothing left in the budget to make the fix, so she wrote to executive producer Steven Soderbergh: "We need $5,000 to fix this. Is there any way you could pay for it?"

Soderbergh responded, "I only pay for my own mistakes. This is on you—you're going to have to figure it out."

Zenovich acknowledged, "Why should he pay for that? We messed up. The shot was mislabeled and somehow made it into the final version. Ever since that day, I've been hypervigilant about lower thirds (the subtitles that identify each person or place). Always triple-check everything."

Which Format?

A good format recipe for a documentary might be 16×9, 4K (or 6K, or 8K), 24fps, 4:2:2 (or 4:4:4), 10-bit video, 48 kHz, 24-bit audio (or 32-bit float).

If numbers and technical jargon make your head spin, don't puke on my book; we'll get through this. I'll keep this section short. A detailed list of format options and explanations of technical terms are in Appendix B: Format Definitions. If that sort of geek porn is your favorite part of the book, you may be one of those "exceptional" people I love to interview.

To decide which camera to buy and which settings to use, recognize that "format" includes many things: aspect ratio, frame rate, resolution, color sampling, bit depth, codecs, sound options, and various technical standards. Summarizing preferred formats is like trying to hit a moving target and would probably be obsolete ten minutes after I write them down. The unchanging directive is this: *choose the highest-quality format you can afford or have available to you at the time.* And get your hands on a sample of any distributor's delivery-specifications sheet that lists their format requirements before you begin, to ensure you will be able to output acceptable masters. A filmmaker has three basic aspect-ratio choices: 16×9, 4×3, or widescreen. If you plan to utilize a framing other than 16×9, be aware that some distributors and streamers have restrictions.

Graphic by Gabriel Koerner.

Four aspect ratios compared: 1.78 (16×9), 1.33 (4×3), 1.85 (37×20), 2.39 (12×5).

The higher the quality of video and audio collected and ingested into the editing process, the higher the quality the final product can attain. Anything lower than 4:2:2 10-bit video would probably get kicked back by a distributor's or exhibitor's QC (quality control) check. Shooting in a higher quality format future-proofs your work. 4K (or higher), flat (RAW or Log), with no LUT applied will provide flexibility in reframing and coloring down the road. Final masters are usually finished in both 4K and HD 16×9 using Rec.709 and delivered in Apple ProRes. Shooting in lower formats is occasionally necessary (or it may be all that is available for a crucial piece of stock footage), and then it is upscaled to match the specifications of the rest of the project.

Before shooting, consult with your editor, post-production supervisor, director of photography, and/or distributor so that everybody is on the same page. Distributor spec sheets list preferred frame rates, resolution, color space, audio, track configurations, how to name your files, and required paperwork. When you shoot in the highest quality possible (i.e., the least-compressed codec available from your camera), calculate your data rate so you won't run out of hard-drive storage or SD (secure digital) card space. Be sure that your editing system's hard-drive storage and camera's SD cards are large enough to accommodate your preferences. Having to stop filming to download a camera's memory cards wastes valuable shoot time.

The bottom line is this: distributors care about format, but audiences don't. For a viewer, it's all about content. You might use a five-year-old camera with an older codec, but if your story is compelling, you will sell the film. If you use the latest top-of-the-line technology, yet the story is not engaging, it's a harder sell. Audiences watch and recommend movies based on how they make them feel, not choice of camera.

Delivery Masters

ProRes is often chosen as a final delivery format (ProRes 4444 XQ, ProRes 4444, or ProRes 422 HQ). Avid DNxHD 10bit 220/185/175 is also used. H.264 is a compressed delivery format utilized for uploading to online sites like YouTube or Vimeo. You can downconvert to H.264 from a higher-resolution ProRes master. As part of your delivery materials, gather items such as transcript, subtitling files, music cue sheet, artwork, photos, press materials, release forms, all contracts, and so on. At the top of that list will be a film's preferred delivery format specifications. Your feature and trailer will both need to meet the distributor's standards, so do not ignore the technical options at the beginning. Okay, the grueling technical part is over. Take a breath.

Crew

On *Trekkies* and *Six Days in Roswell*, I traveled with a crew of six: director, producer, camera, sound, host, and assistant. As you add more cameras, the crew grows. If you are working with big-name talent, they might feel something's not right if the crew is too small. But the advantage of a small team is you can move quickly, stay under the radar, and adapt to changing opportunities. Frederick Wiseman records his own sound and works with only one cameraperson and one assistant. Many times, I handled all six crew positions shooting solo. I have to be super organized while multi-tasking: simultaneously framing the shot, setting focus and exposure, riding sound levels, asking questions, collecting release signatures, and managing digital media. When I'm doing it all, it's easy to make mistakes, like overmodulating an audio level, forgetting to turn off the autofocus, or not adjusting the exposure when lighting changes. Make checklists. The FAA requires pilots to use written pre-flight checklists because accidents happen when they don't. Practice at home with your equipment—ideally before every shoot. That way, you can concentrate on the shoot without fumbling for buttons and menus in front of your subjects.

Even when I have a director of photography (and sometimes multiple camera operators), I often operate one camera myself. Even though a sound recordist collects isolated sound from all the subjects, each camera also records onboard sound from a mounted shotgun mic. This not only serves as a backup track, but it also helps make it easier to sync the video with the hero (best quality) sound recordings. While the director is focusing on setting up the shot, the producer and assistant make sure paperwork is signed, or they track down a neighbor who is using a hammer, or a gardener with a leaf blower, to ask them to hold off until after the shoot. Sometimes that means twenty bucks and a smile. One time during shooting on my film

Suckers (2001), we had to designate a "cricket wrangler." We learned that if we banged on a wall just right, this shrill, elusive cricket would stop chirping for just long enough to get the shot.

Camera Equipment

Use the best cameras you can get your hands on. You don't need expensive equipment. You can shoot on your iPhone in a pinch. Or you can use the latest, expensive, full-frame XDCAM. Just make sure you will be able to finish in a format acceptable to distributors.

Some cameras, such as DSLRs (digital single-lens reflex cameras) and mirrorless cameras, allow you to change lenses. Many video cameras come with only one zoom lens attached. A zoom lens provides versatility in a fast-moving documentary environment. The downside is that the image may not be as crisp as a removable prime lens, but the lens clarity difference is nominal. Being nimble and versatile is the key. I opt for the convenience of a zoom lens for documentary shoots.

My typical equipment package is three video cameras (one is usually a GoPro). If one camera fails, I have redundancy. If you have a camera dolly, add movement. A cheap way is to use a slider, which allows for a limited range of movement. I have also seen filmmakers set a camera on a toy trolly and slowly move it across a table or the floor. Use the zoom to reframe when needed but avoid continual zooming. Occasionally, when you feel a big moment coming, a slow zoom accentuates the drama. I sometimes shoot interviews hand-held, allowing flexibility to adjust a shot at any time or to add movement. However, I opt for a tripod whenever possible because hand-held bumps can ruin a shot. Shaking increases as your arms get tired. As your mother always said, "Don't be a big shot; use a tripod."

Sound Equipment

Spend money on good microphones. They don't have to be the best, but they have to be quality. Boomy sound is like overcooked pasta—a sure sign of an amateur. It is the audio equivalent of an image being out of focus.

Don't rely on the camera's built-in mic. Buy a decent shotgun mic, attach it to the camera mount, and use it to override the built-in mic. The longer the mic, the longer the interference tube, which is designed to cancel out unwanted sound. Also, the longer the mic, the more accurate the direction must be. Rode or Deity make good entry-level products. The shotgun can provide excellent sound when you are on the move or near a subject. For interviews, you need at least two good-quality, wireless lavalier microphones. If you have three or more simultaneous subjects, you will need more mics and a portable location mixer. For wireless radio mics, I use a typical ENG kit (electronic news gathering), like the Sennheiser EW wireless system. These kits come with low-quality mics, so I upgrade to Tram TR50 lavalier microphones. Sometimes, I also bring cabling to be able to hardwire mics in case of frequency interference or a radio mic failure.

Get familiar with what works and what doesn't before you get there. Watch tutorials. Practice placing a mic well, to avoid wind noise and clothes rustling. Attach the mic as close to the subject's mouth as possible. Men with long beards can cause scratchy sound if a beard rubs against the mic. Attach the mic securely so it doesn't come loose during the interview and fall out of the usable pick-up zone. Use fresh batteries and monitor the quality as you shoot.

Wireless mics use specifically allowed frequencies. Radio frequency interference is common in densely populated areas and sports arenas. There's a person at every stadium assigning wireless microphone channels. It looks like an auction where people are screaming, desperately trying to get channels. These folks are like door bouncers, and a $100 slipped in a handshake sometimes gets you into the dance club faster.

Planning Ahead

Try to anticipate anything that could go wrong. If you have sufficient budget, bring backup equipment, extra mics, ample SD cards, duplicates of every cable, replacement bulbs, and extra batteries. For a mega-budget shoot where you are interviewing big-name talent, bring a generator. If you only have Michael Jordan for one day, you don't want to lose the opportunity due to an unexpected power outage.

How you back up footage can be crucial. If possible, get data off the cards onto a hard drive before you leave the location. And then copy the data again, twice. Use a program dedicated to backing up, one that checks for missing or corrupt files, such as Hedge or ShotPut Pro. Have an excessively organized system for downloading and transferring. You will invariably shoot with SD cards out of order, and mistakes happen. Don't put all sets of backup drives in the same bag. Store the duplicate drives in different locations, just in case you get burglarized, the office burns down, or there's a flood. When I was cutting *Trekkies 2*, the insurance company's completion bond (a guarantee that we would deliver the movie on budget and by a specific date) required us to store source material off-site in a protected vault.

Lighting Equipment

When I was on a panel with documentarian Will Gazecki, he said when they started shooting *Waco: The Rules of Engagement* (1997), there were so many television cameras covering the event it seemed like there was no way their project could stand out from the crowd, "Until I realized we should do it on film. Then it becomes cinema, it becomes a piece of art." For Gazecki, shooting on film wasn't meant literally; it was more about how to approach a subject.

If you want a documentary to appear cinematic and beautiful, light it like a movie, which takes time and resources. Many documentaries are shot quickly, under harsh conditions, and lighting suffers. A "television look" comes from a uniform overall lighting scheme that allows quick shooting from any direction. It looks flat because contrast is reduced. Cinematic lighting embraces contrast, creates moody dark areas, has perfectly exposed highlights, and there is camera movement.

An inexpensive way to capture beautiful footage is to use sunlight. Natural sunlight used well makes people look their best. When indoors, my go-to staging is to sit an interviewee near a window and let ambient sunlight hit them from the side. This lateral key light creates strong highlights and shadows. If needed, I use a bounce card to fill in shadows. This natural lighting also offers a low-pressure environment for people to feel comfortable.

Frederick Wiseman rarely lights a scene, only doing so when it's too dark to shoot. Usually, that means swapping higher-wattage lightbulbs in the existing lamps. Most of the time, on a guerrilla shoot, I use no additional lights because they add one suitcase too many. Occasionally, I've had to make an exception. When I interviewed Peter Gilmore, leader of the Satanists, he preferred to stay in his dark Satanic chamber. When I do travel with a small lighting package, it consists of three lights: a soft key light to use from one side, a softer fill to use from the other side, and sometimes an accent to hit from above and behind to separate them from the background. Or I use the third light to give the background an accent. On *Trekkies*, director of photography Harris Done added primary colors to the background with a gel (in a nod to the vivid color schemes used on the original *Star Trek*). On *Trekkies 2*, director of photography David Doyle used a fourth light, a soft China ball that he placed low, or on the ground, which gently filled in wrinkles and added a subtle twinkle in the subjects' eyes, livening them. Whether you travel with a single soft light or a large kit, develop a style and stick with it so that it's one less thing to think about on shoot day.

Visual Style

Low-budget documentaries sometimes leave visual style to chance, merely recording whatever they encounter. An artist considers every aspect of a frame and plans all the design elements. Freida Lee Mock has found that limited funds help shape the production by forcing her to plan as much as possible. Mock prefers not "hosing down a scene," which is easy with video. "I started filmmaking using 16mm film," she said, "where one ten-minute reel was costly on a limited budget. I occasionally found myself with one roll to capture a sequence. Figuring out how to get everything you need in a scene from ten minutes of film is a great exercise because you work back from that. I still try to use that discipline when shooting digitally, as I prefer not facing hundreds of hours of dailies."

There's a scene in *Maya Lin: A Strong Clear Vision* (1995) where Lin was designing her first house in Williamstown, Massachusetts. "We captured the story with limited film stock," she said. "And it's a favorite scene. How long can a scene last? Ten minutes of putting a roof on a house can be

Three images from Maya Lin: A Strong Clear Vision *(1995).*

boring. It may be ten seconds in the final cut—but you want it to be a brilliant ten seconds." Mock framed her shot with a close-up of Lin walking across a white expanse to reveal the undulating shape of the roof against the background of the mountain. "The design of the roof is exactly the shape of the mountain. It moves like a wave. It says a lot about how Maya the artist designs with reference to surrounding landscapes and natural forms. If you look at the Vietnam Memorial, you can see that same aesthetic at work."

Shaunak Sen began filming *All That Breathes* (2022) in a rough, hand-held style. Halfway into the three-year project, he realized that "the characters themselves were contemplative and meditative, and the film had to have a form that allowed you to contemplate things and think about things. Plus, it had to be beautiful." To give the film a smoother, more fluid look, Sen threw out eighteen months' worth of filming, brought in a tripod, and started over.[1] Imagine, if he had just read my book, the way you are right now, it could have saved him a year and a half of anguish.

Errol Morris admits he never wanted to be a documentarian. "I wanted to be a filmmaker. Documentaries were one vehicle to that end. I was interested in drama." When asked about his style as a documentarian, he said, "It's hard to know what style comes out of, but I had an enormous love of Poverty Row film noir. Still do." Poverty Row refers to Hollywood films produced by B-movie studios during the 1920s to the 1950s. Morris added, "I was asked by *The New York Times* why *Citizen Kane* was the greatest film ever made, and I said, 'Well, that's easy. It isn't.' And they asked, 'Well, what is?' I suggested Edgar Ulmer's *Detour* (1945)."

Film noire lighting of actor Tom Neal in Detour *(1945).*

Re-enactments

After completing his first film, *Gates of Heaven* (1978), Morris survived by working as a private detective, which is how he saved money to make his next film, *Vernon, Florida* (1981) (along with support from the Public Broadcasting Laboratory, who he said, "had very little understanding of me or the film"). After that project, Morris was still out of work. "No one wanted to hire me to do anything. My films were not a calling card. Documentary was not terribly popular." Morris often jokingly quotes a line from *Conan the Barbarian* (1982) where the Black Lotus Street Peddler says, "It used to be just another snake cult. Now they're everywhere." Today, as documentaries have become pervasive, they have also become more formulaic and predictable. "When I came of age as a filmmaker," Morris said, "the opportunities to do things that were stranger and less standard was much greater."

In 1985, Morris finally raised enough money to travel to Dallas to interview psychiatrist Dr. James Grigson, who played a role in capital murder trials. Grigson would testify and make predictions that an accused murderer would, in all probability, kill again in the future, in which case the death penalty could be imposed. Grigson suggested Morris interview the people he had helped sentence to death. One of those convicted killers was Randall Dale Adams, on death row for the murder of Dallas police officer Robert Wood. As Morris was sitting in a basement library in Austin, Texas, reading the transcript of Adams's murder trial, he began to realize something was wrong with the story, and he became curious as to whether Adams was innocent. "As I was reading, Adams kept talking repeatedly about 'the kid, the kid, the kid.' It became clear the kid was David Ray Harris. And it also became clear that if I were to tell the story, I needed to find the kid. I recalled this Robert Mitchum film noir movie, *Out of the Past* (1947), where Mitchum's character says, 'All I can see is the frame. I'm going in there now to look at the picture.' And that was certainly true of this case. What role had the kid played?"

Errol Morris filmed highly stylized re-enactments in The Thin Blue Line *(1988).*

Morris's focus switched from making a film about Dr. Grigson to investigating Adams's story. Morris's varied interests in peculiar people, murderers, crime, investigation, literature, drama, and film noir coalesced into a style birthed in *The Thin Blue Line* (1988). Morris broke the rules, and by doing so, he established new ones. The film is cinematic and highly stylized, with slow-motion re-enactments. Working with visual artist and production designer Ted Bafaloukos, Morris created storyboards depicting precisely what he wanted. Morris said, "The question is, was there one person or two in the car when it was stopped by this pair of Dallas police officers, Teresa Turco and Robert Wood? You could abstract it in various different ways."

Rashomon (1950) is a film by Akira Kurosawa that portrays a rape and murder as told by four witnesses, who each tell conflicting stories of what happened. Morris said, "Was I influenced by *Rashomon*? Probably. I certainly had seen it. I love Kurosawa." In 2008, Morris analyzed the elasticity of memory in an essay about *Rashomon* in *The New York Times*.

> We remember selectively, just as we perceive selectively. We have to go back over perceived and remembered events, in order to figure

out what happened, what really happened. . . . The brain is not a Reality-Recorder. There is no perfect replica of reality inside our brains. The brain elides, confabulates, conflates, denies, suppresses, evades, confuses and distorts. It has its own agenda and can even work at cross-purposes with our conscious selves.[2]

Morris allowed that various contradictory accounts can provide clues as to which is the truthful account. "Sometimes you read about *Rashomon* as if it's an essay on the subjectivity of truth, which is something that I do not believe and find abhorrent. There is one truth, and we may not be able to find it, but we pursue it. And in the case of *The Thin Blue Line*, there was a clear, powerful truth that emerged." Morris pursued the truth. The story told in court to convict Adams was false. Morris has also warned that a re-enactment must be presented as such: "If someone presents a scene as a real event, and it has been produced after the fact, it's a re-enactment that's a deceptive practice. It's a false claim. It's a lie."[3]

Set Design

With documentary shoots, you usually have to work creatively with whatever you find in front of you when you get to the location Vérité and low-budget films have to get creative with what they encounter in the real world. Look for backgrounds that enhance the story or give perspective about the subject. Move distracting objects out of the shot and feature important objects in the foreground.

When producer Thomas Tull told Davis Guggenheim, "I want to do a movie about the electric guitar," it was Guggenheim's idea to bring Jack White, The Edge, and Jimmy Page together to tell the story through their eyes in *It Might Get Loud* (2008). In a movie where Guggenheim had rock stars sitting together and sharing their experiences as artists, he said, "A question you ask all the time is, how much do you affect how something looks? I had to pick the color and the lighting to make the scene look authentic and real, but also beautiful and sort of hip because these guys were cool. So it's case by case. You never want to go too far to make the viewer think, *Hey, why are they doing that?* Or, *That's not what these characters would do.*"

Guitarists Jack White, Jimmy Page, and The Edge in It Might Get Loud *(2008).*

A common fallback position has become to shoot everybody in front of a green screen and decide later about backgrounds. For high-budget shows, sometimes sets are built and backdrops are carried with the equipment package, or locations are heavily art-directed.

Travel

After post-production costs, travel is often my most significant expense. One way I funded travel for *The Nature of Existence* was to piggyback on other travel. When I was invited to screen *Trekkies 2* at a *Star Trek* convention in Israel, I put local resources to work. When I was ushered on stage for an introduction, I said, "Hi, everybody. I'm starting my new documentary, and I need a Rabbi!" They found a Rabbi in Jerusalem for me to interview, and I was off and running.

One key to getting great footage is to hire a local guide who can translate and keep you out of trouble. Hiring a driver with his own car is relatively inexpensive in many countries. Tip well, and turn the guide into your pal. That motivates them to locate whatever you need. When I wanted to interview a Sikh scholar in India (he told me, "Sikh means student, learner or disciple. Therefore, everyone is a Sikh."), or the twenty-fourth-generation Taoist Master at Mount Tai in China ("Tao is the source of everything."), my guides found them and made introductions—plus they got the release signed.

Journeying around the world, I always travel respectfully and keep a low profile. I have heard of more than one case of drunk, loud tourists creating a scene and getting arrested. I don't complain or behave obnoxiously. I learn basic words of the local language, smile, and thank and compliment everyone.

Be alert for camera-gear thieves. When I was in Rome, stopping between the train station and a taxi stand to make a phone call, somebody walked off with my pelican case. The lesson I learned was to put cameras in nondescript cases or a backpack that does not advertise as "expensive camera." When I was in a taxi in Rio de Janeiro and I had a camera on my lap, I opened the window. The driver rolled the window back up and said, "They'll reach right in and take that out of your hands."

Get up to date on vaccinations more than a month before you travel because becoming fully effective may take several weeks (or months with vaccines requiring multiple shots). The last thing you want is a debilitating bout of typhoid when you are out in the middle of nowhere. Check with the CDC website for current recommendations and requirements for areas you will visit. Definitely consider vaccines that you are not current on:

tetanus booster (every ten years), typhoid (you get five years with the tablets versus only two years with the injected version), hepatitis A and B, a polio booster, meningococcal vaccine, mpox (essentially a smallpox vaccine), the measles/mumps/rubella update, and the latest flu and COVID-19 updates. Some areas require yellow fever or Japanese encephalitis shots. Malaria tablets are a consideration for some tropical regions. Look into a shingles vaccine for those over fifty, as the stress of travel can awaken a dormant varicella-zoster (chickenpox) virus. Pharmacies have many of these vaccines in stock. Costco is often the cheapest. You may have to go to a travel-specific clinic or hospital for less-common vaccines like typhoid, Japanese encephalitis, and yellow fever. I sometimes bring probiotics or Travelan to help prevent traveler's diarrhea. If you're not sure about the water, pick up a filtered water bottle, such as Grayl, Astrea, or Sawyer, which can remove bacteria, viruses, and contaminants.

Bring currency to exchange for local cash, but make sure the bills are clean and the most recent dates available, with no creases, folds, smudges, or markings. Exchanges pay less for, or balk entirely at, older, defaced, or wrinkled bills. Shop around for the best exchange rates. Airports give the worst prices. You get a reasonably accurate rate from ATMs when you withdraw local money with your bank card, but they charge a fee (around five dollars) for each transaction. Never use a debit card with a pin to make a purchase because if the card and pin are stolen, it allows access to your bank. It's much harder to get money back that has been drained from your account than from fraudulent credit card purchases—you haven't paid for those yet, and credit card companies don't hold you responsible for purchases made after you report a card lost or stolen.

Make a color scan (back and front) of credit cards, travel documents, passport, and visa. Keep multiple copies of the scans separate. If you lose your wallet, the number or website to cancel credit cards is on the back. Print out color copies of your passport to carry in your wallet for when hotels ask for your passport; they are okay with a copy. Aside from when I'm at customs, I never let my original passport out of my hands. Check to be sure your passport is not within six months of expiration, or you may be prevented from traveling.

Hotels have more accountability than private rentals found at Vrbo.com, homestay.com, booking.com, or airbnb.com. However, I have found some of the most unique places by booking private rentals, like a treehouse in Bali or a penthouse in Paris. I often use booking sites to research prices and read reviews, such as agoda.com, hotels.com, hotelscombined.com, Google .com/travel/hotels, or tripadviser.com. Whenever possible, once I select a hotel, I book directly with the hotel's own website. It's sometimes better to eliminate the middleman, who takes a commission, and it's easier to make changes or get refunds from the hotel. Once I arrive, I make friends with the manager and ask directly about a discount if I were to extend my stay.

Before you unpack your bags, examine your hotel room to make sure everything is acceptable, in case you decide to switch. Keep your suitcases off the floor and the beds; use a suitcase stand, or if there's a bathtub, set the bags inside—to avoid hitchhiking bugs. Check bed corners and headboards. If you find bugs, change rooms. In all my years of traveling, at hundreds of locations, I have encountered bedbugs three times. They exist but are less common than you might think. No need to be paranoid.

Before departure, photograph each suitcase (exterior and interior contents) in case you have to describe it when lost. Create a detailed list of what is in each bag (with serial numbers to provide to police or an insurance company). Put your name, address, email, and phone number inside the bags as well as on indestructible tags. Slip in a baggage tracking device, such as Tile or Apple AirTag. Zip-tie luggage closed before you hand it over at the airline counter and pack a nail clipper (no scissors allowed) in an accessible pocket to cut zip ties upon arrival. Bring extra zip ties for each travel leg. Pack camera cards and a set of backup drives in your carry-on. When airlines made me check a camera case, I sometimes took the camera out and carried it by hand, along with a battery. So, in a pinch, with a luggage mishap, I'd be immediately ready to shoot when I got to the other side.

For international travel with a lot of equipment, apply online for a merchandise passport, called a Carnet (pronounced kar-nay). Get it stamped in customs each time you enter or exit a country. Where they have strict import/export laws, this helps avoid paying duties on your equipment. Also, use your list to pack bags exactly the same each time, so the weight doesn't change. That way, you won't have to scramble at the airport, moving things around. For the region you will visit, download a language translation application and activate that country's local taxi and transport services in addition to Uber and Lyft, such as Grab, Gojek, or DiDi.

Look into travel insurance, medical for yourself as well as loss and damage for equipment. Check which of your credit cards automatically provides insurance (e.g., when the entire airfare is charged to the card) and what it covers (medical, dental, prescription, transportation, legal, etc.). Be prepared in case you find yourself in a situation where you need medical transport out of there.

Permission

When shooting in most film-savvy cities, film permits are required if filming within the city's jurisdiction (both public and private property), particularly if it is for anything intended for profit. Permits are a source of income for a city. Most of the time, I have shot documentaries guerrilla-style. If police or security show up, it's time to apologize profusely, pack up, and leave with the footage. If it's a one-of-a-kind opportunity, an expensive talent, or a time-sensitive window, get the permit; don't take a chance on getting shut down before you're done.

When Davis Guggenheim was filming *An Inconvenient Truth* (2006), he wanted to capture Al Gore going through the TSA security process. When he asked for permission, he was told, "Absolutely not. You are not allowed to film the TSA. We can't reveal our methods and practices." So Guggenheim put a camera in his backpack and timed it so that he was five minutes ahead of Gore. Then he sat and waited with his camera and filmed Gore going through security. He recalled, "No one stopped me. And a lot of people talk about this moment in the film. When people watched the movie, the reaction was, 'He was vice president. I can't believe he goes through security!'"

On that same trip to Beijing, after Guggenheim filmed Gore on the airplane working on his slide show, Guggenheim handed his bag to producer Lesley Chilcott and filmed Gore getting off the aircraft. He described what happened next.

The moment Al Gore passes through a TSA metal detector in An Inconvenient Truth *(2006).*

Al went all the way through customs and out onto the street with me following. And he got in the car, and they drove away. I stopped filming and put the camera down. I realized I was outside without my passport and customs approval. (He laughs.) I was panicked. Customs is not designed to go backward, and no one spoke English. I kept saying, "No, my backpack is *inside*. My passport is *inside*." I thought I was going to go to a Chinese jail. Finally, Lesley Chilcott came out, and she had my passport. It took me an hour and a half to find a way back through. It was terrifying to be on the street in Beijing without a wallet or a passport, holding a camera, in a surveillance state.

It's always best to get permission before surprising somebody, but sometimes just showing up works. Michael Moore is famous for walking into corporate headquarters and asking to see the boss. And then he films them kicking him out. One of my goals for *The Nature of Existence* was to interview physicist Stephen Hawking, probably the most famous living scientist at the time. The best I could get was a nebulous "Maybe" from one of his assistants who answered Hawking's email. Since I had reason to be in England for my appointment with Richard Dawkins, I gambled and showed up in Cambridge, in the lobby of the Centre for Mathematical Sciences.

I called the assistant. "We're here."

He said, "Where?"

"Downstairs."

"What? Wait."

A few minutes later, we were greeted by somebody else, Judith Croasdell, Hawking's enforcer and long-time personal assistant, an English woman in her late fifties, who was all business.

She said, "You can't just turn up."

I said, "I'm so sorry, there must have been a misunderstanding. Do you think it would be possible, since we are here, to ask Professor Hawking a few questions."

Her brow furrowed as she grumbled, "Hmm." She took my questions about the origin of the universe upstairs. When she returned, she said, "I ran your questions by Stephen. He thought about it. He started going through the answers, and said the main answer is an explanation of the 'anthropic principle.' But then he decided not to do the interview."

The anthropic principle, first proposed in 1957 by astronomer Robert Dicke and further developed in 1973 by physicist Brandon Carter, says, of course, our universe has the conditions that are perfect for the existence of life, otherwise, we wouldn't be here to observe them. Or, in other words, consciousness is a natural outcome of the presence of the type of matter that exists in our universe—which may be one of an infinite variety of universes, each with a different set of physical laws.

I asked, "Why doesn't he want to do the interview?"

Stephen had said, "I'm tired of the God question."

I guess he got that question a lot.

Media versus Tourist

In some countries, such as China, India, or Cuba, if you travel on a media visa, they may require you to hire a government minder, a censor who is supposed to make sure you don't disparage their country. I have gotten around that by traveling with a tourist visa. That is much harder to do with a crew of six and many bags of equipment. A full-sized professional crew from a big network has to get clearance. Sometimes, there's no way around that. To pull off the tourist gambit, you have to look the part. You and your equipment can't appear too sophisticated. And if you do come in with a larger crew, don't bunch up together. Spread out and look like single, average travelers. Nevertheless, you have to be careful. If you pull out a large camera, you become a focus of attention. Sometimes, a small, high-quality, mirrorless camera such as a Sony A7S can be discreet enough. But getting good sound could require a separate recording unit.

I was surprised that once my co-producer/composer Billy Sullivan and I got into China, nobody questioned our right to be there, tried to stop us, or refused to answer questions. Ironically, we were hassled most in the United States and the United Kingdom, where we constantly heard, "Hey, you can't shoot here!" I attributed it to the increasing prevalence at the time of reality shows in the West; people were more on guard and aware of potential humiliation caused by cameras.

When I went through Heathrow Airport, I suggested we get shots of me going through the airport. My camera operator was shooting on a moving walkway, approaching the customs area, with a gorgeous sunset behind me. We weren't obvious, but if you have your camera in your hands near customs, they get all panicky. The British customs agents grabbed us. They looked through our bags, found notes from previous interviews, and hit us with hard questions: "Who's the Rabbi?!"

Composer/producer/camera operator Billy Sullivan with Chinese guards, outside the Confucious Mansion in Qufu, China, while filming The Nature of Existence *(2010).*

They were playing good cop, bad cop. One of the agents would walk out, and the other would sit down and casually ask, "So, now that he's gone, tell me about the Rabbi. And why do you have a map of Princeton University?" We were glad rubber gloves never came into the mix. Eventually, they realized we were no threat and sent us on our way, but not until they made us erase the incriminating pretty sunset.

If you plan on filming at landmarks, getting clearance can be difficult because they want to monetize the sites, and if they think you are a professional or a news organization with deep pockets, they will tap you for big money. At Stonehenge, the English Heritage commission wanted $2,000 to allow us in for two hours before they opened for tourists. I said we'd get back to them. Then we went in as tourists for $10. Similarly, the Taj Mahal wouldn't let me bring in a camera or microphone that looked professional. I had to take the camera apart to make it look smaller and smuggle a good microphone in my underwear and the cables in my socks. Travel light, be brave, and get what you need.

CHAPTER FOUR

Interviewing

Interviews are the main ingredient in the documentary recipe.

Your interview questions are as important as the outline. They mirror and support each other. For *The Nature of Existence*, I wrote the toughest questions I could think of and tested them on friends, often without their permission. Some questions blossomed, such as, "What is our purpose?" Everybody likes to chew on that one. Other questions fell away when answers were generic or similar. For example, questions about the importance of religion have been debated to death. We all know about the good of charity work and the evil caused by the Inquisition. Documentarians need to break new ground. The following principles apply to most any interview situation, including news features, and podcasts, as well as documentaries.

The Face of the Film

How will you present the story? Will one person be guiding the audience? A main protagonist? A narrator? Will it be you? Nobody? Maybe a series of graphics? Perhaps the interviewees will tell the story, their sound bites handing off the narrative baton to each other. To facilitate that, it helps to ask every interviewee the same core questions so you can intercut answers about the same idea or event, as told by multiple individuals. In *Wild Wild Country* (2018), several witnesses tell the story of Indian cult leader Bhagwan Shree Rajneesh (a.k.a. Osho).

One of the narrators in Wild Wild Country *(2018) is Jane Stork, former follower of controversial Indian guru Rajneesh.*

In *Trekkies*, the guide is Denise Crosby, who was part of the *Star Trek* world. Even though I also conducted interviews, the viewer feels Crosby is the guiding presence throughout once that paradigm is set from the beginning. In *Super Size Me* (2004), Morgan Spurlock is the filmmaker, host, and subject, on a journey to test the limits of his body's reaction to junk food. Werner Herzog is often the voice and sometimes the face guiding his audience, as in *Encounters at the End of the World* (2007). Luc Jacquet's documentary *March of the Penguins* (2005) was initially dubbed with first-person dialogue for the French release, as if the penguins were telling their story. For the English version, it was changed to a third-person narrator in the form of the recognizable voice of Morgan Freeman. Many documentaries have no narrator. Jessica Kingdon's *Ascension* (2021) has no interviews, commentary, or explanation. The scenes stand on their own, presented as a visual essay on capitalism in China.

The films of Ken Burns never have a host. Some of his more contemporary films don't even have narrators, such as *The Central Park Five* (2013), because the story is closer to the present moment, and many potential storytellers are still alive. However, most of Burns's films are narrated. He said it's because "I've always believed in telling stories where there is no war between the word and the picture; they should get along. I don't subscribe to the idea that somehow it's not pure to have a narrator." When he is 98 percent through the editing process, Burns brings in a professional narrator (usually Peter Coyote or Keith David), and when they lock a cut, it requires some adjusting because the pacing of the new voice changes relationships to shots and timing. "We never let narrators see the script ahead of time. We don't ask them to speak to picture. We want them to speak to meaning."

Choosing Interviewees

When I was pitching and selling reality show pilots, I realized that sizzle reels are mostly about casting. The network development executives are primarily looking for captivating *persons*. Setting and premise are important but secondary. Find the narcissists. Reality shows select participants who are among the most narcissistic people you will ever see. Even for documentaries, the best interviewees are open books, genuine, honest, and free of self-filters. Anybody overly worried about how they will come off will be on guard, trying to pre-edit their appearance. Humans are all narcissistic to some degree. Try to cultivate that aspect in your subjects.

When Davis Guggenheim was looking for subjects for *Waiting for Superman* (2010), he started by filming fifty different children, then he narrowed it to twenty, then ten, and then a final five. A great story boils down to characters who want something. These kids desperately wanted school admission slots; there were real obstacles so the stakes were huge for them.

Star Casting

There are so many channels, outlets, and platforms. How do you cut through the clutter and motivate viewers to select your film? It may depend upon your big "gets." A distributor won't pick up a documentary because a few big names pop up in occasional interviews, but distributors do take social-media followings into account. If it is appropriate to your topic to add names, approach famous actors, authors, scientists, or others who are interested in your topic or are part of the world you are documenting. Your host could be a well-known person with an interest in the subject. Leonardo DiCaprio likes taking part in and supporting environmental documentaries, as evidenced by *The 11th Hour* (2007), *Cowspiracy: The Sustainability Secret* (2014), and *Ice on Fire* (2019).

In Freida Lee Mock's *Return with Honor* (1998), a friend showed the finished film to Tom Hanks, who asked, "Why haven't I heard about this story? Why hasn't this been told?" Hanks loved the movie enough to come on board with his company as a presenter. Mock said, "Today, this often happens with documentaries where executive producers are important supporters of the project and help attract press interest."

Access Is Key

Once I succeed in interviewing that first big name, it helps make all the other people I approach feel like they are in good company. To get the first one, I try to find somebody with whom I have a personal connection. Maybe a friend knows somebody who could ask on my behalf or introduce me. In lieu of that, I switch to shotgun mode and send emails to as many big names as I can locate contacts for until I get a response. Managers and agents are usually not helpful. Their job is to prevent you from contacting clients. When you can, go around the gatekeepers. A better avenue is when a star has their own production company or website with contact information. You are much more likely to get an answer through direct contact than representatives.

When ESPN brought a Lance Armstrong documentary idea to Marina Zenovich, she asked, "Why make a film about Lance Armstrong? Didn't Alex Gibney already do this?"

The ESPN executive said, "He's willing to talk. He wants to be interviewed. Enough time has passed."

When Zenovich thought further about it and about films where the filmmakers were in the right place at the right time, such as *Weiner* (2016), she realized it's all about access—and that's what ESPN was offering. "I wasn't thinking I wanted to do something about Lance Armstrong. But once I got into it, it

Photograph by Keri Oberly.

Lance Armstrong, interviewed by Marina Zenovich for LANCE *(2020).*

felt like the perfect subject for me. There was so much to delve into." She added that access sometimes works best when you get it, but the person isn't fully happy that they're giving it to you "because then there's a bit of tension, and that can make a scene sizzle."

Persist

If there is a crucial interview, don't give up easily. Be patient. Keep trying. Be the nice pest. As *The Truth About Marriage* (2020) shoot progressed, I discovered most psychologists specializing in marriage referenced research done by one particular researcher: Dr. John Gottman, who (with his wife Dr. Julie Schwartz Gottman) is arguably the biggest name in marriage therapy. I felt like I couldn't finish the film until I interviewed him. I looked up contact information on The Gottman Institute website and sent multiple emails over several months but got no response. I was frustrated but tried another approach. I found a phone number for their public relations representative, Katie Reynolds. I called, got her voicemail, and left a message.

Reynolds was kind enough to call back, but she had bad news. "The Gottmans are only in the office a few days per month. Their time is tightly booked. And they never really do interviews."

Sometimes, if you can keep them talking, you can change a no to a maybe. Or if you can persuade them to identify the problem standing in the way, you can offer solutions. As I talked, I explained, "I'm a filmmaker, I also work in television, and I make documentaries. My first documentary was about *Star Trek* fans, it's called—"

She interrupted, "Oh, John *loves Star Trek!*" Suddenly, I had a way in. She softened and said she would present my request. I wrote a letter to Dr. Gottman (and laid the *Star Trek* stuff on thick). My request was approved, and I flew to Seattle for my key interview.

Control the Eyeline

Dialogue has the most impact when the eyeline is as close to the camera lens as possible. But telling subjects to look at the camera and talk can make them feel awkward. A solution is for the interviewer to sit as close to the camera lens as possible. That way, you have a natural conversation while keeping the eyeline close to the lens. For variety, alternate which side of the camera you are on. Avoid interviewing somebody in profile unless you want viewers to feel disconnected. Clear the set of other eyes or questioners. Otherwise, the subject's eyes will shift around, darting back and forth between you and whoever is behind you, making them look nervous.

While filming *Trekkies*, we had only one 16mm camera. To get coverage, we had to restage questions, reaction shots, and cutaways after the interview ended. For my documentaries that followed, I began using multiple angles, which provide more cutting options to tighten, trim, and re-order material. Sam Pollard cautions, "Sometimes you can become overly confident. I've been guilty of this, where you say, 'I only need one shot to tell this story.' But you should have covered yourself with a second angle." You never know what you're going to need in the editing room. The smart filmmaker will get coverage.

Typically, I frame three angles on the interview subject: close, medium, and wide. It can be challenging to frame a wide shot that doesn't see the other cameras, and this angle sometimes works as a side angle (which I use sparingly). The shots have to be different enough to allow intercutting. I will use them to remove pauses and speed things up. If I am part of the story, I might use one camera to film myself interacting and asking questions. With multiple cameras, it can be confusing trying to keep eyelines on the same side of all the cameras. I have messed this up more than once. Sometimes, you can get away with "jumping the line," especially when the room's geography is clearly established from the start. Whatever style choices you use, be consistent.

After making *The Thin Blue Line* (1998), Errol Morris said he became interested in eye contact. But with the camera off to the side, he felt that the interviewee loses a direct visual connection with the viewer. So, Morris designed his "Interrotron," a mirror system that allows interviewees to look directly into the camera lens while also seeing the interviewer, a kind of "true first person." Morris said he's not even sure exactly what the effect is. "It has a whole number of unintended consequences that weren't really part of the plan, or wasn't something I imagined initially. But it became apparent the more I used it that somehow the whole environment in which you were shooting disappeared, and just two faces were talking to each other, almost in limbo. It focused it in some strange, magical way."

Morris said he wished he had patented the Interrotron, but he didn't realize an invention has to be patented within one year from the first public notification. After *A Brief History of Time* (1991) was released, *The New York Times Magazine* ran an article showing Morris shooting with an Interrotron on *Fast, Cheap & Out of Control* (1997). Morris said, "Maybe it was my usual suspicion about whether I've really come up with something special. In fact, I had something quite unique. God knows how many people use it now."

Topiary gardener George Mendonça, looking into Errol Morris's Interrotron, in Fast, Cheap & Out of Control *(1997).*

Framing

The typical way to balance a shot is to position an interviewee in the frame at eye level, to one side of the frame, leaving negative space (open space) in the direction they are looking. Avoid putting them dead center, unless it's an extreme close-up, or you have an Interrotron, or you want to intentionally try unusual framing or odd angles. In *The Comedy Store* (2020), Mike Binder put almost everybody on the wrong side of the frame—where it felt appropriate for comedians, whose lives seemed out of balance. Often, we rebalanced the framing by sliding in archival photos over the negative space.

Comedian Martin Lawrence, framing balanced by negative space in front of him, in The Comedy Store, *"Episode Two: The Comedy Strike" (2020).*

Comedian Whitney Cummings, unbalanced framing due to negative space behind her, in The Comedy Store, *"Episode Two: The Comedy Strike" (2020).*

Errol Morris frames canted angles in Fast, Cheap & Out of Control *(1997).*

If you have wild ideas for odd framing, be daring. A low angle makes the subject seem heroic (though you risk looking up their nose). A high angle diminishes them. An off-kilter angle conveys that the profiled world is eccentric. You don't have to play it safe. But whatever style you choose, be consistent.

New avenues for interviewing are constantly opening up, such as using footage of a subject in a Zoom app window. A problem with Internet interviews is that a grainy, badly framed image with questionable lighting and sound calls attention to itself. To excuse the inferior quality of video-conferencing footage, the filming process can to be introduced as part of the documentary narrative, where the interviewer might be filmed watching the interviewee on a computer screen. A workaround when you are unable to be at the same location as the interviewee is to hire a crew on the other end to film the subject while you use video conferencing to be present to conduct the interview.

Scout Locations

Whenever possible, find out in advance what you will be dealing with at your next location. Will you need lights or a bounce card? Do you need to match daylight, or incandescent, or fluorescent lighting? Is the sound going to be affected by an airplane landing path? Is there a good backup location nearby? If it's impossible to get there in advance, have somebody send photos. Even cinéma vérité exponent Frederick Wiseman spends a day in advance at the location to get a sense of geography. But then he is shooting quickly so as not to miss anything. In *Hospital* (1970), there is a scene where a young man is projectile vomiting because he was given a dose of ipecac to throw up an overdose of mescaline. Wiseman said, "As far as I'm concerned, that was one of the best scenes in any of my movies. But if it had happened on a day when I was wandering around the emergency ward doing preparatory research, I'd have been very unhappy to have missed it. I learned quickly that you have to be ready to shoot at a moment's notice."

When I arranged to interview Rollo Maughfling, the Archdruid of Stonehenge, it was lucky that I went to Stonehenge to scout and shoot my stand-ups the day before because it rained the next day. On an average sunny day at Stonehenge, hordes of tourists are circling the stones. We were the only ones there that rainy day—which, in a way, was perfect, having no errant tourists spoiling the background. Plus, the clouds added a portentous mood. I interviewed Archdruid Maughfling from under a rickety umbrella. A good lavalier microphone has a tight pick-up pattern, and it didn't pick up the sound of the rain. Soaked at the halfway point, we decided to dry off and wait for a break in the clouds. Maughfling suggested we drive from Salisbury to Dorset to view the Cerne Abbas Giant—a colossal figure of a naked, erect man that had been carved into the hillside centuries ago. The rain slowed by the time we reached Cerne Abbas, and we finished the interview using this different background. We would have missed an extraordinary opportunity had it been a nice day.

Archdruid Rollo Maughfling, interviewed at Stonehenge for The Nature of Existence *(2010).*

Listening Is Your Best Skill

Some interviewees are succinct sound-bite machines, and others like to circle around and chew on their answers. I try to arrange it so interviewees don't have anything scheduled afterward so we can keep going if they get on a roll. Some of my longest interviews started with them asking, "How long is this going to take?" And judging from their tone, they were hoping it would be brief, but once the interview was underway, it lasted several hours. Expressing one's point of view to a willing listener is one of life's greatest joys, and that pleasure is what a good documentarian provides. Listen as though hearing everything for the first time, as the audience will be. You must seem genuinely interested, and this will motivate your interviewee. When your reaction is genuine, the interviewee is given a sense of satisfaction. It makes them feel good, and they want to repeat that feeling, again and again.

Marina Zenovich began her career as an actor, and she brought forward her experience as a performer into her style as a documentarian. She is on camera in her films *Independent's Day* (1998), *Who Is Bernard Tapie?* (2001), and *Estonia Dreams of Eurovision!* (2002). In college, she was a drama major but switched to broadcast journalism. "I was a late bloomer and didn't know what I wanted to do. I found documentary suited my personality, which is incredibly curious, relentless, and passionate." She also discovered that her training as an actor, which is all about listening and reacting, was a great skill when interviewing people. "Most people don't listen. So when people feel they're really being heard, they tend to open up."

Shut Up!

Silence is the interviewer's most powerful tool. After you ask a question, don't rush to fill in the awkward pause; let the interviewee do it. If you fill the space, it gives them time to second guess their answer and play it safe. After asking a customer if he wants to buy the car today, the sales manager tells his sales team in *Suckers*, "The first one to speak loses." Ask a question, and then clamp your mouth shut and wait, no matter what happens. You will be surprised at the reward.

Liz Garbus recalled times when she was in a cell with an inmate at Angola (Louisiana State Penitentiary). "Early on in my films, there was a learning curve for me, to be able to be with characters, in vérité films in particular, or during interviews, and be in silence with them, being open to not knowing where it might go, and allowing myself to go into a journey that may be a little uncomfortable. In an interview, let the silence have its own space and see where things go next."

Errol Morris said the way he encourages interviewees to open up is by being willing to listen. "You talk to people. You ask questions. Or, if you're me, avoid asking questions, you accumulate evidence, and you think." Morris's interview style began to emerge even before Morris was making films, when he was interviewing mass murderers in Northern California.

> Part of my style was to leave the tape recorder running. There was a game I played with myself, to see how infrequently my voice would appear on the recording. So, for example, if I was using a one-hour cassette that was 30 minutes on one side, 30 minutes on the other side, could I go through the full hour without saying anything? Remaining completely silent. Just "encouraging" people to continue talking. I was most proud of the interviews where I said the least. I was very much interested in the stream-of-consciousness narration, where the person talks and talks and continues talking— much more monologue than interview. Certainly that technique very much influenced *Gates of Heaven* and *Vernon, Florida* and everything I did subsequently.[1]

Stay Out of It

Don't interrupt. Avoid overtalking or overlapping. Leave room between utterances. Continue to remain silent when they are in the middle of a response, or you suspect something is yet to be said. "And then what?" is a good prompt. Suppress your natural instinct to say "yeah" or "right" or "um hm." Wait until they are done speaking. This gives you better editorial options than when your voice is all over the audio track. Sometimes, their addendum is the nugget you were waiting for, but you cut it off because you didn't realize in the moment what you will need later. An exception would be if you are also on camera and your responses are part of a natural give-and-take. Conversely, if they are going off on a clearly non-useful tangent, that's when you interrupt and guide them back to the subject at hand.

Eliminate Lead-Ins

Don't pre-characterize questions with, "Now I'm going to ask a difficult question." Or, "Let me ask you something." Don't say, "This is a funny question." That's the joke-teller's mistake to preface with, "This is a funny story." You've set the bar high and will probably fail to reach it. Ask a question with no pre-qualifiers. Also, don't start making guesses as to what the answer might be. If you ask, "Why are crime rates in the city dropping?" don't start offering suggestions: "Is it because of the increase in police funding? Is it because more people are moving to other states? Or . . ." Shut up and let your subject answer.

Put Interviewees at Ease

Do compliment their responses: "That's a great answer." Make them feel good about their contribution: "I love that perspective. That was so insightful." When they feel like the interview is going well, they relax, lower their guard, and open up more.

To make your subjects feel comfortable, say something like, "If you make a mistake or say something wrong, we can take it out."

Don't say, "Just be yourself," or they will start to think about what that means.

Flattery works. Begin by pre-thanking them for taking part, and then compliment them on their work, accomplishments, books, or even the tasteful decor of their office. We like people who compliment us; it's human nature. You will probably get better material from a subject who likes you. Also, say their names; people love hearing their own name.

One technique to help avoid a sea of talking heads is to interview people while doing tasks they would normally be doing (making breakfast, painting, driving, etc.). Create an environment in their natural habitat that allows them to feel loose enough to open up. Sitting in a maze of tripods and lighting stands may take someone out of their normal zone. Once they relax, that's when the best stuff comes. For variety, interview people in couples or groups. Look for opposing viewpoints and get them to discuss the issue.

You will help put them at ease by being a level-headed, respectful person. Do the research before you get there, so when asking questions, they feel you know the subject. And due to that, they assume you will treat them fairly. Zenovich sometimes reveals something vulnerable about herself, which makes others feel safe to be vulnerable. When she was interviewing Zak Williams about his father for *Robin Williams: Come Inside My Mind* (2018), she first talked about when her own dad died. "I got super emotional. It's like you're trying to light a match within yourself in order to ignite a spark within someone else. And when it's good and you connect on that emotional level, there's nothing better." Zenovich also suggested, "You have to be empathetic, there can't be any judgment. Treat the interview like a date. Be interested, open, and loving toward the person, wanting them to open up and share their story. Reflect their emotions back to them. I'm always trying to bring out the best in people. I think they can sense that. And so they *want* to open up."

Avoid Superiority

When I was at the 1997 Hamptons International Film Festival, documentarian D.A. Pennebaker (or "Penny," as his co-documentarian and wife Chris Hegedus called him) was on a panel with me called "The Truth About Documentaries." Pennebaker and Hegedus's latest film, *Moon Over Broadway* (1997), was showing at the festival. It was their follow–up

Documentarians George Nierenberg, D.A. Pennebaker, Michèle Ohayon, Chris Hegedus, Roger Nygard, Tim Kirkman, Brent Sims, 1997 Hamptons International Film Festival.

to *The War Room* (1993). And on the topic of how to get interviewees to talk, he said, "The dumber you seem to your subjects, the harder they try to help make things go right for you. All is lost if you say something too intelligent in front of them." Nobody likes a smarty pants. Don't give away your game.

Pre-Interviewing

It can save time to pre-interview candidates. This can be helpful if time is limited and you need to identify the most ideal topics and answers in advance. I pre-interviewed people for *Trekkies* and *Six Days in Roswell* because both were shot on film, which is expensive; we couldn't let it roll endlessly, as is often done with video. I spoke in advance with the subjects, identified quotes we wanted, and filmed those sentences as efficiently as possible.

With video, I rarely do pre-interviews. I would rather throw out entire useless interviews than miss something that is never captured again. Zenovich said she never pre-interviews; she wants to hear everything for the first time "because the look on my face is different than if I'm hearing it for the second time, and the person can see that. When it's genuinely new to me, they get even more engaged in telling their story." Spontaneity comes from the interviewer. If you do conduct a pre-interview, save the most pressing or searching questions for on-camera to keep responses natural. Sometimes, even they are surprised at what comes out of their mouths, and those moments are magical.

Guide the Responses

Get the sound bites you need. Don't settle for generalities. If they give a general comment, ask for a specific example or a story to illustrate. If you miss something, tell them to repeat it. If they stumbled or were long-winded, have them say it again more concisely. Ask the question again if needed. Sometimes, say, "This is such an important idea, I want to have you cover that point one more time." I may tell them what I'm looking for, what was missing, or that it was a bit convoluted and we need it more concise. If necessary, I feed them a concise version of the sentence I would like them to say. They will appreciate it. They want to look good.

Zenovich listens for complete sentences during interviews as if she's already in the editing room "because if I don't get what's needed, it's my fault. It's like directing actors, trying to get someone to go somewhere emotionally." She will prompt them, "Could you say that again, but slow down?" Or, "Oh, my God, this is huge. Why are you treating this like it's not a big deal? Will you do me a favor? Close your eyes and go back to that moment. And then start over and tell me again."

During the Q&A after a screening of *The Fire Within: A Requiem for Katia and Maurice Krafft* (2022), Werner Herzog said that while making *Little Dieter Needs to Fly* (1997), he interviewed Dieter Dengler, the protagonist who had been held captive in Laos during the Vietnam War. When he asked Dengler to describe a key, gruesome moment before he was rescued, his first telling was forty-two minutes. Herzog didn't interrupt, but it was too long for a short moment in the documentary, and the account was full of unimportant details. Herzog asked Dengler to tell the story again, five or six times, because he was trying to get at a "condensed form of truth. [It was] condensed for the film and has a truth of poetry. I'm trying to dig into a deeper stratum of truth."

Finesse the Questions

Ask a concise, single, direct question. Avoid multiple questions or two-part questions, or long, rambling questions with qualifiers. The interviewee will only remember and answer the last part of a multi-part question.

A disarming way to phrase a question is to preface it with, "Say more about...." Or, "Talk about...." This is an open-ended way to get interviewees onto a subject. "Talk about what it's like being a Twins fan." "Talk about when you were arrested." "Talk about preparing for the wedding." "Talk about the best thing about being a lawyer."

Avoid questions that result in a yes or no. If you ask, "Do you like being a doctor?" You get a "Yes." Then silence. Instead, give an open-ended prompt. "Talk about what it's like being in an emergency room."

Sometimes, you must explain to subjects that they need to include your question in their answer so they will make a complete statement. If you ask, "Why do you like football?" They might launch with a fragment, giving a useless sound bite: "Because it's so much fun." What is the "it" in that sentence? If necessary, feed them a beginning for their response, such as: "Start your answer by saying, 'The reason I like the Vikings is because. . . .'"

Ask *Why?*

"Why" is the number one word in your toolkit. "Why are you a thoracic surgeon?" An answer goes to the heart of their belief. "Why did you commit this crime?" "Why is your research such a breakthrough?" "Why do you believe you were abducted by aliens?" "Why are you a Trekkie?" "Why are there multiple religions?" Why, why, why!

When considering what motivates the human beings he profiles, Errol Morris said, "It's hard to know why people do the things that they do." But he pointed to a passage, which he said has helped him understand human motivations, from the beginning of Edgar Allan Poe's *The Black Cat* (1843):

> And then came, as if to my final and irrevocable overthrow, the spirit of PERVERSENESS. Of this spirit philosophy takes no account. Yet I am not more sure that my soul lives, than I am that perverseness is one of the primitive impulses of the human heart—one of the indivisible primary faculties, or sentiments, which give direction to the character of Man. Who has not, a hundred times, found himself committing a vile or a silly action, for no other reason than because he knows he should not? Have we not a perpetual inclination, in the teeth of our best judgment, to violate that which is Law, merely because we understand it to be such? This spirit of perverseness, I say, came to my final overthrow. It was this unfathomable longing of the soul to vex itself—to offer violence to its own nature—to do wrong for the wrong's sake only—that urged me to continue.

Seek the Emotion

Journalists often ask about feelings: "How did that make you feel?" Capturing emotions on camera is the money shot. Journalists want people to express motivations, ideas, and feelings. People are not always qualified to describe some complex topic accurately, but *everybody* is qualified to talk about their emotions. "How did you feel when the Challenger space shuttle exploded?" "Talk about how you felt when you were fired." "Talk about how it made you feel to carry a baby out of that burning house."

When Marina Zenovich was interviewing Lance Armstrong, she needed to have him talk about his experience with cancer, but it was a story he had told many times. Zenovich worried, "How am I going to get him to tell this as if it's the first time?" She interviewed Armstrong eight times, and she brought up the subject during one of the earlier interviews.

"Let's talk about cancer."

Armstrong replied, "Oh, I don't want to talk about that right now."

She hadn't expected him to stonewall. She was thrown off her plan. She thought, *What are we going to talk about? What am I going to do?* Armstrong kept looking at his watch. "It was his way of letting me know his time was limited." Zenovich remembered about another cyclist named Jan Ullrich, a close friend of Armstrong's, who had been on drugs and nearly died until Armstrong, and others, interceded.

Scrambling for something to talk about, she said, "Talk to me about Jan." Armstrong wasn't expecting this subject, and you could see that it took him to a place he didn't expect to go. He was quiet for a bit and then started talking, and suddenly, his eyes began to tear up.

Something in the moment hadn't worked, so Zenovich grabbed for another approach, and she touched the core of an undercurrent that Armstrong was trying to suppress: that this could have happened to him. It was the only time Armstrong cried in all the interviews.

"It was this amazing emotional moment that none of us were expecting," said Zenovich. "And it was beautiful." She said, when doing interviews, "I'm so genuine and open, almost to the point of being naive. I was thrilled that we hit that emotional moment. I'm always trying to get to that deeper level, which is probably why I love interviewing so much because I love going there. When Lance finally talked about cancer in another interview, it was because we had engaged enough for him to see that I cared and wanted the best out of him. He saw that I had good intentions. And then it was like he was talking about it for the first time."

When they finished the interview where Armstrong cried, Zenovich went into the next room, and Armstrong's manager said, "You got the cry."

Zenovich thought to herself, *Yes, that's what we do! We're in the emotion business.*

What to Ask

Ask what you are curious about—the audience will also be curious. Start with easy questions about facts to warm them up. "Talk about how many books you have sold." Move to opinions and feelings later, when they get relaxed. "Talk about how your mother feels about your work." Bury the controversial question in the middle. While filming *The Nature of Existence*, I started with questions that have clearer answers, such as, "How old is the Universe?" Cosmologists pretty much agree it's around 13.787 billion years old. Later, I would ask matter-of-factly, in the same tone as the innocuous questions, "Is masturbation a sin?" Eventually, you have to get to the big questions. That's the reason you are there. Ask what it is you want to know. If you are interviewing a murderer, you have to ask about the murder at some point.

Sam Pollard puts his questions on three-by-five cards. He tries to make an interview feel like a relaxed conversation, where subjects are simply expressing themselves. "Most of the time, they give you the information you need during the conversation. If they don't, I'll go back and have them give me something more specific."

Davis Guggenheim avoids chronological, organized interviews. He makes a list of things to cover and leaves it in his pocket. At the end, he opens the paper and usually discovers he's covered everything, but he did so in a more interesting way than if he had rattled off his questions. Guggenheim said, "The best interviews are after something more elusive, which is energy, flow, and the subject opening up in surprising ways. You want an interviewee to get lost in a great conversation. The worst thought is, *Okay, next question.* Because if you think, *Next question*, you've interrupted the flow and gone back to zero. The result is that you get an interview like something on a morning show."

When producer Jonathan Vogler goes into an interview, he has two types of enquiry questions he knows the answers to and questions he doesn't. Sometimes, a documentary filmmaker needs someone to provide specific answers to function as a linkage to carry the story that has been built in the outline. But then, when you ask questions you don't know the answer to, you leave room for learning. You might even change your outline because you've uncovered something new.

How to Ask Questions

Set the tone. Your demeanor as the interviewer will guide the result. The energy that you put out is what you will get back. If there's someone who's quiet and needs leading, bring your energy up until they match it. If that doesn't work, go ahead and coach them.

Maintain eye contact. Be specific, direct, and deliberate. Your confidence in your questions encourages your subjects to submit to your prompts. Nod, but remain silent. Don't end a question with "or," or, "and . . . um." End cleanly, and then wait. Ask follow-up questions to an interesting answer. Don't simply read questions.

Be Bold

Don't be afraid of crises and emotions. Rush right into powerful situations. The camera gives you authority; it empowers you to be assertive, and people accept that—they expect it. No apologies are necessary. You are the boss in an interview, and they will obey when your camera is on and you are giving instructions and asking questions.

When I was in Loreto, Italy, touring the Basilica della Santa Casa, I bumped into the Archbishop of Manfredonia. I approached and asked for an impromptu interview. He agreed but became less and less interested as I pressed him with tough questions about religion. When you have some-body on camera, it's almost impossible for them to quit. They feel they must keep answering as long as you keep firing questions. Because it was an impromptu interview, the recording ran out of space after twenty minutes.

During the pause while I reloaded, he fled. I was lucky to get what I did. Start every interview with an empty memory card and a full battery.

Ending an Interview

When concluding, ask, "Is there anything we missed?" Or, "Is there anything you would like to add?" Some of the best quotes come after the interview is over and they suggest something you had not thought of. Afterward, thank them, and always say that it was a successful interview, whether it was or not. They don't know and will be wondering. Make them feel good about taking part. You will need their support later, and this will give them a good feeling about being involved.

Documentarians Make Friends

I have learned an immense amount during the making of my documentaries. And I have stayed in touch with many of those interviewed. I have made friends around the world because they felt my genuine interest while I listened, something that rarely happens in our lives. One of the perks of being a documentary filmmaker is that your friend list increases. Imagine spending a few hours with scientists, gurus, athletes, experts, *Star Trek* fans, UFO enthusiasts, wrestlers, pizza chefs, and many others and asking about their lives. It was particularly satisfying to talk to psychologists, asking them the most challenging questions that were troubling me, and because I had a camera, our sessions were free!

Ken Burns has found new friends and mentors on almost every film. For *Brooklyn Bridge* (1981), it was Lewis Mumford, the social critic. It was the Shaker Eldresses, who were still alive in their nineties, for his film *The Shakers: Hands to Work, Hearts to God* (1984). He got to know Robert Penn Warren on *Huey Long* (1985), Shelby Foote in *The Civil War* (1990), and in *Jazz* (2001), he said it was Wynton Marsalis, "a mentor who was younger than me. And it's because we've been open to them and their knowledge of the particular subject. And then we keep them. They're friends for life. There's something familial about the way we've organized ourselves."

82

CHAPTER FIVE

Pitching

Ask people for their money.

I've had a bit of luck talking investors out of their money. It helps if you clean up and put on a nice shirt. Don't make sideways, darting glances. Nobody invests in shifty people. Many "committed" investors talk a big game and then back out when it comes time to write a check. It's a numbers game; be prepared to talk to a lot of rich folks. They've got plenty of money, and there's no reason they can't wager some on an exciting investment such as your movie.

Write a Proposal

Even though each of my films' funding sources was different, the process was similar. Don't pitch until you have figured out your film's story because story is what sells. My first step is to write a one-page synopsis, beginning with a logline, which is one or two sentences that concisely explain the entire story. In the synopsis, use bold and colorful descriptions. Describe the protagonist(s), goal(s), obstacle(s), antagonist(s), the climax, and the ending. When any of these elements are missing, such as in a concept documentary, you may have to rely entirely upon a killer theme and a captivating core question that you will answer.

Keep it short. If your pitch doesn't excite in the first three lines buyers' and distributors' eyes will glaze over, and your chances of getting a check decline with each sentence. If development and acquisition executives cannot quickly grasp the conflict and main characters in a few sentences, they will not be able to concisely pitch it to *their* bosses. Later, a marketing department will struggle with how to sell it.

Investors and buyers don't know what they want until you tell them. They are rooting for your pitch to succeed because they want to get excited by a fantastic idea. They hope you will convince them because it ends their search. Approach with confidence, as if you are doing them a favor. You are going to fill their pockets with money and make them a part of something so special they will take great pride in the finished product and subsequent accolades.

The Pitch Deck

A pitch deck (a.k.a. lookbook) is a visual presentation that lays out essential information about your project, supported by enticing photos. Search the Internet for examples of pitch decks from other projects for a sense of what they look like. It can be a digital presentation using PowerPoint or InDesign, or a PDF, or a glossy printed book to page through during the meeting. A pitch deck could be anywhere between eight and eighty pages. The deck will answer questions anyone interested in the film will ask. There's a title page, a logline, a page with a longer description, and a section with the characters. If it's a series, break it down episode by episode. For example, if it's a backward-looking profile on a person, team, or event, present all the big moments. Perhaps include a timeline. If it's a vérité documentary, build up the colorful characters and the important scenes you plan to capture. The pitch deck is a forecasting of what the documentary will be.

List other comparable (successful) documentaries. How much money did these comps make? Include supporting evidence, such as core audiences who will seek out your film. What market is salivating for your topic? Who will be your big interview gets? Who are the star names? How big is their (and your) combined social media following? For investors, add up budget versus potential revenue streams, and show your investor's healthy share of returns. A typical profit split is fifty–fifty, with half the net income to the investors and half to the filmmakers.

Prepare a Budget

Somewhere in your proposal is the bottom line. It's your financial ask. Get your hands on budget templates, think about everything you need to spend on to accomplish your goals, and add it up. You can't do everything yourself; you need a crew. The last thing you want to do is realize you should have hired somebody better qualified than you but it's too late.

There are three types of budgets to work with: the core budget, the total production budget, and the investor (or buyer) budget.

The Core Budget

The core budget contains the lean-and-mean hard costs. What unavoidable expenditures will it take to finish? You may be able to persuade the crew to work for free (or deferred salaries). But there are expenses you can't avoid, such as equipment purchases, hard drives, travel costs, film festival submission fees, and so on. Even if you put a film on credit cards, you still owe that money.

As different as all my documentaries were, their basic hard costs (not including deferments) were similar, between $120,000 and $145,000. That's not to say you couldn't do it for much less. If you own a camera, mics, a computer for editing, and there is no traveling, you can finish a film for a fraction of that. But be sure to budget for purchasing copies of this book for your entire crew.

The Total Production Budget

Even though *Trekkies* cost $120,000 in hard cash, the total budget was $505,937 when all deferments were paid. When you add to your core budget what it will cost once you pay off deferments, plus any other financial promises, you will have your total production budget. You won't be in "profit" until you pay off all your obligations. Include your own deferment. If you are working for somebody else, a weekly rate with a minimum guarantee is better than a deferment or a flat rate because, more often than not, documentary projects take longer than expected, and with a flat rate, you might end up working part of the job for free.

One downside to using crew deferments is that you usually have to promise larger amounts than their normal salary when a crew agrees to this gamble. When negotiating deferments, treat it like real money. As easy as it is to be generous with money that doesn't yet exist, the goal is to have that money in the bank someday, and if you've promised someone a hundred thousand dollars, that's a hundred thousand real dollars you owe.

Keep in mind that a deferment is different from a profit share. Never give anybody a share of profits (a.k.a. back-end points) if it can be avoided. Otherwise, when you have a successful film, you will be married to these partners for life. Filmmaker Les Blank once advised me, "Be sure to cap it off." When Blank made *The Blues Accordin' to Lightnin' Hopkins* (1968), he owed Hopkins a share of royalties forever. He said, "I gave him a percentage. The guy's been dead for years, and I'm still paying his wife."

Below are budget breakdowns for each of my documentaries.

Trekkies
Hard costs: $120,000
Deferred expenses: $385,937
Total production budget: $505,937

Six Days in Roswell
Hard costs: $130,000
Deferred expenses: $90,000
Total production budget: $220,000

Trekkies 2
Hard costs: $325,000
Deferred expenses: $0 (paid in original hard costs)
Above-the-line (partners' profit): $775,000
Total production budget: $1.1 million

The Nature of Existence
Hard costs: $125,000
Deferred expenses: $500,000

Marketing, PR, and theatrical distribution: $100,000
Total production budget: $725,000

The Truth About Marriage
Hard costs: $145,000
Deferred expenses: $250,000
Marketing, PR, and digital distribution: $50,000
Total production budget: $495,000

Most films never get into profit and deferments are never paid, so the number that matters most is hard costs. However, contracts and paperwork are ready for when you hit the jackpot. With a film that takes off, you are in the rarified position of paying everybody and putting smiles on their faces. If you don't have contracts in place ahead of time, you will likely experience the worst buzzkill of your life (with accompanying lawsuits) when everybody disagrees on what they deserve.

The Investor Budget

When I approach investors (or networks/platforms), I don't give them budget one or two; I provide them with budget three, which adds appropriate salaries for the above-the-line director and producers, a built-in profit for the production company, and contingencies. A feature-length documentary budget for cable or a streaming platform normally ranges between $750,000 and $1 million. It can be much more if the film has a large crew and lots of research and effects. How do I justify asking for $1 million? Because if I am going to spend a year (or more) of my life dedicated to finishing a film, I need to be appropriately compensated with a full-year salary.

High-Budget Documentaries

Film agent Glen Reynolds's experience is that most documentaries he sees are in the $200,000 to $400,000 budget range. Reynolds said, "To go beyond that is pretty gutsy. If you convince someone to give you $1 million

Michael Jordan vs. Bryon Russell, just before Jordan's game-six winning-shot in the The Last Dance *(2020).*

to make a documentary, you're probably someone who's made two or three movies in that budget range that worked before. Maybe you have work-shopped it at the Sundance Lab so you have a certain percentage chance of being in Sundance next year."

When your first documentary hits the jackpot, and you get offers to move up to the big leagues, budgets rise. The five-episode series *The Comedy Store* (2020) cost about $1 million per episode. *The Last Dance* (2020) cost closer to $2 million per episode. The eleven-part BBC series *Planet Earth* (2006) advertised that they had a production budget of $25 million, or $2.27 million per episode. That project took five years, with 2,000 shoot days and over 200 locations. The more you shoot, the more it becomes about media management. Everything starts to balloon: more cameras, more operators, more editors, more assistant editors, more storage, everything is multiplying.

When budgeting a documentary for cable or a streamer, categories are calculated in percentages. Whatever the budget, 30 percent comes off the top for the above-the-line recipients: production company, producers, director, star talent, and sometimes a writer. Everybody else is below-the-line, from cinematographer to office staff to editor. Shooting gets 20 percent. Post production, clip licensing, and music (whether composer or library) are 40 percent. Licensed songs would be separate. Editing is the most consistent and steady expense (which is one good reason to consider becoming an editor). An editing burn rate of $10,000 per week is not unusual. Depending on the quantity of clips and archival footage, licensing could be huge, or it could be zero. The last 10 percent goes to office, legal, and miscellaneous.

The Sizzle Reel

Now that you have your budget and pitch deck, what's next? Start shooting! Don't wait for somebody to validate your idea. *You* will validate it by making it real. Everybody selling docu-projects has pitch decks and sizzle reels. To compete, you must do the same. A sizzle reel is a visual sample of your idea edited together from any of the following: footage you have shot, stock footage, photos, animation, graphics, or clips borrowed from YouTube and other movies. Make it dynamic, give the stills digitally added movement, and animate storyboards and title cards. Add sound effects and music that builds with the images to a strong climax. With some initial footage, you can create a visual sample of your terrific idea, which is a much stronger selling point than a solely verbal pitch. If you haven't got any footage, you can create a "mood reel," made entirely from borrowed footage, cut together to present a feeling of what your project will be like.

Never speak as *if* you will make your film—you *are* making the film. When you talk about it, call it a project, not a pitch. A project is an endeavor in progress, not a maybe. A proposal is a bunch of papers; a documentary is tangible and happening. Sometimes, you have to start filming, and as you work toward your goals, others will join because people like getting on board a project already in motion. Plus, you will get a sense after your first interview if your idea is a winner. When you feel it, you can sell it; you can sell that excitement to investors more passionately.

The Pitch

There are only so many topics, and many ideas have already been done, but new generations come along and put a different spin on them. Marina Zenovich said, "If you have a great story, with compelling characters, with access, something no one else is doing, you can probably sell it."

Don't hit up your funding sources before you are ready. You only get one chance to make a first impression. Wait until you can answer every question: story, profilees, budget, marketing, and distribution. Then you are ready to approach funding sources: streamers, networks, production companies, investors, foundations, dentists, friends, parents, corporations, grants, and charities. If you are represented by an agency or production company, they will set up meetings.

Executives don't get fired for saying no; they get fired for saying yes to the wrong thing. Jonathan Vogler suggested, "Show them something that makes them feel as comfortable as possible that you're going to be able to deliver." The sizzle reel and the pitch deck show them the content you will provide. They can see and hear what it will be like. This makes it a lower risk.

Ken Burns's advice is, "Underwriters have to feel confidence in your sincerity. Given my reputation, I suppose I could walk into a streaming service or a premium cable and get what I need to make a $30 million ten-part series," he said. "But they wouldn't give me ten and a half years, which was what it took to make *The Vietnam War*. They would have wanted it in two to three years." At the beginning of that series, Burns credits and thanks nine foundations and fourteen other entities and individuals for contributing funding. Burns needs the ability to change direction, as he continually researches, so he utilizes grants and the public broadcasting model to avoid "intercession by the so-called suits."

Once you are in the room, Rachel Grady cautions, "Never tell them there's any chance it will be boring. Keep it engaging. There needs to be a reason for people to keep watching. The most important thing is to believe in the story from the bottom of your heart; and usually, if you do, it's contagious. It's about translating all of that energy and excitement to get someone to financially support it."

Davis Guggenheim tries to get buyers to feel his excitement and to experience the story. "I want to immerse them in what it might be like to watch the movie. Whether that means me talking and gesticulating or cutting a ten-minute series of scenes that can immerse them in the story." He waits until he finds a project that makes *him* enthusiastic. "If I'm excited and fascinated, then the people I'm pitching to will be excited and fascinated. I've failed if I haven't communicated my excitement." Enthusiasm closes deals. A wealthy investor who owns 200 quick-oil-change franchises doesn't need all that money, and what you can sell is something people don't have: a chance to rub elbows with exciting show business types while participating in your exhilarating journey and sharing in the accolades. Everybody wants to get on a train that's going someplace fun.

Michael Tollin advises: "During a pitch, always take yes for an answer. Some people just keep talking; shut up already. They said, 'yes,' they're nodding vertically. It looks good. Get out too early rather than too late."

Sam Pollard was hired by a company called This Machine Filmworks to co-direct a documentary with Charles Blow about his book *The Devil You Know: A Black Power Manifesto* (2021). The production company set up meetings with ten streamers (in this case, on Zoom) over two weeks. The story was about African Americans reverse-migrating to the South to recapture political and economic power and collectively dismantle white supremacy. They had a pitch deck that they sent to the streamers beforehand. Pollard said the simple secret is to come up with a pitch they're going to fall in love with. "They have to love the idea, but they also have to love you." The pitch was carefully organized and choreographed: who would go first, who would go second, and what each would say. Blow talked about his vision when he wrote the book, and he and Pollard described conceptually how they would turn it into a film. HBO quickly bought the pitch, and the documentary aired in 2023, titled *South to Black Power*. When I asked Pollard if it helps to write a best-selling book first, he said, "It don't hurt. It don't hurt, quite honestly."

In a pitch, expect buyers to ask every question you would ask, and be prepared for their objections.

If they say, "Documentaries never make money."

You say, "Look at the comparable films, the worldwide market is strong, and with our budget, it's a low threshold to profit."

"Who would want to see it?"

"I've fully researched every aspect, and the core audience is huge. Look at these statistics based on similarly themed films."

If they say, "Sure, great idea, but what do we need you for?"

Show them why nobody can do it without you. "I've already got the people lined up and the rights signed off. Some of the main interviews are in the can. I have already collected archival footage. I have a head start. Nobody can catch me."

What Are Buyers Looking For?

Your job is to surprise and excite the executives. According to Davis Guggenheim, "The streamers are content hungry for a great piece of material, and when it comes up, they battle for it." Executives may have seemingly arbitrary reasons why they turn down a pitch. They might say, "We're not making films about that right now." Or, "We're looking for something different." Sometimes, they're looking for a specific type of content or a subject matter that fits an algorithm. Other times they're looking to work with people or directors they think are hot.

Michael Pollard suggested, "Unless you have some major celebrity, or it's a true crime story, it's difficult to raise the funds. If you have a true crime story, it's almost like money in the bank."[1] Liz Garbus acknowledged that there is a dominance of celebrity in documentaries. She said that when she made *Harry & Meghan* (2022), she wasn't purely interested in them as celebrities. "I was interested in what their journey told us about colonialism, history, and the figure of the biracial American coming into this organism that has been part of empire, and now commonwealth, for hundreds of years. The streamers are certainly pushing toward celebrity. And I think for us as storytellers, it's about trying to find the meat on the bones that make it worth us showing up for work."

Garbus also warned not to try to predict what streamer executives want. She acknowledged that a film like *Navalny* (2022) would obviously muster wide interest; it had a thriller dynamic and geopolitical reverberations. When you consider the Academy Award-nominated film *All That Breathes* (2022), it's hard to figure out why a documentary about trying to save injured birds in New Delhi works.

A cinematic image from All That Breathes *(2023).*

Garbus asked, "Would you say streamers would be interested in such a film if you pitched it on paper? No. But it was at Sundance and then nominated for an Oscar. It's a quiet, gorgeous film. And through the efforts of two brothers, you learn so much about a different world. It's about a thrilling arc. It's about unforgettable characters. It's about a visual style that's different. So I don't think anything should be off the table. Once we start talking about formulas, we'll be dead in the water."

Michael Tollin produced a six-hour docuseries called *Justice, USA* (2023). It took seven years from inception to finally getting a greenlight from OWN, and then the series premiered on MAX. "A tiny percentage of the things we engage in actually come to fruition," said Tollin. I asked about his criteria for saying yes to developing a project. He asks himself three questions: "Is this a project that might have a social impact? Is this a project that's going to be fun? Is this a project that will involve people that I'll enjoy spending my time with?" If the answer is yes to all three, he goes forward without regrets.

Be an Owner

Ken Burns says creative control is "it" for him. He has insisted on autonomy and owning his projects so he can be free to make the films he chooses. After the success of *The Civil War* (1990), producers in Hollywood made tantalizing offers. When Burns told them he was doing a documentary about baseball, they said, "Oh, great, how long will it be? Ninety minutes? Two hours?"

Burns said, "No, I think it's going to be eighteen hours."

They replied, "Oh, nobody will watch that."

Baseball (1994) garnered a bigger audience than *The Civil War.*

After that, the same people came back and said, "What are you doing now?"

Burns said, "Jazz."

This time, they said, "Um, you know stuff with black people doesn't sell, right?"

Burns just shook his head and said, "Whatever you say."

After that, he stopped entertaining those sorts of overtures. "They're just people in the marketplace," he said. "They call their business 'The Industry.' They might put silhouettes of palm trees on their stationery, but they're factory smokestacks. I was just looking for my own way to do it." For Burns, the solution was retreating to New Hampshire in 1979 to continue his own creative process, living in the same house ever since, working in the same kind of handmade fashion with an intimate group of people. Burns said, "I still get rejected all the time while asking people to fund projects. I'm always trying to get the budget fully raised by the time we lock the film. It's always a race."

Duke Ellington in Ken Burns's Jazz *(2001), "Episode Four: The True Welcome: 1929–1934."*

The owner of a film is usually the person or entity that provides the money. However, filmmakers can hang on to ownership (and creative control) if they negotiate well. This is a clause in a sample investor agreement where an investor gets a 12.5 percent share but the producer retains ownership:

> Producer shall be the sole and exclusive owner of the copyright in the Picture and shall have the exclusive right to develop and produce the Picture and to cut, edit, modify, use, exploit, advertise, exhibit, and otherwise turn to account any or all of the foregoing in or for any and all media, now known or hereafter devised, throughout the universe, in perpetuity, as Producer in its sole and complete discretion determines. To the full extent allowed under any applicable law, Investor hereby waives or assigns to Producer its so-called "moral rights" or "*droit moral.*" In the event Producer is dissolved, Investor shall have a twelve and one-half percent (12.5 percent) equity interest in the Picture. In the event Producer is dissolved, Producer shall execute all documents required by Investor, if requested in writing, to evidence such ownership interest, and if Producer fails to do so, Producer appoints Investor as its attorney in fact for such purposes (and such appointment is irrevocable and a power coupled with an interest).

If you can't keep 100 percent ownership, negotiate to be a co-owner with the financier or other partners. Ideally, you want the revenue stream to flow directly to you first and then to your partners. You don't want to be chasing them for your share of the financial waterfall; better if they have to chase you. If you are not an owner and the owners go bankrupt or disappear, you might find yourself out of luck. An excellent path to wealth is to accumulate as many passive income streams as possible. Every project, documentary, book, song, remake, series, or spinoff you own or are a part owner of is a property you can keep re-licensing and creating new passive income streams.

You can only accept investors' money once you have a place to deposit it. You first need to create a legal framework, such as a corporation, LLC (Limited Liability Company), or partnership because banks usually ask for documentation before opening an account in the name of a business. Then this entity that you create (and own) will own the film.

For *Trekkies*, we formed a general partnership called Trekkies Productions, and we transferred all rights to that company. When I made *Suckers*, the producers formed a company called Genius Squad, Inc. specifically to handle the financial needs for the film and to accept investor funds. I had no ownership; however, the corporation they set up had an obligation to pay back my financial investment in the film and my deferred salary (neither of which was ever fully paid). Two decades later, the producers decided to shut down their companies, and they were about to discard the film—and send it into the public domain if they dissolved the chain of title (which is composed of all the documents and agreements that show ownership rights). I persuaded the producers to sell the movie to me (since they were throwing it away). To acquire ownership, I had to pin down the copyright chain of title to prove I would be the new owner. It took months to track everything down, but then I filed copyright assignment forms. I collected the film and sound elements that still existed and then spent my own money to restore the film.

Don't get too far ahead and form an entity before you need it. It creates a lot of yearly paperwork and is an expensive annoyance if you set it up too soon. Depending on the state, you may also need a business license. Research the process thoroughly. Ask your attorney and accountant for guidance. Be ready to set up your business framework the moment you confirm the first investment check is real.

Financing Sources

There are not many second-time film investors. They learn their lesson the first time; it is a difficult business in which to profit. A sole investor is the ideal situation. It's easier to answer to one master than several investors with differing opinions. When you accept an investor's money, try to stipulate that they are passive participants with no control over business or creative decisions.

Rachel Grady said, when she develops projects and looks for money, "We do what everybody does; we go to the streamers. There's a lot of financing now in private equity. Everybody's trying to get into the nonfiction game. The hard part is coming up with the idea. The selling of it is not as hard as it used to be." Film rep Glen Reynolds pointed out one problem with streamers. "You usually have to have already made a film with them before you can make another film with them. And it's tough to break in. They don't like to take risks on unproven filmmakers. Financiers want to be in a no-risk business when they can get it."

Many of Freida Lee Mock's independent projects have been supported by grants and donations. She said, "*Maya Lin* competed well and landed sufficient grant submissions to finish the film." Everybody is usually stuck self-financing unless they already have a name, or are good at talking wealthy people out of money, or if they can stand at a freeway offramp to collect enough contributions. Frederick Wiseman started out self-funding *Titicut Follies* (1967). After that, he formed a relationship with PBS, which gave him a portion of his budget for every film, which made it easier to get the rest of the money from foundation grants and other sources. He says he advises young documentary filmmakers, "Marry rich."

Self-Funding

The ideal situation is to be the sole owner of a project, beholden to nobody. Mock concurred, "There is something amazing about controlling your own project, where your voice is intentional. You're an auteur. No one's giving you notes. With commissioned projects, there are executives and all the corresponding notes, which can be terrific and challenging." Strings come attached to money. Despite flirting with investors, I self-financed *The Nature of Existence* and *The Truth About Marriage*. One reason I did this, aside from retaining control, was because of the intrinsic joy I derived from the documentary-making journey. In between earning money by directing and editing television shows, I saved enough to go on the road with my camera. I am 100 percent owner of both films and collect all royalties.

Most novice filmmakers are forced to self-fund until their documentary is complete and distributors can see how well it works. When we began production on *Trekkies*, the producers at Neo Motion Pictures put up enough money for one test shoot. I cut a twenty-minute demo, and we screened it for investors, garnering interest. However, we felt the offers were low, and we wanted to hold onto the ownership, so we continued self-funding. In the long run, it paid off. I own 25 percent, and we can now re-license and re-release it forever. Be an owner.

CHAPTER SIX

Contracts

Paper everything.

Handshake deals end relationships. If you co-write or co-create a project, or work collaboratively in some way, utilize a deal memo that sets forth in principle what each person's responsibilities and revenues will be. You can find forms online and by working with a production attorney. Contract forms are often updated, and deals are constantly changing, so you should work with a qualified, licensed legal expert. I am not an attorney, and this book is not a source of contracts or bona fide legal advice. Based on what I have encountered, I will share some ideas to keep in mind as you navigate these waters.

Greed Kills Deals

Everybody imagines how the business works and the future will be laid out, but it rarely goes that way. When money is set on the table, each partner begins rationalizing why they deserve a little more than their comrades. They may even be correct, but there is only 100 percent available. Sometimes, this leads to a deal collapsing, and everybody loses. When we began work on *Trekkies*, we hadn't thoroughly envisioned each of our participations. Once the issue arose, the three producers wanted a full share in addition to Denise Crosby and me, creating a five-way (20 percent) split. Crosby put her foot down; she wanted a one-third share. We compromised at 25 percent to Crosby, me, producer Keith Border, and another quarter to the production company. The three producers split their 50 percent three ways, receiving 16.66 percent each.

The Collaboration Agreement

Once we agreed on a money split—the biggest issue—we wrote a one-page collaboration agreement. It listed ownership, profit share percentages, salaries, and credits. And there was a sentence that said: "Any other points, credits, deferrals, payments, or provisions not listed here, and all deals for sale or licensing of the film, must be mutually agreed upon by all three Film-makers." Crosby, Border, and I were defined as the three decision-making filmmakers.

The effect of our first document was to give each filmmaker financial veto power. Nothing seems to enforce good behavior more than when somebody has a veto over your financial affairs. What always brought us back to the table was that we had to agree or we could lose everything.

As offers for our film started heating up, we turned this first memorandum over to our attorneys. They upgraded it to a three-page co-administration/co-production agreement, which laid out more precisely the duties, credits, salaries, deferments, ownership percentages, creative control, what we intended to do with the project, what would happen if an investor came on board, the definition of gross receipts, and how income and profits would be split. It re-emphasized that anything not specified would require mutual agreement.

Partnership

If you are making a documentary, you are starting a business. Once a distribution deal closed, we realized we needed an even more comprehensive contract that covered every possible eventuality. A partnership agreement is a foundational contract. An LLC has an operating agreement. A corporation has bylaws. Each form of document details how you would govern internal operations: What is the company's purpose? Who are the officers or members? How will the business be managed? What is the length of the term? Who has decision-making ability? How much compensation for each? How much capital does each contribute? How will profits and losses or other distributions be allocated? How is ownership divided? How will ownership of the film pass to heirs?

We decided to form a general partnership. My attorney, Todd Stern, and his associate, Alan Kirios, drafted a thirty-two-page partnership agreement. Trekkies Productions became the entity that owned the project and was able to license rights to the film. Partnerships don't send out 1099s to the partners; income is reflected on a Schedule K-1 form as a share of profits. The partnership acts as a pass-through entity, a conduit for money, with no payroll taxes or withholdings necessary.

To open an account, our bank required a fictitious business name statement, a notice of publication in a newspaper, an employer tax identification number, our executed partnership agreement, two forms of identification for each partner, and one dollar for an opening balance. Some banks were willing to proceed without the partnership agreement in hand (which was helpful because we were still revising it).

One of the most essential things a comprehensive agreement does is specify what happens when you close down a business. Without that road-map, you might have a big, expensive, legal wreck to clean up. Much like a marriage, when there is a divorce, the mess is easier to unwind when there is a contract.

Investment Agreement

You need a legal framework when an investor is ready to sign a check over to your business, partnership, LLC, or corporation. An investment agreement details how much money will be invested, when it will be paid to your business entity, the rate of return to the investor, how net profits will be defined and distributed, credit, salary, ownership, accounting rights, various other legal boilerplate, and anything else you negotiate.

An important sentence to include is some version of: "Investor acknowledges and agrees that Investor is hereby making a high-risk investment and that Investor can afford the total loss of the contribution." Have an attorney draft the document to prevent misunderstandings. Most investors are savvy enough to have an attorney representing their side, so you better have one looking out for you. Lawyers are not paid to be fair to both sides.

Ideally, you want investors to be passive participants, where you are calling the shots, but if they want to be involved creatively, make sure they only get "consultation" and not "approval." You, the filmmaker, the artist, should have final creative approval. If you are quick to give up control, the film will no longer be yours, and you may have to make all their changes. Instead, offer them all the fun stuff, such as a guarantee they will be invited to all events that are under your control (wrap party premiere film festivals, industry screenings, etc.).

One good incentive is to offer to pay back out of the first proceeds an investor's monetary contribution plus 10 percent. A typical payback priority starts by first reimbursing hard cash expenditures (including investor funds, sometimes plus this 10 percent), then the filmmaker deferments, then a fifty-fifty profit split. You will be in an even better position if you can negotiate to split the first dollar of income right away, perhaps 50 percent paying off toward the investor share and 50 percent toward paying filmmaker deferments. First, ask for the better deal; you can always fall back. Don't be insulted by ridiculous offers; it's just business. I have had an investor ask for 75 percent of the profits. Try to hold their profit share down as low as possible, closer to 10 percent. Get as high a number for your side as you can. It all comes down to how badly you need that investor's money. After you finish shooting, if you turn to an investor for finishing funds, a typical last-money-in deal will probably require payback as first-money-out plus 10 to 25 percent, paid ahead of the original investment, possibly with producer credit and profit points thrown in.

Often, there is an agreement to define the split of proceeds on a *pro-rata* or *pari passu* basis. *Pro rata* is Latin for "in proportion," meaning that each stakeholder gets a proportion of a dollar of revenue according to what percentage their share of compensation is to the total of all shares. If the investor's compensation is 35 percent of the total payback obligations, the investor would get thirty-five cents from every dollar of revenue. *Pari passu* is Latin for "equal footing," meaning each party receives the same share, regardless of their percentage of the total compensation. In this case, if five dollars of revenue comes in, and there are five parties, each gets one dollar.

Crew Deal Memos

All crew members should sign a deal memo: director, producer, editor, camera, sound, composer, publicist, and so on. The main point of discussion and clarification is pay rate. People typically get paid weeks after a job, memories get hazy, and issues arise. Ensure every contract for a creative contribution, like website designer or poster artist, contains a "work for hire" clause that says you will be the sole and exclusive owner of all copyright and other rights in and to the material they create and any results and proceeds therefrom. If their work is not designated a work made for hire, they may be able to claim later that they own the work they created for you.

Non-Disparagement Agreement and Nondisclosure Agreement (NDA)

I once hired a website designer who finished a site, was paid, and then a month later demanded $10,000 more. When I declined to accede to his demand, he took down the website, refusing to restore it until his demands were met. I used the Internet Wayback Machine at archive.org to recapture the information and then paid someone else, who was more reliable, to reconstitute the site for less. Before making any final payments, make sure you get all the keys and passwords to your website, and change them immediately once the work is done so nobody can shake you down.

Another time, I hired an editor whose work was not acceptable. When I terminated his employment, he took it personally and started writing scathing reviews about the film online. Hell hath no fury like a fired crew member—now with plenty of free time to try to mess with you. He ceased when I pointed out I could do the same about him and his filmmaker roommate/landlord and everybody he knew. Adding a non-disparagement clause to your agreements helps prevent this sort of behavior. Also, consider including a nondisclosure clause, with a financial penalty for violating it, to prevent crew from revealing confidential and proprietary information to competitors while, or after, they work for you.

Studios and networks regularly add these clauses to deal memos. When I sold a reality pilot to the TNT network, the cast agreements they required contained strict confidentiality paragraphs that included a $250,000 payment assessed in liquidated damages per each confidentiality breach, plus disgorgement of any income the participant may have received in connection with the breach. Networks don't want cast or crew posting photos, videos, or plot details on social media or badmouthing shows the networks are financing and promoting. Incidental non-derogatory mentions might be allowed, but otherwise, they want advance approval for disclosures. In the age of social media, everybody likes to blab as soon as possible, but contractually, discipline may be required.

Music Contracts

Music rights are considered to have two "sides": writers' share and recording artists' share. A music synchronization license covers the composition (the writer's share), and a master-use license covers the recording (the publisher's share). When prerecorded songs are licensed in movies, a payment has to be negotiated with the owners of both sides.

For the score, sometimes a composer keeps only the writer's rights (sync license), and the producer acquires the publishing rights (master-use license). Or the producer and composer might negotiate to share a percentage of the publishing rights. I typically ask for a fifty-fifty split of master-use publishing rights to new music that a composer creates for my films. When a film airs, it triggers music royalty payments via a PRO (performing rights organization), such as BMI (Broadcast Music, Inc.) or ASCAP (American Society of Composers, Authors, and Publishers). Also, if the same music cue is used again by a composer in another project, it triggers additional royalty payments. To collect your royalties, you need to set up an account in advance at one of these PROs. The music cue sheet that you create and deliver to a distributor lays out who gets paid for each cue and in what proportion.

A composer contract will specify who owns the composed music, the services required, compensation, delivery date, making changes (how many rounds of notes are allowed), recording expenses (who will pay), credit, exclusivity (or non-exclusivity), soundtrack royalties, and so on. If a film's score is not a work for hire, if it is "needle-drop" music (licensed from a music library), a licensing contract will specify nonexclusive use of that music throughout the universe in perpetuity specifically for that film, and/or trailers, and/or promotional materials, and possibly even for derivative works and sequels (depending on what is negotiated).

Some rights can't be negotiated away, such as rights of *droit moral*, a French term meaning a creator has some rights that are always protected. One example would be a prohibition against a filmmaker changing a composer's work (other than editing for timing purposes) or taking an artist's name off a work without the artist's permission.

Archival Clearance

If you intend to use stock footage, photographs, artwork, or anything not clearly in the public domain, get permission from owners, for protection against lawsuits. The "fair use" doctrine of Section 107 of the U.S. Copyright Act allows limited portions of a work (video, audio, images, text) to be excerpted or quoted. This applies to commentary, criticism, parody, news reporting, teaching, research, and scholarship. The amount used has to be very small in relation to the total amount of the original work. The excerpted material must be directly related to the content it is inserted within, and the use of the material must not adversely impact the market value of the original work. If you make a documentary about the use of wardrobe in cinema, if one segment is about the use of hats in movies, and if you use short clips in a montage as examples of people wearing hats in movies to make the point, you have a solid, legal argument to support your fair use of the clips.

Sometimes a strategic decision is made not to try to clear a clip. Maybe it's because there is a good chance that if the owner is alerted, there is a certainty they will refuse or they will charge a price beyond what the production can afford. First, a copy of the clip has to be procured from an open source like YouTube or a Blu-ray because once a producer asks the owner for a copy of the clip, they are on the owner's radar. Now that they have empowered the owner, the production either has to pay the license fee or not use the clip. Asking for a price and then deciding not to pay it drastically increases legal risk; it places the production in a weak position with respect to making a fair use argument. Abiding by fair use rules does not protect anyone from being sued, but it is a defense that can be offered. A signed release is a much stronger defense. Copyright rules can vary from country to country, so even if you rely on fair use in the United States, it may not cover a project in some foreign territories.

When a production makes the decision to use unlicensed clips, they hire an attorney to review the usage. If the legal firm concludes the use qualifies under fair use, they write an analysis that says the use of the clip has qualified. Then, the producer files this document with the rest of the delivery items and hopes that the insurance company, a future buyer, and any future court will accept this opinion. Often, the giant organization that owns the material you excerpted never notices or cares. And chances are good that their productions are doing the same thing. But what if they do object? They may demand money or send a cease and desist letter. Then the production's lawyer responds with a letter that says: "Here are all the reasons it qualifies as fair use." Maybe they go away. Or maybe they keep fighting. A production has to weigh which would be more expensive, the license fee or the legal fees to defend its use (or the costs of editing out the clips). If an insurance company initially accepts the fair use argument and insures the project, the insurance company pays the legal fees for defense, up to a point, minus a deductible.

Life Rights and Exclusivity

Lock down the rights to whoever or whatever you are filming or pitching. If you decide to spend months or years filming somebody, a group of people, or an institution, you would be wise to get a sign-off that says you have exclusive rights to this story and the materials you create to document and promote it—at least for some reasonable period of time. You don't want to spend months pitching a project or years working on a film only to have the subjects of the film work with somebody else who cuts you out of the project.

Often, filmmakers find themselves in a situation where there is another project in development or in production that is similar to theirs. There may be nothing you can do except try to be first or better. There is another option.

When Marina Zenovich was working on a Robin Williams documentary for CNN, she heard that Alex Gibney had a competing project at HBO.

Zenovich called Gibney (her friend and mentor) and said, "Are you making a documentary about Robin Williams? Because I'm making a documentary about Robin Williams."

Gibney said, "Yes, how far along are you?"

She said, "Oh, I'm way far along."

She admitted she didn't know who was further along, but she feared Gibney was. "What else was I going to say? He was going to get it done before me." So they joined forces and merged their projects, with Gibney producing and Zenovich directing, a win for both.

Cast and Interviewee Releases

Always use a solid release form, and never pay interviewees. One aspect in a documentary producer's favor is that union wages for interviewees are not required unless the filmmakers opt to voluntarily make their documentary a SAG (Screen Actors Guild) film. However, that could cost a lot of money. Independent documentaries would rarely get made if filmmakers had to pay interviewees. However, shooting scripted re-enactments is a different situation and could fall under SAG's jurisdiction if you are using union actors.

Because we worked outside the studio system on *Trekkies*, below the radar, we were able to make it for less than if a big studio had produced the film, in which case all the actors might have expected to get paid. Denise Crosby said that the *Star Trek* actors had never felt well treated by Paramount and were particularly on guard about being screwed over. She recalled how during the first season of *Star Trek: The Next Generation* (1987–1994), at Christmas, the cast of *Cheers* (1982–1993) were given Range Rovers and big-screen TVs. What did Paramount give *The Next Generation* cast? Glass tumblers with the Paramount logo. Not even a nice single-malt Scotch to fill the tumbler.

Now, I will contradict myself. I admit I have given interviewees money on occasion. When a druid I interviewed near Odiham Castle in Hampshire, England, ran out of petrol for his motorcycle, I gave him gas money to get home. When interviewing somebody who is impoverished, if you feel like helping them out, there's nothing wrong with that. What you don't want to do is set a precedent that forces you to pay all interviewees.

Every interviewee (or a parent or guardian if the interviewee is under eighteen) must sign a release form. Get the release signed in advance! You never want to have to chase somebody and beg for a signature afterward. Take a photo of the person to go along with the release form, or jot down on the form a physical description of the person (describing how they looked on camera) to help with identification. Two hundred interviews later, it gets hard to remember who was who.

This form should cover every potential type of contribution you might encounter. In Ken Burns's Vietnam documentary, President Lyndon Johnson says about the Gulf of Tonkin Resolution, what you want is something "like grandma's nightshirt, it covers everything."[1] In addition to image and voice, include words, likeness, material, artwork, photographs, camerawork, photography, drawings, editing, intellectual material, or other contributions. Obviously, most eventualities will not be relevant for a typical interview, but if they do burst into song (like the filk [science fiction folk] singer in *Trekkies*) or they show you their photos or artwork (like the folk artists in *The Nature of Existence*), you will be covered. If they do start singing, the general release can cover the performance but not the writer of the music, which requires a separate (sync license) agreement. Have the usage extend throughout the universe in perpetuity, to websites, social media, any advertising or publicity, posters, promotional materials, videos, including bonus material, outtakes, raw footage, or portions thereof, derivative works, or any other projects or material, so you can use or license the material for any other projects, sequels, books, or anything else that comes later. Somebody you interview might become a character in a bigger story later. In 2015, I interviewed Noel Biederman, CEO of AshleyMadison.com, for my marriage documentary. Two months later, a hacker breached their website and publicly released client names. This caused massive turmoil for the company and the site's users. Eight years later, an archivist working on a Netflix docuseries, called *Ashley Madison: Sex, Lies & Scandal*, contacted me and offered $85 per second for interview footage and $60 per second for B-roll for my interview footage. Because I had saved my raw files and had a comprehensive release, I was able to re-license footage and collect a $4,000 windfall. Appendix A contains a sample of a release form I have used.

When you put a release form in front of people and ask them to sign, most do so immediately without question. Out of the thousands of individuals who have signed my release forms, only three have taken the time to read the release thoroughly. And if there is something that does not apply or they object to and you agree to the change, you could cross it off, and then both initial the change.

Generally, anybody in a public place is fair game if you don't show their face clearly and if you don't stop and dwell on them. You should never feature somebody captured randomly in public and imply something about them, especially if it could be perceived as negative. When shooting in a specific place, like at a concert or public event, announce and post signs that say you are filming. Take a photo of the sign to prove you posted it. The sign should read something like this:

PLEASE NOTE: THIS AREA IS BEING FILMED AS PART OF THE MOTION PICTURE _____ AND YOU MAY POSSIBLY APPEAR IN THE FOOTAGE. YOUR ENTERING INTO THIS AREA MEANS YOU CONSENT TO APPEARING IN THE FOOTAGE OF THIS MOTION PICTURE.

In a pinch, have an interviewee sign off verbally to the camera at the beginning of an interview, saying the words "I consent to be interviewed." Neither this nor a posted sign are nearly as good as a signed form, but it's better than nothing.

There is so much to coordinate during the whirlwind of production, there will be times when you're tempted to overlook paperwork. It's far easier to do the paperwork during production than try to hunt it down after the film is completed. People may hold you up for a lot of money at that point when they know their signature is needed for you to get distribution, or worse, they refuse to sign. Some distributors want everything released and signed off, every musical note cleared, and to see your birth certificate to prove you're you. Some smaller distributors are more lax, willing to accept that you signed their distribution contract with waivers declaring everything is cleared, so if any legal issue comes up, it will fall on your shoulders. Most distributors require that a film's producer purchase E&O insurance (producers' errors and omissions insurance or multimedia risk insurance), which covers producers and distributors against lawsuits. If you don't get a needed form or contract signed, you might arrive at a soul-crushing point where the film you worked so hard on is denied distribution. Do the paperwork. That's not a request.

CHAPTER SEVEN

Post Production

Documentaries are discovered in the editing room.

Your project is your baby, and you want to get it to the editing room where you can make it beautiful. Nobody likes ugly babies, except their parents, and you want to sell more than two tickets. To a large extent, editing is about being methodological and organized in the face of mountains of footage. If you are good at organizing your garage, you might just have what it takes to be a good documentary editor. Also crucial is that the editor has to fully understand the story in order to be able to write the final draft in the edit. Sometimes, the filmmaker is the editor. Other times a director works with several editors. The director-editor relationship is so essential that filmmakers often repeatedly work with the same editors. Errol Morris has worked with editor Steven Hathaway for the last ten years. Davis Guggenheim feels that editors are his equal partners. "I'm sort of a co-writer, where the editor and I are writing the movie together." Frederick Wiseman prefers to solely edit his films "because I want the movie to be a reflection of my voice only."

Marina Zenovich believes the editing room should be respected as a sacred space "because you never want to make anyone feel bad. You want to boost each other up because it's such a vulnerable creative space. You need to be able to say, 'I know this sounds crazy, but what if we try this?' You give each other space to come up with ideas and work off each other. The relationship between director and editor is best when they have a certain chemistry. It's how you get along with someone, how they make you feel, how they inspire you."

For comprehensive editing guidelines, refer to my book *Cut to the Monkey* (2021).

Find the Narrative Arc

How do you know when you've got enough footage to tell the story? Wiseman's shoots have varied from four to twelve weeks. He said, "You know how many hours of rushes you have, how long you've been away from your wife and children. The mattress in the motel is uncomfortable. I have to make a decision that I have enough footage." His goal is to create a dramatic structure from 100 to 150 hours of footage. "I try to figure out how the sequences might be thematically related in the editing. I'm attracted by the idea of imposing a form on my experience." Wiseman said there are some shoot days where he doesn't get anything good, "but six months later in the editing room, because of other choices you made in editing, a scene suddenly has value where originally it had none." The challenge is to distill an overload of interviews down to a logical narrative that doesn't overstay its welcome. It's tempting to feel entitled to two-plus hours for your very important subject, but you will try an audience's patience if you exceed ninety minutes.

Sam Pollard says that on every film, he puts story cards on the wall. He moves scenes around while building the structure. "Sometimes the ending becomes the beginning, and the beginning becomes the ending, and the middle becomes the first act. It's a dance." The cards will help make it apparent where the narrative thread is strong and where there are holes. What to keep or remove becomes evident as the shape of the acts comes into focus.

Start with the Ending

A film may ultimately deviate from the plan, but having a three-act structure with an ending in place is a solid way to begin. One good approach is to find the ending and work backward. You may not know all the details of your conclusion, and it may shift as you shoot, but you must know where to look for it. If you are asking a question, solving a mystery, or searching for something, you have to get there somehow.

Some stories have built-in endings such as a verdict, finding the sought-after person, or winning the big game. A story that establishes the promise of a climactic finale, right at the start, has a better chance of holding an audience to the end. D.A. Pennebaker and Chris Hegedus's *The War Room* (1993) had a definite ending: either a win or a loss for Bill Clinton's presidential campaign. Their gamble ended with an election-night victory. Crime documentaries have arrests, indictments, verdicts, and retrials that can provide resolutions, though not always closure. *The Thin Blue Line* (1988) brought this style to the forefront and led to Randall Dale Adams's release from prison. Errol Morris lamented, "I'll never find a case quite like *The Thin Blue Line* again. It's like all the stars aligned. You don't ever find a case that wraps up quite so neatly. Not in my experience." Other examples of this type of documentary that followed are *Making a Murderer* (2015–TBD), *The Jinx: The Life and Deaths of Robert Durst* (2015), and *The Inventor: Out for Blood in Silicon Valley* (2019).

Sports documentaries, such as *The Last Dance* (2020), end with winning or losing. *Grizzly Man* (2005) ends with death. With *Free Solo* (2018), even though you know Alex Honnold survived his daredevil climb, watching how he does it is gripping. When Liz Garbus was working on a past-tense story where she knew the ending, such as *What Happened, Miss Simone?* (2016) or *Bobby Fischer Against the World* (2011), she said, "I'm looking for narrative elements, of personal struggles or accomplishments that illuminate an individual's journey as well as telling us something about the historical moment or social context. With a vérité film, I'm looking for a journey too. Those arcs may ultimately be the spine around which we structure the film in the edit and determine what to shoot and what not to shoot." In Freida Lee Mock's film *G-Dog* (2012), Homeboy Industries faced the danger of closing when they realized they needed to lay off 400 employees. One of the young men Father Greg Boyle

Father Greg Boyle speaking to his employees at Homeboy Industries in G-Dog (2012).

One of Father Greg Boyle's employees in in G-Dog (2012).

helped get off the streets dramatizes this plot point when he says: "There's an old saying, show me a place of struggle, and I will show you a place of strength." The conflict and turning point of the film were set: Will the organization survive, and will the at-risk kids get a second chance in life?

The ending of a biography is clear from the start; the film examines how somebody's life played out. *The Kid Stays in the Picture* (2002) was based on Hollywood producer Robert Evans's autobiography. Viewers watched to see how he succeeded in Hollywood. *Three Identical Strangers* (2018) asked what happened to triplets separated at birth. *Crumb* (1994) profiled an odd-ball cartoonist who hit it big with one particular "Keep on Truckin'" comic.

Quest documentaries like *Roger and Me* (1989) and *Searching for Sugar Man* (2012) end when the filmmakers find the sought-after person or don't. Filmmakers Malik Bendjelloul and Simon Chinn followed two obsessed Sugar Man fans who tracked down the once-celebrated Sixto Rodriguez. Michael Moore failed to get to his target, Roger B. Smith, chairman and CEO of General Motors. Moore solved his story-ending problem by interviewing an empty chair.

Davis Guggenheim was presented with a challenge when Participant Media asked "Can you make a film about public education?" Guggenheim declined, not seeing an obvious story inherent in the subject. But then he read an editorial by Thomas Friedman about the SEED School of Maryland, which had an admissions lottery. They used a random bingo selector, and if your ball rolled down the chute, you got into the school. That was a breakthrough for Guggenheim, who saw conflict and stakes: "Suddenly, I knew my third act. It was a plot device, but it was also a thematic container for the idea that a child's future is decided by how a bingo ball bounces. I constructed the narrative of *Waiting for Superman* backward, building to that point."

Rachel Grady said she works intuitively; she knows she's found an ending when it feels satisfying. Perhaps there's a catharsis for the main character; something they care about goes well or poorly. Or sometimes it is simply: and life goes on. "If you're trying too hard to tie it up in a bow, it may come across as too pat and fake. You might shoot something while you're in the field and realize it was the ending; you just know it in your heart. And then you work toward that feeling."

In the world of vérité, getting to a satisfying ending can be harder. In Albert and David Maysles's *Grey Gardens* (1975), the audience watches to

An inmate plays solo trombone in the exer-   *The inmates perform on stage at the end*
cise yard in Frederick Wiseman's Titicut   *of Frederick Wiseman's* Titicut Follies
Follies *(1967).*   *(1967).*

the end to find out if two apparently delusional women will survive living in a decrepit house (and world) that is falling down around them. Frederick Wiseman has no checklist that he goes through. "I'm sitting there and looking at the screen, and I try various alternatives, and I say to myself, 'Well, I think this one works.' Someone else might make a different choice." As subjective or random as his process may seem, Wiseman acknowledged there is always a specific meaning attached to his endings, representing his choice of how to end the film. Wiseman found a memorable ending for *Titicut Follies* (1967) by closing with a musical performance, where the inmates at the State Prison for the Criminally Insane in Bridgewater, Massachusetts, put on a talent show.

Editing is Writing

Sam Pollard has a background as an editor on narrative films, such as Spike Lee's *Mo' Better Blues* (1990) and Ernest R. Dickerson's *Juice* (1992). Because of this experience, Pollard thinks dramatically as he works on documentaries. He considers: *What's the dramatic high point of this sequence? How do I change the tone and texture from one sequence to the next?* Pollard is looking to create ups and downs, emotional highs and lows, to avoid having an unvarying tempo.

    Once Pollard has completed a first assembly, he asks himself: *Now, how do we make it into a film? How do we make it engaging?* He said, of his first cut of *The League* (2023), about the Negro baseball leagues: "It was all there. But was it exciting? No. Was it really engaging? No. It was: *Here's the history of the Negro Leagues.* And so we went back in to reshape and re-edit, and change music, move things around, add and subtract voices, to give it more dynamics and drama." When he showed the next cut to his executive producers, they pushed him to make it even more dramatic and exciting. "The documentary process is collaborative. You lay out the foundation of the house, and then you build the house, but then you've got to figure out how to make it into a beautiful house."

The documentary that made Marina Zenovich go, "Oh, I want to do that!" was Alan Berliner's *Nobody's Business* (1996), a simple—yet superbly poignant—portrait of Berliner's crotchety father, Oscar Berliner. A moment created through editing that greatly affected Zenovich was when Alan Berliner's mother recalls Oscar Berliner asking Alan as a child, "Would you rather have mother happy away from us, or unhappy and with us?"

Young Alan responded, "Unhappy and with us."

The film then cuts to a shot of a house on a cliff crumbling into the ocean.

"When I saw that," Zenovich recalled, "I was like, *Oh my god, I want to do this.* That was my moment. That's what I'm chasing now, that sort of deep emotion with visuals that serve it."

A series of shots from Nobody's Business *(1996).*

A documentarian thinks about editing while shooting. Nothing but talking heads gets old fast. Will there be B-roll, stock footage, photos, newspaper articles, re-enactments, animation? To be able to shape a story, the editor needs cutaways: insert shots, close-ups, establishing shots, exteriors, and portrait shots. A portrait shows a subject walking, standing, or sitting, looking to the lens, maybe doing and saying nothing. It could be used as an interstitial shot or an introduction the first time you see them. These options will be needed later. When a moment feels dull during shooting, Frederick Wiseman pans over and picks up cutaways of people making notes, turning their heads, sharpening a pencil, or scratching their heads. He protects himself against missing interesting conversations by keeping the sound recorder running. If the action suddenly gets interesting, he pans back, without missing the audio lead-in to the moment.

Begin an edit by putting like with like. Collect all the pieces on similar topics into one bin, and soon these coalesce into chunks, and then segments, and maybe polished chapters. One of the challenges to creating an elegant flow is finding the links, the transitions from shot to shot and from segment to segment. The footage is a puzzle where all the pieces do not necessarily fit, but you must find a way to combine them. One way to lay the groundwork for the links is to ask theme questions so you can intercut answers, building sound-bite trains, where interviewees finish each other's sentences. Or juxtapose opposing statements for maximum contrast.

Pacing is deciding when to reveal the next plot point—and the answer is probably sooner. Lead the audience and keep them from getting ahead of the story. If they can predict what's next, they will lose interest. The audience has to fully understand why you presented something, but at the same time, you have to move fast enough to surprise them with your next cut.

Ken Burns loves nothing better than an edit session that makes a scene better and more complicated. Although Burns has the ultimate say, the editors are at the frontline, choosing the images. "Yelling is forbidden," says Burns. "It's hugely important to me that the process be joyous as well as hard. Sometimes we've got a scene that works, and we don't want to touch it, but then we learn new and sometimes contradictory information, and we dismantle it. If you find out information that makes a scene less stable, you've got to figure out how to make that instability part of the story. Sometimes that scene ends up not as good as it once was, but it's truer to what actually happened."

Burns's writing and editing process is somewhat unique. He and his team begin by interviewing scholars and experts. The writers usually do not participate at this point; they might look at questions and suggest things, but the filmmakers shoot without a script. Then, the writer reviews the interviews and begins researching and writing a script. "We might have fifty interviews done by the time we give it to the writer, who throws quotes into various places," said Burns. "Usually, every talking head gets moved at least once, if not twenty times, during the editing process. We want to be corrigible to the end."

When the script's first draft is done, it is sent to scholars. Burns and his team will chop it up; they may go through twenty drafts. "The script becomes a conversation among me, the writer, my co-directors and co-producers, and our scholars—who are not window dressing. In fact, we've been humbled, in some cases humiliated, by a subject we thought we knew. We never stop researching, and we never stop writing."

They call the initial editing process a blind assembly. "We listen to it almost as a radio play, with me as the narrator and people in the office reading first-person voices (if that film has first-person voices)." All the talking heads are jump-cut together, and the editors don't begin adding pictures until drafts three, four, or five of the script. And then it takes another year or two of editing to refine the film (particularly on a big series). "Any time you see a talking head in our film, its location is sort of a happy accident of trial and error."

Compassion and Fairness

Documentarians provide a soapbox for individuals, who can choose to speak their minds or not. Some make a great point, and some don't. There is always a danger of a film edging into overt ridicule or mockery. I try not to include anything that an interviewee would feel upset about. I want them to be pleased to be in the film. Sometimes people change their minds about what they said. There is no foolproof rule.

Frederick Wiseman says he never considers anything except the following questions: *Does it work? Is the complexity of the situation adequately represented? Is what's going on in the sequence clear?*

Rachel Grady says the process constantly puts her morals and ethics to the test. "I have to grapple with filming real life and meeting people when they're vulnerable. It challenges me, and it keeps me on my toes." A documentary is a reflection of who the filmmaker is as a person.

Alex Gibney said the standard he applies is: "I try to imagine myself screening the film for them, with them sitting on the chair right next to me, so that I can look and I can defend every frame and say this is why I think this is fair."[1]

Ken Burns considers how to reciprocate appropriately "when you're taking from somebody, an interview subject, or a photograph, or a story." He is supremely careful about how stills and footage are used. "And that kind of delicacy is as if you're handling nitroglycerin. That's how we attend to almost every film we've worked on, with varying degrees of urgency to that fragility. For example, our Holocaust scenes don't have the worst material we've seen. If they did, that risks revictimizing the victims."

Trekkies has very little narration, aside from Denise Crosby's brief set-up, and there is no overt comment on the fans and their lifestyles. Because viewers judge for themselves, they tend to project motives onto the filmmakers that coincide with their own attitudes. If they are intolerant of alternate lifestyles, they may see the film as an indictment. If they are open-minded or approve of how the profilees live their lives, they may see the film's presentation as sympathetic. If you, as a filmmaker, convey your position overtly, that will frame how the viewer perceives the footage. If you let the viewer absorb the information and make their own decision, they will color it through the lens of their own experiences.

Liz Garbus said she absolutely considers how her subjects feel. "I'm human, and they're human, and we've entered into a relationship." Early in her career, she read Janet Malcolm's essay, "The Journalist and the Murderer," where Malcolm wrote, "Every journalist . . . is a kind of confidence man, preying on people's vanity, ignorance, or loneliness, gaining their trust and betraying them without remorse."[2] Garbus said the filmmaker-interviewee relationship has a power dynamic that has to be managed. "Subjects see storytellers and their microphones as ways to right the wrongs in their lives."

Garbus made the documentary *There's Something Wrong with Aunt Diane* (2011), which is about a woman who drove the wrong way down the Potomac Parkway on a sunny Sunday afternoon with her son, daughter, and three nieces. Everybody died except her son. Three gentlemen in an oncoming car also died. A toxicology test said Diane Schuler had the equivalent of ten shots of vodka and high levels of THC in her bloodstream. Her husband, who was not in the car, was absolutely sure there had to be a mix-up or some conspiracy because he believed his wife would never do that. Garbus said, "My relationship with the husband, his hopes, his dreams, his pain, his suffering, it weighed heavily on me, as it should. I tried to manage expectations because it's important for subjects who embark on documentaries with filmmakers to have a realistic sense of what might or might not happen. In this case, I was clear about my perspective that the simplest explanation is usually the right one and that it would be hard to believe that there was a conspiracy. But I would, of course, do thorough fact-checking. And if there were irregularities, they would certainly become part of the film." Garbus couldn't promise more than that, no matter what result a person was hoping for. And ultimately, what Garbus found made it more understandable how Schuler ended up causing a deadly crash that afternoon.

Test Screening

After seeing *Trekkies*, actor Walter Koenig's criticism of the film was, "You should have had more of me in the film! But that's my actor's ego talking." I laughed and agreed. I especially missed him in the segment about the memories of the first convention. I explained how, unfortunately, because he was one of our first interviewees, our theme questions had yet to evolve fully, so we neglected to ask him about his first convention experience. Koenig's criticism is typically the number one criticism I have received from interviewees. After sitting for a couple hours and then seeing only two minutes in the film—or maybe even just one quote—it's often a shock how little remains.

Sometimes you have to remove segments you love because they don't fit the overall scheme. The way that becomes clear is by watching rough cuts with an audience. Don't rely on yourself and a few buddies to tell you you've got a great movie. Studios test movies for a reason. Film rep Glen Reynolds said, "I've been around several films that got into Sundance that would never have gotten in on the first cut before testing. Have five or six screenings of ten people, ranging from editors to your barista to your Aunt Joy. Sometimes you find common issues among people, something you might need to address that you wouldn't have thought of. Some people get caught up in the belief, 'It's my vision, and I know it works, so I don't need to do that.' But that's a mistake."

An audience can't tell you how to fix your movie, but they will show you where the problems are. You will feel where it drags when you observe people screening your film. Ask specific questions about the weaknesses you suspect your film has. If they confirm your suspicions, work on fixing those issues. If you disagree with their criticisms, go with your instinct. The film is your vision, not theirs. Liz Garbus said, "Tuning out the noise and listening to my gut is something I constantly have to remind myself to do. If you don't listen to your gut, you're lost because there will always be a sea of voices telling you different things. If you're the filmmaker, you need to be tuned in to that voice."

Freida Lee Mock wondered what people would have said if Picasso had done test screenings for his portraits. What if someone had said, "Oh, Dora Maar's right eyeball looks weird. Shouldn't it be closer to her nose?" Or, "*Guernica* is too busy. There are too many animals and soldiers lying upside down."With *Maya Lin: A Strong Clear Vision* (1995), Mock's only screenings included those who worked on the film. For later films, Mock showed fine cuts to three or four friends who were not in the industry and whose opinions she valued. "Typically, I find out what's not clear. I don't change much, but it's often an issue of clarity."

Music Choices

Sam Pollard cuts without music at first. "I try to build things and then have the music work with the scene." If you edit with music in place, it can hide problems. Adding music to a completed scene should support the natural emotions that the footage already evokes.

Many documentaries use no score at all. Frederick Wiseman avoids adding a score. At most, there may be incidental or source music, such as in *Model* (1981), where music plays in the studios where the models are working.

After I add a temporary score pulled from movie soundtracks, songs, or library music, my composer and I watch the film together and discuss all the places where I placed temp music. This is called a spotting session. That music is then replaced with an original score by the composer. A documentary composer needs a diverse set of skills to avoid falling into one sound throughout; sometimes, you have to shake the audience up with something different.

Composer Billy Sullivan (right) at work with guitarist Pierre Karlsson (left) on the score for The Truth About Marriage *(2020).*

Ken Burns approaches music differently. He records music early, well before a scene is edited. The music brings an emotional impact that he is trying to preserve by making the music primary. "We want music to be something more than just what's added at the end to amplify emotions you hope are there." For *The Civil War* (1990), Burns went through hymnals and popular sheet music from that era, collected around thirty-five songs, and recorded each in thirty different ways. "We don't score the films; we edit to the music. We will change a line of narration to get out of the way of a musical phrase. My brother Ric [Burns] once said, 'All the other art forms, when they die and go to heaven, aspire to be music.'"

Licensing existing songs can be expensive, unless you make a deal with a performer who is not signed to a label and controls all the song rights. $5,000 is common for songs without much notoriety. A Frank Sinatra song might cost $50,000. An independent artist might give you the rights for $100. There are also sources of royalty-free library music online. Read the agreements carefully to ensure all the rights you need are fully cleared. Sometimes, if you can go directly to a recording artist, or they are a big supporter of your film's topic, they might be willing to create a song for your film. While making *Trekkies*, we discovered that Fred Schneider of The B-52s was a *Star Trek* fan. For *Trekkies 2*, Producer Michael Leahy contacted Schneider, and we were thrilled when he agreed to record an opening song.

On-Line Editing

If you have plenty of hard-drive space that allows editing on a one-to-one basis at full resolution, on-lining is no longer an issue. When compressing footage, which may be necessary when shooting hundreds of hours of footage, an online session to up-res the final version will be needed after locking a cut. This used to be a step that had to be done at a post-production facility, but it's now easy to online footage in your edit bay. Make sure you have a plan in place for a post-production workflow when you set up a project so you don't back yourself into a corner. Consult with your assistant editor, distributor spec sheets, and/or post-production supervisor before beginning.

Color Correction

Include money in the budget for color correction, done by a qualified technician who can deliver beautiful images that fall within the technical parameters required by distributors and broadcasters. A good colorist can hide many sins, do basic effects work, and fix many of the problems you have identified in your offline edit.

Digital Effects

Fixes that are more elaborate than can be done in your online and color sessions will require a digital-effects artist. Have all your effects shots in place before the color-correction pass. Sometimes, you have to blur or remove faces or products that are not cleared. You may need to remove booms, reflections, and blemishes, or add diagrams, clean up archival footage, give new footage an old look, create text, letters, or social-media posts, or change anything your creativity and budget can imagine.

Graphics

A digital artist can create a graphics package that includes a unique style for identifications, transitions, chapter cards, and perhaps animation. Place lower thirds (identifications at the bottom of the frame) in a way that they fill the negative space in the frame. Graphics can set up a topic or present a question, statistic, location, or any information that re-centers the focus and helps viewers follow the progression of ideas. I have found that chapter cards help give the audience mile markers as to where the film's story is, intellectually or psychologically. Be careful of over-

Graphics by Gabriel Koerner.

Love and divorce graphics created for The Truth About Marriage *(2020).*

using text graphics as a Band-Aid to replace information you didn't film that would be better served via interviewee sound bites. If you don't have a sound bite that you need, to help make a transition or tie two sequences together, and if your interviewees are still available, Sam Pollard recommends reaching out to them to record the audio. Sometimes they can do it right on their iPhone memo application and forward the voice files to you.

Animation

When you need to present complex ideas, show what people are thinking, recreate past or future events, or fill holes that you don't have any other way of addressing, animation opens up a world of possibilities. *Good Night Oppy* (2022) is a documentary in support of the CGI (computer-generated imagery) animation that depicts the experiences of NASA's anthropomorphized Mars rovers. For *The Truth About Marriage* (2020), I hired four different animators and divided up segments according to their specialties. I needed

Animation by artist Brittney Sherwood.

Dating app footage created for The Truth About Marriage *(2020)*

Animation by artist James Morr.

Sperm training footage created for The Truth About Marriage *(2020)*

computer-based graphics for chapter cards and explanatory graphics. One artist animated hand-drawn cartoons, and another utilized stop-motion with clay figures. This is a labor-intensive endeavor and can be expensive. I have found that artists like to be busy, and they appreciate being able to express their art. Even if the budget is low, if you approach them honestly with the compensation you can afford, they say yes more often than not.

The Ken Burns Effect

Animatics are created by taking photographs or drawings and adding movement either by filming or digitally scanning them, then zooming, tilting, or panning across the image, to isolate details or convey a sense of movement. Sometimes the process is used for sizzle reels or during preproduction to animate storyboard images, or to pre-visualize effects shots, or to plan the look and feel of the final animation.

Ken Burns is famous for his use of photographs. He treats every archival photo as a master shot, containing a long shot, a medium shot, a close-up, and an extreme close-up. He said he feels that he can often pull more truth out of a photograph than out of motion pictures. "With footage, Babe Ruth running around the bases is basically all you can talk about. But if you've got a beautiful still photograph, like a Karsh photograph, you can talk about Babe Ruth running the bases. You can talk about his unhappy childhood on the wharves of Baltimore. You can talk about his relationships, his failings, his humor. You can talk about anything. A photo is a tabula rasa into which you carefully try to pour the story and the meaning you're discovering."

Burns attended Hampshire College, a radically experimental school, and fell under the sway of social-documentary still-photographers Jerome Liebling and Elaine Mayes. Burns said, "They reminded me there is as much drama in what is and what was than anything the human imagination can dream up. Suddenly, at eighteen years old, I found myself wanting to make documentary films." His college thesis (division three examination) was a thirty-minute film called *Working in Rural New England* (1975), made for Old Sturbridge Village, in which the last shot is a pan across a painting.

In 2002, Steve Jobs showed Burns something his engineers had been working on: the ability to pan and zoom on photographs in a computer. Jobs told Burns, "Our working title is The Ken Burns Effect." This digital effect became a simplistic version of Burns's signature style: a complex use of movement on camera, combined with first-person voices, myriad levels of sound effects, and contemporary music, along with the use of photographs, footage, live cinematography, and/or interviews.

Burns gets full-resolution copies of prints when he wants to do elaborate moves and zooms. Sometimes, stock footage houses offer only lower-resolution copies of the photos until you pay for them. Burns said the problem with using temporary versions is that "we don't get in as close or do moves that are as daring. When you do an extreme close-up, it's so blurred and unrecognizable that in early editing you tend not to use it because it just doesn't seem like it's working."

Burns also started using digital maps to help tell the stories of *The Vietnam War* (2017), such as the battle in the Ia Drang Valley, and then for *Benjamin Franklin* (2022). Burns also realized he could use CGI maps to help illustrate *The American Revolution* (2025). "The British positions were moving west through Long Island to what is now Brooklyn. And the American positions were in Brooklyn Heights. And I could dramatize the Battle of New York this way. I didn't have to be dependent only on paintings and drawings."

Map from Ken Burns's The Vietnam War, *"Episode Three: The River Styx (January 1964–December 1965)."*

Sound Mix

A good sound-mixing engineer will make sure your film sounds professional. Distributors ask for soundtracks to be delivered in stereo and 5.1 (left, right, center, surround left, surround right, and subwoofer). They may also want a DME mix (separation of the dialogue, music, and sound effects tracks) for potential dubbing and remixing by foreign buyers. A DME is less likely to be needed for documentaries, but it's good to have your mixing company provide these elements for posterity.

Final Masters

Once you marry final sound-mix tracks to a CCM (color-corrected master), you are ready to output a final ProRes master for delivery to a distributor. And you can use that master to create an H.264, a Blu-ray, and a DCP (Digital Cinema Package). Fully back up your project (and all the elements) multiple times. In the future, a distributor may want you to revisit your final cut and output different versions. Be ready for any future needs that may arise.

CHAPTER EIGHT

Selling Your Film

Your film is complete. Now what?

Y ou need money for your next film, so you want to sell the one you just made at a considerable profit, right? A film is an IP (intellectual property). Like a real estate listing or a collectible on eBay, you can put your film property up for sale in hopes of fielding bids greater than what you paid to make it. Your strongest selling point will be the story (unless your documentary is about Billie Eilish or Muhammad Ali or some other famous subject with a built-in core audience). Once you have condensed your film to a logline that grabs attention, you've got a concise selling pitch. Before listing your property for sale, there are a few steps to take.

Copyright

Register your intellectual property with the United States Copyright Office. Until you do this, your ability to protect a project is limited. It's hard to prevent somebody from shooting their own version of your idea if you haven't found a way to lock down rights. Ideas are not copyrightable. Only specific expressions that are captured in a fixed medium can be copyrighted. A written document or a video that you have completed can be copyrighted. If your film is not yet complete, use your outline or pitch proposal to write a document describing the project. Do not call it a synopsis or treatment or imply it is an unfinished work. Title it as a story or as an article written by you. If you are so inspired, it might even make sense to spend the time to write the story as a complete nonfiction book. Then, copyright that work and use it as the basis to adapt for a documentary. It's much less expensive to write and publish a book (self-publish if necessary) than it is to mount a film project.

Whichever document you wish to register, write at the top: "© Copyright (this year) by (your name)." Register this document as a finished literary work with the Copyright Office using Form TX (for text). This will give you the beginning of a basis to protect your project. This will also establish an earlier date of inception than if you wait until the film is complete. The instructions read:

> Use Form TX to register published or unpublished nondramatic literary works, excluding periodicals or serial issues. This class includes a wide variety of works: fiction, nonfiction, poetry, textbooks, reference works, directories, catalogs, advertising copy, compilations of information, and computer programs.[1,2]

Once you finish making the film and have a completed video, copyright the documentary with Form PA (performing arts). Reference it as having an underlying work, your earlier registered text, if you did so. This form is also for screenplays. Form PA's instructions read:

> Use Form PA to register published or unpublished works of the performing arts. This class includes works prepared to be "performed" directly before an audience or indirectly "by means of any device or process." Works of the performing arts include: (1) musical works, including any accompanying words; (2) dramatic works, including any accompanying music; (3) pantomimes and choreographic works; and (4) motion pictures and other audiovisual works.[3,4]

A distributor will ask you to prove you possess the film's copyright. The copyright certificate is a primary document establishing a film's chain of title. If the copyright isn't in your name or your company's name, you may need a contract that transfers rights to you or your company.

Key Art

After the film's title, the poster is your next best means of advertising. The poster will showcase your key art, which should be strong enough to be quickly perceived by eyeballs besieged with multitudes of images clamoring for attention. Consider what sort of image will work when reduced to the size of a thumbnail, which is how most will encounter your film on a VOD (video on demand) storefront. It has to stand out on any type of background, which could be colorful, black, white, or gray. Keep the artwork simple, clean, and uncluttered. All text and font choices should be clearly legible. Leave off website information. Reviewer blurbs, laurels, and credit blocks may be acceptable during a festival run, but that clutter will be cleared away for delivery to a distributor. Avoid explicit nudity or anything overtly sexual. Sex sells, but advertising smarties have for ages been finding ways to keep it subliminal.

Trailer

If you hit the big leagues, studios make their own trailers, but for most distributors, a trailer is a required delivery item. Trailers should be 75 to 120 seconds in length, not longer. The quicker you make your point, the better. It should have a clear multi-act storyline (mirroring your film) that features the main character(s) and the obstacle(s) they face. Think of it as a visual presentation of your logline. Watch other trailers of successful films in a similar genre to see what works. Don't hold back all your best hooks; lead with a strong one. Avoid gore, violence, drug use, or language that would push it out of a rating suitable for all audiences. Leave out websites or social-media URLs. And don't date it by announcing release information. All music must be cleared. Do not release it prematurely (see sections later in this chapter).

Formulate a Sales Strategy

Is it best to launch your documentary at film festivals or get a film agent? Should you go directly to buyers or try to self-distribute? Each approach has merit. The first rule is do not submit a film before it is ready. You only get one first impression. An exception would be screening for film agents, who can help guide you toward completion and preparation for submission. Film rep Glen Reynolds advises, "The only time to show an unfinished movie is if you're in a distressed situation where you have no way out but to sell the movie. I've seen that quite often."

Film Agents

I have sold films on my own as well as worked with a film agent. The real estate metaphor is appropriate again. You can sell your house without representation. *For sale by owner.* But would you do that? Maybe you love the business side of selling. Then go for it; dive in and learn everything. However, if you don't know the actual value of your property and are unaware of all the legal pitfalls that surround every deal, you will probably not make as good a deal as you could working with a pro. A film agent has years of experience and knowledge that you probably do not have.

Many of Glen Reynolds's clients are first-time filmmakers who don't know a good distributor from a bad one. Can you identify the fewer than forty viable distributors out of the several hundred? Even documentary veterans welcome the guidance of an agent; filmmakers often prefer to focus on other creative endeavors. Each time a filmmaker gets to the distribution stage, the world of distributors has probably changed again as players come and go. Reynolds's job is to protect filmmakers and make sure they make good deals. Some distributors refuse to even talk to filmmakers directly. They say, "Get an agent," because they want to utilize this filtering process. Reynolds also consults with filmmakers after they get distribution to troubleshoot problems with distributors downstream.

A film agent is not the same as a talent agent or manager, who might offer to represent your career as a filmmaker. Should you get an agent and/or manager to represent you personally? At some point, yes, but probably not until after you are seen as the person behind a successful project. When offers for jobs start to come in, you may also get offers for personal representation.

Photograph courtesy of Glen Reynolds.

Film agent Glen Reynolds at the Sundance Film Festival.

Talent and literary *agents* focus on fielding job offers and are motivated to book clients as often as possible (to generate maximum commissions). A talent *manager* is choosier, helping clients guide careers. A manager's motivation is to build your value by saying no to detrimental projects, which may cause you to be associated with mediocre work and diminish your value, and saying yes to quality work, which will lead to more quality work. After your film hits it big, when you launch your own company developing multiple projects, a talent or literary agent will become a crucial tool in your arsenal.

The way to approach a film rep is via email or phone with an offer to show your film. As you begin contacting and communicating with film agents, publicists, and distributors, remember they are dealing with hundreds of filmmakers. Put the name of your film plus the topic of your communication in the subject line of every email. Label all emails distinctively so that particular ones will be easy to find when searching back.

Keep your pitch to a film agent brief. Reynolds says, "If somebody sends me a long letter about how great the movie is, I still just need to see the movie. I don't find how someone personally presents themselves is particularly related to how good a movie is." Reynolds doesn't have to think a film is going to Sundance or be suitable for Netflix to get involved, but he has to feel he can find an appropriate home for it. "I tend to go for documentaries that feel like features more than they feel like something for CNN."

Reynolds said he typically represents 75 percent narratives and 25 percent documentaries. He noticed that the quality of documentaries that come across his desk is, on average, higher than narratives. He said it's because "if someone decides to make a documentary, there's a level of care and education that has to be there to craft it. Whereas someone can run around in their backyard with an iPhone camera, a fake knife, and a bottle of ketchup and put together a little horror movie. Documentaries take a lot of time and love and care to get to the point of completion."

There are big agencies, like Creative Artists Agency and William Morris Endeavor, that have divisions that handle film sales. They're less approachable than someone like Reynolds, who works with truly independent films. The big agencies mainly handle Hollywood-based independent films they helped pre-sell or package. If you are fortunate to have a film rep interested in your documentary, remember that the most effective salesperson believes in the product. Don't sign with just anybody. If somebody is blown away by your film, they will push harder and persevere longer than somebody who is lukewarm. You can sense enthusiasm. Approach hiring a film agent like hiring any professional. There are reps out there that are not a value–add. Some focus on quantity over quality, and their association might even taint a film. Have conversations with a few to get the right fit. Reynolds suggests getting referrals and going on IMDb to look up filmmakers who have previously worked with that producer's rep. Ask them, "How was your experience? What happened? Did they call you back when you had a problem?"

Publicists

You say your film is fantastic? Nobody's going to believe you. You're hardly in a position to be objective. That's one reason publicists exist. Anybody can be your "publicist" as long as it's not you. Good publicists are expensive, at about $5,000 to $15,000 per month, but sometimes you can't afford not to hire them. If you spent a lot of money making the film, why aren't you going to spend what's needed for PR?

The best way to succeed is to go with somebody with a good track record. You're paying for them to use their contacts on your behalf. Sylvia Desrochers has been in public relations over twenty-five years, representing filmmakers such as Freida Lee Mock, Sofia Coppola, and John Ridley, and the documentaries *Anita: Speaking Truth to Power* (2013), *Grace Jones: Bloodlight and Bami* (2017), and *The Social Dilemma* (2020). Desrochers said her minimum contract is six weeks because "if it's less than that, there's no point in paying me because I can't really do my job." She prefers two to three months. The more time publicists have, the better the results.

When I asked Desrochers what exactly a publicist does, she said the way she explained it to her parents is that she is the conduit between the filmmaker/studio/film and

Publicist Sylvia Desrochers at MPRM Communications.

the public. She doesn't talk directly to the public; she uses the media to get a message across. She pursues reviews, articles, podcasts, radio shows, talks shows, television morning shows, and so on. Some publicists also get filmmakers into film festival parties so they can rub elbows with people who might be watching their movie. Desrochers will try to sell an angle to journalists so they will write a piece that reflects the story she is trying to influence them to tell. Desrochers admitted, "Publicists are slightly crazy because we're always trying to control things that are uncontrollable. We do our best to point people in the right direction. We work hard to establish the storyline so that it's being amplified. But in the end, I can't control what a critic says about a film." You can't expect results—you hope for results. Everybody is at the whims of media gatekeepers and critics.

Publicists put together a package called a press kit (a.k.a. press notes). It contains information about the film such as synopsis, filmmaker's statement, Q&A with the director, biographies of the filmmaker and cast, credits, photos, and the poster. If the film is about a historical subject or it is an issue documentary, they might include relevant supplemental materials. For example, when Desrochers handled a documentary titled *I Didn't See You There* (2022), because it was a film by a wheelchair-using filmmaker, they wanted to make sure people used the proper language around disability, so they also included a vocabulary list. Publicists email the press notes as a PDF document to the press to use as a resource to ensure they have all the information.

Publicists evaluate a movie and look for a sales hook. They don't try to pitch every single aspect. There might be more than one kernel of what a movie is, but they are looking for ones that will help sell it. Desrochers said when she doesn't have the angle of a famous person or a core group to tie it to, it's harder to pitch. She said, "It's our job to find angles to talk about, and then use all these bits and pieces to pitch it, depending on who I'm talking to." When publicists watch a movie, and it makes them feel something emotional or gets them excited, they try to make the media feel that same excitement so they'll write about it. Desrochers said, "I'm trying to convince someone to see things the way I see them. Publicists are salespeople in the end."

Desrochers represented the documentary *What We Leave Behind* (2022) by Iliana Sosa about her eighty-nine-year-old grandfather, Julián Moreno, in rural Mexico, who made a seventeen-hour bus ride every month from

Mexico to visit family in Texas. Sosa followed him for seven years. Desrochers found several good hooks: *The film is a beautiful, personal portrait of a remarkable man. The story is not one we typically see. The filmmaking style is poetic, with a unique structure with voiceover from Sosa. Sosa is a female filmmaker from an immigrant family. The film has won jury prizes at multiple film festivals.* Desrochers utilized one or more of these angles depending on who she was pitching to.

Working with a publicist is more of a personal relationship than a straight business hire like a production attorney. "At a film festival," Desrochers said, "you'll see your sales agent once or twice, but you see your PR team daily, multiple times. And even on a regular release, you will be talking to us every day. So, it's a very intense relationship." Publicists have different approaches. For Desrochers, she meets the filmmaker first to see if they are someone she wants to work with. Then she watches the film. "I love film, but I love people even more. I feel like I get them, I get along with them, and I get their neuroses."

You don't want to start racking up publicity costs until you have a film festival premiere, a specific event, or a release date to work toward. If your film lands a slot at a big festival, Glen Reynolds strongly recommends hiring a publicist because you are competing for attention with everybody else, and they all have publicists. With smaller festivals, publicists have a harder time generating publicity. "In that case," Reynolds said, "I usually tell filmmakers to hold their fire. If a publicist gets a review from a Seattle newspaper, I will use it and share it with a distributor. But was it worth paying $5,000 to get that? Will it really affect a distributor's decision all that much? It's debatable."

Promote Yourself

You probably think you know who you are. A publicist will make you who you should be. Filmmakers sometimes go into the PR process assuming the end goal is simply getting feature stories and reviews for their film. But filmmakers also have to be good at promoting *themselves*. Audiences want to know about the person who made the film. Behind the film's voice is a filmmaker. Desrochers teaches her clients how to describe themselves. *What are the talking points? What language should they be using? What are they bringing to this story that's unique to them as a storyteller?* She also works on branding, which is having a specific identity for what you're selling, and then repeating it.

Filmmakers need a degree in glad-handing, charismatic speech-making, and how to work a room. Those that don't have that skill are at a disadvantage. Desrochers said many of her clients don't like to be prepped, don't want media training, and don't enjoy doing their interviews. She has to coach them. She described how she has had to push one of her filmmakers to give speeches. "He hates it. I have to fight with him every time. But once I finally get him to do it, he's brilliant. That's why I'm on retainer; my job is to convince him and point him in the right direction so he's doing things that will be most helpful. I'm sensitive to the fact that many people don't want to do this. It's a lot of work, and you have to put yourself out there, but you have no choice. It's part of the job." She also recommends, "If you can't be a good representative of yourself and the film, make friends with a good outgoing producer. You might do this in film school and become a team for the rest of your careers."

Another thing that Desrochers says trips filmmakers up is the question: "What's your film about?" Often, they say: "Well, it's about many things." They're used to thinking about their film in a global way. It can be a challenge to be more specific and crystallize it down to thirty seconds. It's critical to do so because when doing interviews, filmmakers need to be able to talk about themselves and their film in bite-sized chunks. In the film notes, Desrochers includes a brief synopsis, two to three short paragraphs at most; each is one or two sentences. "Make it succinct and elegant. That's more than enough to talk about what a film is and to get people interested." After a description of the film, she writes a positioning paragraph, describing why the film, or what the filmmaker did, is different, some kind of language that sets the film apart, that says why this movie is unique and special, among all others.

To get to an elevator pitch, Desrochers gives her clients an exercise. She tells them to write five to ten things that are important to them as artists and filmmakers. This is the first step in thinking about how to talk about *yourself*—which is different from talking about your film. This is another reason to hire a publicist because it's also about getting your next film. "There can be a danger of being overly associated with just one film. They need to think about what's their long-term goal as a filmmaker. What kind of stories are they looking to tell? Be ready to talk about what's next because it always comes up in interviews, and you don't want to be staring blankly. I don't care if you don't have a script or an idea; make one up that you will use while doing these interviews. Nobody's going to hold you to it and go back and say, 'Hey, you never made that Al Capone film.'"

When I was doing festival Q&As for *The Nature of Existence*, I came up with a ready answer: "For my next documentary, I had to find a topic that was even more inexplicable and challenging than existence itself: marriage." It got a laugh every time. And then I started thinking, *Maybe I really should make that marriage documentary.*

Impact Producers

The impact producer (also impact manager, outreach manager, or social impact producer) has become a big part of some film campaigns. Sylvia Desrochers warned: "Do an issue-oriented documentary without an impact producer at your own risk. For example, if you are doing an environmental film, they connect the film with the organizations aligned with your message, maybe doing group sales or special screenings for those communities. They used to be called the grassroots person. They do a lot of the outreach that publicists used to do as part of the campaigns, but it's become so much bigger in recent years that now it's better to hire someone who focuses on only that." Impact producers work to bring real-world results based on the social issues advocated in a film. They find interested audiences and drive them to films, but they also do work outside and beyond the film's distribution to promote ideas, create social change, organize political activism, do fundraising, sell products, design online campaigns, promote campus engagement, and so on. Their goal is to bring the film's message to a tangible impact on society.

Filmmakers sometimes do the impact work themselves, but they don't always have the time to do it justice or are busy on their next film. If you consider how much you would pay yourself to do the work, and weigh that against the cost of an impact producer, you can calculate the potential ROI (return on investment). An impact producer might be on board from the beginning of production, working through distribution and then promoting for years afterward. For example, if a film advocates utilizing better teaching materials in classrooms, why not provide those better materials and sell them to schools? A successful impact campaign could do just that. A strategy needs to be in place before the film is released. Louie Psihoyos's Academy-Award-winning film *The Cove* (2009) is about activists who had a specific goal to pressure international organizations to ban the capturing and killing of dolphins in Taiji, Japan. The film's website is still tracking the ongoing social impact of the film.[5]

When Desrochers publicized *The Social Dilemma* (2020) at the Sundance Film Festival, she worked with the filmmakers as well as the sales team at Submarine Entertainment—and then when Netflix bought it, she worked with Netflix on the release. The filmmakers had done *Chasing Ice* (2012) and *Chasing Coral* (2017) and knew exactly what they wanted to do for the impact campaign and educational screenings. They already had a team in place, and they worked it out with Netflix when they made the deal. Desrochers said, "If it's somebody's first film, they often have big ideas, but they don't understand the amount of work that goes into an impact campaign. If you're going to do hundreds of extra screenings, who will be handling the scheduling? Who's sending the DCP around?" Often, the answer is to hire an impact producer.

Controlled Screenings

Once you have decided whether you are working with a representative or going it alone, there are two main approaches: distributor screenings and film festival showings. The first strategy is to invite all the acquisition executives to a screening. New York and Los Angeles are where most are based, so that's where screenings should be, or else at key film festivals they will attend. These folks are used to demanding links. They will tell you they are able to screen movies alone on a computer in their office and properly evaluate them. We all know that films play better with an audience (especially when packed with your friends). It's almost impossible to get scouts to show up to your screening unless there is a buzz or big names and if it's the only way you will allow it to be seen. Unless you know the upper-level decision-makers personally, only first-tier scouts will attend. They will tell their bosses, who will tell their bosses, and so on, as it moves up the ladder. The top bosses will not come to you, and at some point, you will be forced to send that link, Blu-ray, or DCP.

Word of mouth is your best ally. You are a biased liar, so the execs have to hear it from another source. Try to avoid sneaking the film to anybody before your premiere. Don't let them make you feel guilty about holding it back. It's their job to go to screenings and festivals, and it's your job to get the lazy bastards off their couches. If you send a link or arrange a screening for a distributor at their office, at best, you will have a small audience of jaded highbrows. You might be blocked by an executive who sees your film and doesn't like it. Leapfrogging over them will be difficult.

Film Festivals

You are probably better off holding back all screenings prior to your festival premiere. There are several benefits to film festivals:

1. It's a lot of fun and a chance to see many great movies for free (programmed filmmakers get a free pass).
2. You will enjoy screening for an audience of your peers.
3. You will meet other filmmakers, network, and build a list of contacts.
4. A distributor can see your film with a receptive audience.
5. Buyers are in a competitive atmosphere.
6. The setting provides avenues to publicize your film and field-test marketing ideas.
7. A big-time reviewer might get behind your film.
8. The film can win acclaim; good work gets noticed and invited to more festivals.

Film Markets

Film markets are where sales agents present films directly to buyers, mainly foreign distributors. Sometimes, these markets are adjuncts to film festivals, like the Marché du Film at Cannes or the European Film Market at the Berlinale. Often, they are standalone entities. One of the biggest is the American Film Market, held in November in Los Angeles, California. Filmmakers and wannabes are not usually participants, although you can find some hanging out at the bar looking to network (or scam newbies). A great deal of business at film markets is pre-selling rights to foreign territories, to finance films that are not yet complete, based chiefly on track records and name talent. Novice filmmakers have no business attending a film market without a film agent representing their interests.

What Are Distributors Looking For?

Will your documentary draw eyeballs to a theater or streamer? That's all that matters to distributors. Tastes, trends, and interests continually change—but good stories are always in demand. For one example, Glen Reynolds found that films about health are tough to sell because there's an oversupply; many people have made films about someone they know with a personal health struggle. He added that distributors recently were hungry for anything to do with aliens. "There's a crazy audience for extraterrestrial stuff. And it's mostly quasi-documentaries because they're following around people that are just making shit up."

Regularly, Reynolds will hear a distributor ask, "Do you have anything in this or that category?" Reynolds said he was pitching Netflix on a documentary, and they said, "We really just want horror, action, or thrillers right now." Reynolds said, "That's what everybody wants, and that's because it's what the audience wants. But filmmakers are mostly making introspective, interesting dramas, the exact opposite of where demand is strongest."

For documentaries, it's easier for Reynolds to place films focusing on a particular niche. The wrong goal for a filmmaker is to say, "I want to make a film that everybody will want to see." It's much better, especially from a marketing perspective, to say, "I want to make a film that this specific sliver of people I can readily identify want to see." Make a film you're passionate about, but to compete, limit your subject matter. Reynolds suggests if you're making a film about sports, narrow it down to something like bicycling. Then, narrow that further to mountain bikers. And then narrow it down to female mountain bikers. And then to a specific person or group.

The more granular, the more of a niche you find, the more specific and easier the audience is to identify. In a related example, Reynolds represented a film about Alden Olmsted, who designed his own BMX bicycle, featured in a quirky little documentary called *30 Bikes: The Story of Homestead Bicycles* (2020). Similarly, if Terry Zwigoff had made a generic documentary

Alden Olmsted locates one of his original frames in 30 Bikes: The Story of Homestead Bicycles *(2020).*

about the underground comix world, his film would probably have only appealed to people interested in that counterculture. By focusing on Robert Crumb, a unique, fascinating, semi-famous person, he found a story within that world that worked for fans but also attracted that much-coveted crossover audience. The documentaries that do the best find a story within the subject matter they're profiling, usually through captivating characters.

Streamers have a subscriber base that needs to be continually fed product on certain subjects. They want something similar to what worked for them in the past—but also unique. It's hard to do similar-yet-unique without being derivative. When Reynolds approaches buyers, he looks for another documentary in their library that's of comparable subject matter but told differently. They'll think, "Yeah, that worked for us. So, this might work too." Reynolds advised, "It's not usually a good pitch to go in and say, 'You've never had anything like this. It's totally different from anything else.'" They want stuff that's known to work. An exception is when they have an emerging audience demographic they want to capture by adding new subjects. And distributor mandates are often very different from film festival programming preferences.

What Are Film Festivals Looking For?

When a festival rejected my first film, they tended to reject all my following films; if they accepted my first submission, they tended to accept all the rest. Some festivals will get you, and some won't. You'll discover which festivals are in sync with your artistic tone. Film festivals have personalities, which makes sense because they're run by people. Each festival has its own dynamic, and each has its own audience that programmers try to service. Publicist Sylvia Desrochers has picked up on some of the festival nuances: "At South by Southwest, their docs tend to be more fun, and they have a lot more music because of the music connection. A lot of issue docs are at Sundance. Cannes only programs a couple of docs; it's not something they focus on. There are more in the market at Cannes, but the traditional festival has very few." The "important" festivals sometimes feel pressure to be "serious," so heavy dramas have a better shot. Smaller festivals can be quirkier.

Programmers also have to consider which films will fill theaters, in order to meet festival revenue requirements. Can you generate a hundred ticket sales from fans, crew, friends, and family, all in addition to whatever unknown interest the general public will have? If you have a local fanbase or a huge extended family in a particular city who will buy tickets, make the festival aware of this.

Michael Rabehl has been the director of programming at the Cinequest Film & Creativity Festival in San Jose since 1996. Rabehl says he likes films that speak to viewers on a personal level and exposes them to other perspectives and experiences. "I'm looking for a film that makes me say, 'Oh my God, I have never seen that before.' I want films that are going to push buttons. I am not afraid to take on a subject. I don't want a safe program. Festivals sometimes go into survival mode and try not to piss off people. I want a program that has the safe zones but also has films that are going to challenge people." Even if Rabehl has seen something like your film before, if you can make him really like the people in your movie, he may still champion it. *Charm Circle* (2022) is a documentary about a family in New York. There is a glut of documentaries about somebody uncovering something in an attic, finding an old video, or looking through old photos and telling their family story. Rabehl said, "The eccentricity of this family and their lives and who they are as people stood out from all the others and was really special as an experience for me."

Rabehl feels the role of programmers is to be supportive of a variety of artists, like a museum curator who would not just display one artistic style. "I want to go to a gallery that has Ansel Adams plus Henri Matisse plus Vincent van Gogh, exhibitions that open me up to different realms. And film festivals should open people up to new points of view. We're not going to program a festival that has all the same kinds of film."

Film Festival Selection Process

Being chosen sometimes depends not just on the film but also the day the submission arrives and the programmer's mood—details out of a film-maker's control. That's why Rabehl says they have two people plus Rabehl on each feature-viewing team. With the shorts teams, eight to ten people screen each film, and then they average the scores. Selected shorts tend to score seven or above, and selected features score eight or above. Before making a selection, Rabehl looks at all the scores and notes for every film. If somebody scored a three, but the notes are exceptional, he will take another look. "We don't go with just the final average. Sometimes we review the information, look at it again, and say, 'This is something we really should do.' There was a film where two people scored it below a five. I ended up programming despite the low rating, and it won the audience award."

Choose Your Premiere Carefully

Every film gets one super-hyped screening. Strategize about which festivals to apply to and in which order. Choose the first festival screening with care because you can only premiere once. A-level festivals usually insist on having premieres. A top festival gets its reputation because it has a strong track record for getting distribution for films. There are thousands of film festivals but only a few where buyers actually attend. It would be malprac-tice not to submit your film to top-level festivals where deals happen, such as the Berlin International Film Festival (a.k.a. the Berlinale), Cannes Film Festival, New York Film Festival, Slamdance Film Festival, South by South-west, Sundance Film Festival, Telluride Film Festival, Toronto International Film Festival, Tribeca Film Festival, and Venice Film Festival. There are also festivals dedicated to documentaries that you should strongly consider, such as Cinéma du Réel, Copenhagen International Documentary Film Festi-val, Documenta Madrid, DOC NYC, DOK Leipzig, Hot Docs Canadian

International Documentary Festival, Hot Springs Documentary Film Festival, IDFA: International Documentary Film Festival Amsterdam, Ji.hlava International Documentary Film Festival, Sheffield DocFest, Silver Docs, Sunny Side of the Doc, Thessaloniki International Film Festival, True/False Film Festival, and Visions du Réel.

Don't neglect regional and mid-level festivals. You may need the leverage of acceptance in one festival to help get into another. Plus, B and C festivals can be cozier and more fun than A-level festivals. The programmers at some regional festivals have cultivated relationships with distributors and will advocate strongly on behalf of films. Michael Rabehl at Cinequest recalled, "We premiered two films last year that I pushed and pushed to distributors. I kept on doing that until they saw the films. HBO responded and put one on their platform. Even though I can't focus on just your movie, if I'm going to put energy into your film, that means I'm also working as a sales agent during your time with us. Go with festivals that have that track record."

Another reason to broaden your submissions is that you can't count on winning the A-level festival lottery. South by Southwest programs 150 features and 100 shorts out of 8,000 submissions. That works out to about a 3.5 percent chance for any given submission. Each year, approximately 4,500 features and 9,500 shorts are submitted to the Sundance Film Festival. Around ninety to 120 features and sixty to seventy shorts make the final cut, fewer than 3 percent of the Sundance feature submissions and 1 percent of the shorts. And of the films that do get in, only about 20 percent are picked up for distribution; that is, half of 1 percent of the films submitted to Sundance find distribution at the festival. Reducing the odds further is the fact that many films arrive with distribution already in place because studios place films at festivals by promising stars will attend, taking away plumb screening slots from unaligned indie films. A typical acceptance rate for a regional festival is higher, around 6 to 10 percent, but still long odds.

I use a shotgun approach to hit as many festivals as I can afford. My films have had a 10 to 15 percent success ratio. If I want to do ten festivals, that means I need to submit to 100. If you only submit to twenty festivals, you may get zero invitations. Submit to at least fifty. You need a strategy for going forward if you don't win the festival lottery.

I start with top festivals and documentary showcases, then add major festivals in or near Los Angeles and New York, where distributors are located. Then I look at other locations and consider, *Is this a place I would like to visit?* Like Fort Lauderdale or Barcelona. *Will this festival add prestige?* Perhaps London or São Paulo. *Do the programmers work their asses off to get my film noticed?* Cinequest or Hamptons. I also investigate exotic festivals but check ratings and reviews and consider how long they've been in business. A festival still in its first couple of years may not have worked out the kinks. Film agent Glen Reynolds says there are many great festivals he can use as a conversation starter: "'Hey, we've got a film in Seattle this week. Do you want to check it out?'" Reynolds added, "It's helpful that there is someone other than me and the filmmaker who likes the movie. It's getting laurel leaves; it's getting some attention."

Beware of festivals that are largely money-making ventures for the originator. That doesn't mean it still can't suit your needs. Sketchier festivals might charge $175 to reject you—or they invite nearly everybody who submits to add another laurel, diluting the value. Be cautious when encountering high submission fees. What can you do about that? Absolutely nothing. Except start your own over-priced festival and bask in the sun on your own festival yacht. Sincere programmers are not getting rich off of submission fees. "No matter what the submission fee is," Cinequest's Michael Rabehl said, "I still make the same wage. You can ask my twenty-one-year-old Passat with fading paint in my driveway."

The best festival experiences are ones where they have all the logistics worked out. The USA Film Festival in Dallas and the Barbados Independent Film Festival staff are some of the nicest folks I have ever met, plus they took care of everything. You don't want to be left waiting and confused at the airport. Don't be a pain in the ass, but also, don't be bashful. Ask in advance to determine what will be taken care of and what won't. Assume nothing.

Photograph courtesy of Michael Rabehl.

Cinequest programmer Michael Rabehl and his beleaguered car.

Avoid Overexposure

After you book your big premiere, enjoy attending every quality festival that invites you. That way, you can build up a collection of reviews. But don't overexpose your film. For example, choose only one festival in Northern California, not three; otherwise, you're diluting your ability to get media attention in the region. Publicist Sylvia Desrochers even cautions filmmakers not to get too much press at film festivals because they don't need an overdose to get acquired by a distributor, and it leaves her with less to work with when the film is released. Desrochers's advice is to get just enough press to sell the movie and no more. "Think about your goals and why you're doing publicity. If you can't tell me why you're getting that coverage, you probably shouldn't be getting it. At festivals, we're going for a handful of breaks. We try for trade reviews and a few key pieces. There's no hard-and-fast rule. There are cases where getting only two things is a huge win."

When the film gets picked up by a distributor, they usually ask filmmakers to stop all festival screenings because there's little upside for a distributor. They will concentrate on promoting audience awareness around one specific release date. The publicity generated months prior at festivals is next to useless for a commercial release. Unless it's the big prizewinner at a top festival, distributors pooh-pooh film festival laurels. Notice how few films in release advertise film festival participation. If laurels and festival reviews on a poster translated into ticket purchases or streamer views, they would be all over it.

Pace yourself. Don't post all your promotional materials right at the start. If you put everything out at the beginning, there's nowhere else to go. Once something is up, there's no pulling it back. Desrochers tells filmmakers to only use two or three photos, so when the film is released later, they'll have more fresh shots available.

Desrochers says a mistake many filmmakers make while doing film festivals is to release a trailer on their website. If their trailer is no longer exclusive, media outlets won't be interested in featuring it, making it harder to promote the release. A publicist will want to be able to place a trailer or a clip with an outlet as an exclusive. Once the publication runs that story with the exclusive material, that's when you can put it on your website or social media.

A sales agent also wants to be able to tell potential distributors there's not already a trailer out there. To promote a film for festivals, before a commercial release, Desrochers prefers to use a short clip instead of a trailer. "When a film doesn't work well with clips, if it's a foreign language or the pacing is slow, in select cases, we'll do a teaser." A teaser is a lightly edited sample from the movie. It is different from a trailer. The key is to make sure to call it a teaser to preserve the publicity value of your future trailer.

One reason in favor of having a teaser is that you will need something for film festival submissions. Festival programmer Mike Rabehl watches 900 movies over ten months. When the final deadline approaches, it's impossible to remember all the details from films that came in early, so when Rabehl revisits high-scoring films, he says, "The films with trailers were easier for me to say, 'Oh, yes! I loved that movie!' and remember why. While we wish we had amazing memories and perfect recall, trailers quickly remind us why we loved the films."

Websites

Once a film is in the tail end of its campaign, that's a good time to put everything you've got online. A film's website can be a one-stop shop for everything anybody could want to know about your project: poster, glowing reviewer quotes, logline, short synopsis, press information, trailer, and release information (links to where it can be rented or streamed). Include high-resolution color photos that a writer or reviewer could download. Make the site simple, clean, lively, and concise.

Launch a Presence on Social Media

Social-media accounts are often a delivery requirement. A filmmaker should defensively secure space on each social-media platform and begin having a presence, even if there is minimal content. Post a few key things, like festival reviews. You need to have these accounts to be ready to hand over to a social-media campaign manager and/or distributor. Publicists used to handle a film's social-media, but the scope of film campaigns has expanded dramatically. Sylvia Desrochers's company, MPRM Communications, offers the services of a social-media specialist to run social-media campaigns alongside the publicist. This is becoming indispensable for a commercial release. Desrochers said it's less important to run an extensive social-media campaign for film festivals unless you have an issue-driven film. In that case, you may want to start building a following during the festivals because it's a long road to cultivating those audiences. Putting money into social-media advertising buys is also a cost-effective alternative when filmmakers can't afford a publicist.

"Organic posts" are the updates you do yourself until you are ready to start spending money. Campaigns have gone from being organic conversations to mostly paid ads. Some filmmakers can do it themselves, but most are not skilled in the nuances of maximizing an ad spend or don't want to deal with it. A social-media manager will take over and pretend to be you and continue what will appear to be organic posting. They will then schedule which ideas and thought-starters to focus on each week. They design and create new content, spend budgeted amounts to boost posts, and place ads on social media to draw attention to the film, aiming to yield a positive return on investment. Boosting an organic post means paying for it to show up as a sponsored post in the feeds of targeted people who you consider to be open to your subject matter. A distributor may be doing media buys, and your campaign manager coordinates placements with them. Filmmakers hope they will get a distributor who will cover all the advertising and marketing expenses, but especially with documentaries, filmmakers have to be prepared to pay for much of that themselves.

A specialist starts putting materials together several weeks in advance, even though the social-media campaign doesn't begin until a few days before the film comes out. Your publicist will probably be done a week after the film's release date, but the social-media manager will stay on for months longer, especially if the film will be on VOD, where it has a long tail and they are trying to push audiences to it. Desrochers said she has seen people spend only $500 and get effective results. Some social-media budgets are $30,000. She advises a minimum ad spend of at least $1,000. "It's important to work with someone to help you determine a plan," she said, "because with some films, no matter how much you spend, there's an upward limit to how many people are actually going to respond."

The Film Festival Budget

To succeed on the festival circuit, a $10,000 budget is not extravagant; it may even be just a start. When submitting *The Truth About Marriage* to 200 festivals, I spent $7,000 on entry fees alone. If you are broke, you can ask for a submission discount or a fee waiver, which is often granted. However, I don't recommend it. Cinequest programmer Michael Rabehl looks at submission fees this way: For the average film of ninety minutes to two hours, you're paying three people ten or twenty bucks per hour to watch your movie. Rabehl said, "If somebody pays an entry fee, they are like clients. They have hired us to do a job, they're supporting the festival, and their film gets viewed. That's our policy. You're not guaranteed a viewing if you don't pay a fee." If you ask for a waiver, you are risking your film getting a lower viewing priority.

You could spend more submitting a short film to festivals than you spent making it, especially when you add another $1,500 for creating DCPs and $5,000 for travel expenses. Not every festival covers travel. I know people who have done fifty festivals with their short film and enjoyed the run, and it was helpful to their careers. There are a handful of distribution avenues for shorts, but they are not something distributors usually pick up, so your ROI with a short is not likely to put you in the black.

What if you beat the odds and get into the Sundance Film Festival? You can save money by sleeping on condo couches, doing minimal PR, and hoping for a miracle. The reality is that you are competing with what everybody else is doing (and spending). Sylvia Desrochers said a publicist for a feature documentary at Sundance costs about $10,000. "If you're trying to get into those elite festivals, you need to set aside a good chunk of money to do the festival in a meaningful way." Then, add the costs of bringing in your stars. You have to fly them, house them, add ground transportation, and sometimes pay for hair and makeup. Desrochers recommends holding at least $30,000 for festivals. "I've seen people do things with far less. I get people that call and say, 'I have $1,500 for PR.' I'm like, 'Well, that's great, but I can't really help you. And I don't know who to refer you to because none of my colleagues can do much for that. You should just do a nice social-media campaign and put that money into boosting your ads.' But if somebody can come up with at least $3,000 to $5,000, there's probably a freelance publicist who could help."

Festival Submission Strategies

Film festivals are run by people, and people have agendas. If you have big-name stars, producers, or directors, you'll have an easier time getting past gatekeepers. Like distributors, festivals love star names because the media are more likely to cover star-studded events and spread the word to the ticket-buying public.

There are things you *can* do to improve your film's chances of being selected:

1. Do not submit either too soon or at the last minute. Submit during the Goldilocks period, about two or three months before the regular deadline. If it's too early, it may be forgotten. At some festivals, when submissions come in at the final deadline crush of hundreds (or thousands) of films, it may not be physically possible to give every film proper consideration. No matter when you submit, always follow up to make sure it was received.

2. Don't ignore your logline and synopsis. Make it concise, give it personality, engage the reader, and be sure it represents the film accurately. Run drafts by others to make sure it's working. Programmer Michael Rabehl doesn't read the synopsis and director's notes until after he watches a movie. If he's on the fence, a bad, boring, depressing, or badly written synopsis might talk him out of programming it.

3. Submit a finished-looking version of the film. When programmers see timecode, hear obvious temp music, or see missing credits, they see a movie that might not be ready in time. Give them no reason to reject you. If they accept your unfinished film, and you try to cancel at the last minute after they've scheduled it, they can probably still screen your half-assed version because there's a clause in the submission agreement saying you have given them authorization to do so.

4. Make sure your film's story grabs people in the first few minutes, or it may not be viewed past the first act. A harried screener will sometimes watch the beginning and, if not impressed, dip into the middle here and there and jump to the conclusion. Programmers want your film to be great because accepting it gets them closer to finishing their job. They are also looking for any reason to stop watching and move on to the next one.

5. An eye-grabbing photo and captivating artwork is essential.
6. Gently lobby the festivals. Call, write, and remind them what an asset you and your film and your stars are and the huge numbers of people you will draw to their festival. They are selling a product (their festival), and if your film will help them do so, it's got a better chance. Have big names lobby on your behalf. This is another area where a film rep can help.
7. Work with a festival strategist, who specializes in submission success. Film agents know this landscape. Some publicists can help.

Once you begin the submission process, your film begins aging. You can't screen at three festivals this month, wait eight months, and start over again as if it's a fresh product. People know you are submitting old goods, and it will count against you.

Festival Rejection Syndrome Is Normal

Everybody has high hopes and believes their film is the worthiest submission. The sheer number of entries creates a competitive atmosphere that's not always about recognizing quality. Accept that you win some and lose some. If you don't get in, move on; it's nothing personal. Michael Rabehl has gotten letters from filmmakers who looked at Vimeo stats and accused programmers of not watching the film. Cinequest's viewing teams sometimes use VPNs, so Vimeo stats will not necessarily reflect that it was viewed in a particular city. Never write angry letters. Never badmouth programmers or reviewers on social media. That only hurts you for the next round because people remember. Write your angry letter and throw it away. Abraham Lincoln famously wrote "hot letters" and then put them aside until he cooled off.[6,7]

Have contingency plans. Film rep Glen Reynolds often has to talk directors off the ledge. A festival run is not necessary to get a distributor. If the film is in a festival in Cleveland or Chicago, the distributors are not likely to be in attendance. They will still get the film directly from Glen Reynolds, either via Blu-ray or web link (with a password). At that point, they're going to make an assessment: *Is this a great movie? Is it marketable? Who's in it?*

Who's the audience? What're the demographics? What's the trailer like? How does the poster look? And way down at the bottom of the list is the fact that it was in the St. Louis International Film Festival. In Reynolds's evaluation, "The only reason they care about Sundance or South by Southwest is because those have become places where top movies sell, and their competitors will be there watching in the room. So they've also got to be in the audience and make timely decisions." Most films leave even those festivals without distribution. It's not a fait accompli that you get in and it's done. There is a place for your film, and it is the perfect place. You just need to find it. It could be the first festival or the last distributor you approach. Don't give up. Know that this place exists.

Managing Filmmaker Delusion

Almost every filmmaker is headed for some kind of disappointment at a film festival where some of their competitors are winning awards or getting deals. When *Trekkies* was in competition at the 1997 Hamptons International Film Festival, we felt like we lost big in the documentary competition, and losing is not fun. In our category, Michèle Ohayon's *Colors Straight Up* (1997) won the audience-favorite award and a special jury citation. Robert Pulcini and Shari Springer Berman's *Off the Menu* (1997) won the juried prize. It was the first time I'd been amongst a group of filmmakers vying for awards, and I noticed a phenomenon. Without exception, all the non-winning (i.e., losing) filmmakers I encountered were upset, resentful, or depressed. Understandably. Darren Stein, who directed the narrative *Sparkler* (1997), one of the most talked about films at the festival, practically burst into tears. He, like everybody else, felt certain his film was a shoo-in. Director Tim Chey was distraught that *Fakin' Da Funk*

Los Angeles inner-city teenagers pursue the performing arts in Colors Straight Up *(1997).*

(1997) had lost. He felt he had let down his actors, Pam Grier and Ernie Hudson, who had flown in for the event. You can't bank on awards recognition. Even without awards, you can definitely sell your film. The belief in yourself and your project keeps you going through the ups and downs. It's what got your film made in the first place. The filmmaker's delusion is a massive benefit—a weakness turned into a strength—that helps push you and your film toward success.

The opportunities for disappointment continue with the film's release. Publicist Sylvia Desrochers said, "There's no campaign where everything goes right. And even people who are generally happy, I can name moments in the campaign when they were disappointed or things didn't go our way. Being an armchair psychologist is a huge part of my job. I spend a ton of time managing expectations. I try to explain the landscape to filmmakers, and the challenges we face. So much of it is dependent on luck and timing."

Desrochers warned that one danger that documentaries fall into more than narratives is that sometimes reviews are about what critics wish had been made as opposed to the film that was actually made. They might say, "I wanted to see a film that focused on this other part of the subject's life, but that's not what this filmmaker chose to do, and I don't like that." It's unfair because they're not looking at the film for what it is. They're looking at it based on the film they think *they* would make about the subject matter. There's not much a filmmaker can do about that except stay true to their own vision and understand that all films get criticism.

Desrochers handled a film at DOC NYC called *My Sister Liv* (2022) about a teenage suicide epidemic. She thought it would be a tough sell because of the difficult subject matter. "I can't predict success. But that film did much better than I thought it would because many people in the press had experienced that issue in their lives in some way. They were responding in a very human way. And then it's heartbreaking when other films are overlooked. With some of our pet environmental films, where the filmmakers feel like this is the most important issue of our time, they wonder, 'Why don't people care more?' And I can only say, 'I wish they did.'"

Desrochers said she had a client with a film at Sundance who said to her, "I really think I just need someone to hold my hand."

She said, "I was impressed because most people don't admit that. That's part of what they're looking for in a publicist."

When I asked filmmaker Marina Zenovich how she deals with rejection, she joked, "A lot of ice cream." Then she admitted, "It's really upsetting. But what can you do? You have to pick yourself up and keep going. And that's what's good about being a parent, because you're telling your child that they have to learn—and you're learning this at the same time—that life doesn't always work the way you want it to." Even with her impressive track record of successful films, it was a struggle to find distribution for her latest film, *Jerry Brown: The Disrupter* (2022). She raised $400,000 to make the film, much of it from Jerry Brown supporters.

When Zenovich was looking for finishing funds, she was talking to someone whom she asked to donate, and he said, "Wait, why should I donate instead of invest?"

She said, "Well, I could tell you to invest, but I don't think I'm going to be able to pay you back. I might be able to, but it'll be a process of many years. But if you donate, you'll get a tax write-off now."

She took the film to the San Francisco International Film Festival and DOC NYC, utilized a publicist in each city, and hired a sales agent. Many distributors passed, giving reasons such as, "I love the film, but our docs didn't perform this year, so we're going to pass." Or, "I love the film, but it's too niche." Or when a streamer was thinking internationally, they said, "It's too specific to American politics, even though it's a portrait of a politician not a political film."

Zenovich dusted herself off and soldiered on. "I've made this passion project that people love about an important American character. It's inspiring and uplifting after this horrible moment in time for democracy in our country. I'm lucky that I got to finish the film, and I know we're going to sell it and it's going to get out there. But rejection is hard. Getting any distribution is a win. Because what do you want? You want everyone to see your film and be inspired by it." Ultimately, Zenovich found a home for the film at PBS on the *American Masters* series.

Liz Garbus told of a similar attitude: "I mope around for a little while. And then I pick myself up and start doing the next thing. For me, it's the high of storytelling. I can't not be engaged in it for very long. When I go to bed at night, I'm thinking about how to crack a challenge or how to make something better. It's my lifeblood. If I'm not engaged in a story, I'm looking for one. It's how I'm wired."

When Davis Guggenheim brought a feature script written by David Ayers called *Training Day* (2001) to Warner Bros., he fought for them to cast Denzel Washington. When they did, Guggenheim was fired off his own movie. "I never met Denzel. He just didn't want me for arbitrary reasons. That would have been my big break, and I was so disillusioned by how quickly the Hollywood system can love you one moment and then discard you the next because a movie star has a whim. I was so devastated and heartbroken. I couldn't get out of bed for six months." While licking his wounds, Guggenheim bought a camera and started filming a documentary where he followed public school teachers, called *The First Year* (2001). Making a documentary became the antidote to his depression. "I loved the people in my movie; teachers that slugged it out every day and believed in something. I was so emptied out, and here I was, going to these public schools, driving to Compton and Watts in East LA, but coming home really happy. I was using all these years of being a director and applying that to the nonfiction world. It was like, 'Oh my God, I'm in heaven.' It felt like the lights turned on, and I was so happy."

Build Film Festival Hype

Film festivals have a publicity team, but they focus on the festival as a whole rather than only your film. Programmer Michael Rabehl recalled how the people with the top ten films at a prior Cinequest all had publicists, and they appeared on the top ten list for the *San Francisco Chronicle* and the *San Jose Mercury News*. Publicists focus on getting those films out to the media.

Publicists work hand in hand with a sales agent. And a filmmaker who stays engaged with them throughout the process has greater success. Don't expect somebody to do things for you. Stay involved the entire way. They are part of your team and should be fighting for you, believing in you, and working with you.

Everybody at a festival has access to the same press lists. Make sure you do, too. Canvass the local media outlets in the city hosting the festival. They are faced with covering dozens or hundreds of films, and you want yours to be one of the chosen few. A timely email or phone call may bring your film to the top of the pile. Contact them on the pretext of alerting them to you or your stars and profilees' availability for interviews. Journalists are often grateful for the lead. You aren't bothering them. It's their job to write about this event, and you are there to help.

If you've got a track record, flaunt it. If you're related to somebody famous, use that. If you've got a lot of money, spend it. If you've got a dead horse, beat it. If you have none of the above, rely on your creativity and your cheap, clever PR ideas. Blanket the town with irresistible solicitations to your film's screening. Give away flyers, postcards, key rings, refrigerator magnets, T-shirts, lollypops, whatever it takes to get your film the attention it deserves.

Collect the Good Reviews

When I finished my first feature film, *High Strung* (1991), Richard von Busack at the *Santa Clara Valley Metro* (now *Metro Silicon Valley*) gave it a really nice review for the festival premiere: "Inventive camerawork and extremely funny monologues . . . cruelly funny." However, when the film was released commercially in San Jose several months later, his review did a complete 180-degree turn and savaged the film. Same guy. Same film. It was like night and day. WTF? Sometimes, you just have to laugh, let it go, and focus on the successes. As you attend festivals, collect all your rave-review blurbs, pretend the bad reviews never existed, and keep moving forward.

Time to Sell

Once everybody has seen your film, a bidding war ensues, driving up the price, and you make a killing. Or so you hope. This is what everything is leading toward. Davis Guggenheim warned, "People who have come up with a great idea for a film and have the talent to pull it off aren't necessarily skilled in negotiating their distribution deal. And so it's a good idea to get some help. Whether it's another filmmaker who says, 'Hey, you shouldn't settle for less than this.' Or a lawyer who you hire to negotiate on your behalf." A good sales agent will bring distributors to this point and handle negotiations. But you are the only person who knows what is right for your movie. Be the one making the decisions.

CHAPTER NINE

Distribution

Locking the final cut is only the halfway point.

A typical documentary takes twelve to eighteen months to complete. Sometimes, it is much longer. But once you have finished, you may be surprised to find you still need more money for distribution. You may have to spend more on marketing than the original production budget. Try to save 30 percent above your production budget (some believe that should be 50 percent, or even 200 percent) to spend on marketing and distribution, just in case you have to do everything yourself. Even if you land a major distributor, your days of promotional spending are not over.

Distribution Options

Is it worthwhile to book theaters, hire publicists, and spend your money on marketing? If you were willing to spend $200,000 making a documentary, aren't you willing to spend whatever it takes for it to be seen? The theatrical-spend rule of thumb is that for every dollar spent in advertising, you get one dollar back in box office gross. If you choose to release your film directly to video, which is what happens to most films, digital releases also need a marketing and advertising budget. But a major problem for the direct-to-video scenario is one of perception. Virtually anybody can put their film on the Internet, making it hard to stand out from a glut of mediocrity. A film isn't appreciated as "cinema" unless it has been in movie theaters or is treated to that level of marketing. A theatrical run results in articles and reviews and a resulting product awareness and possibly awards. Direct-to-digital only generates that sort of awareness if a streamer spends enough on marketing to substantially raise a film's profile.

Submission Strategy

When film rep Glen Reynolds gets a press kit from a filmmaker, he breaks it into pieces and uses the data in different ways. Distributors create a one-page "sell-sheet" to pitch a film to platforms, so Reynolds makes a sell-sheet in advance to demonstrate to distributors how a film is a viable, sellable product. A sell-sheet has a poster on it or some great image(s) from the film, maybe some laurel leaves and reviewer quotes, cast, genre, logline, and bullet points listing key marketing, publicity, and commercial aspects about the film, such as social-media numbers, core audience, or any other criteria that will help promote the movie. It is a condensed, bite-sized, one-page document so buyers can quickly see why the film will appeal. Get your hands on sell-sheet examples for use as a template for layout, font, and formatting.

Reynolds also works with clients to improve their teaser and/or trailer, or uses clips from the movie, or both. His first step is to call buyers to pitch the film and share what it's about and whether it's in a festival. And then he sends the movie to buyers via link or Blu-ray. Sometimes, he first teases

The Truth About Marriage

Synopsis: Award-winning documentarian Roger Nygard explains why relationships fail; and provides scientifically researched tips on how to find one that goes the distance.

Key Selling Points

- OFFICIAL SELECTION at 20+ international film festivals.
- WINNER Best Documentary: Hollywood Reel Independent Film Festival, Trenton Film Festival, Worldfest Houston.
- Audience appetite for relationship insider tips is insatiable.
- Cast social media fan base (combined): 1.6 mil.

Genre: Documentary

Key Cast/Relationship Experts

- John Gottman, Ph.D., & Julie Schwartz, Ph.D.; 40+ books, 1-mil copies.
- Neil Strauss, best-selling author, *The Game*; 2.5-million copies.
- Steven B. Ward, author, Host of VH1's, *Tough Love*.
- Christopher Ryan, Ph.D., author, *Sex at Dawn; Ted Talk*, 2.2-mil views.
- Matt Ridley, author, *The Red Queen*; 1-million copies.
- Pat Allen, Ph.D., famous guru & author, *Getting to 'I Do'*; 32nd printing.

Additional Film Information

- Tagline: All the relationship secrets nobody tells you.
- Roger Nygard directed the award-winning, *Trekkies*, a Paramount Classics top performing documentary; $7 mil gross revenue.
- Nygard has written the book The Truth About Marriage to be promoted & released simultaneously.

TEMP ARTWORK

VOD, DVD & BD Release Date
Valentine's Day
February 14, 2020

Marketing Overview

- Copies are already being requested by marriage professionals.
- Presented humorously, it gives easy-to-apply relationship tools.
- The film appeals to those in love, searching for love, or wondering why their love went wrong – pretty much everyone!

Sample sell sheet for The Truth About Marriage *(2020).*

with a clip, then next week a trailer, another week a quote, then a review. He doesn't dump everything on a distributor and say, "Here's the movie and a bunch of marketing." He doles it out bit by bit, using new items as reasons to follow up later. Instead of saying, "Hey, did you watch the film yet?" he's sharing something different each time. With every contact he makes, he's trying to take them another step toward watching the movie.

As the submissions commence, Reynolds maintains a database to track what each buyer has received, viewing status, and response. He allows film-maker clients access to the database he keeps for their film so they don't have to wonder what's happening; they can monitor real-time updates. Reynolds submits to all the buyers within a short period of time. He doesn't send it to just one entity, because if Netflix offers $20,000, you need to know what Hulu, MAX, Disney+, or Showtime might offer. According to Reynolds, most of the hundreds of distributors are not viable choices: "If I'm representing a non-Sundance movie, and maybe there is a possibility of something theatrical, but probably it's more likely straight to digital, in that case, I'm probably going to submit to about fifteen distributors and eight streamers."

Distribution Deals

Reynolds suggested four reasons to go with a distributor, even a small one, instead of putting out a film yourself.

1. Filmmakers cannot personally place their film on some platforms, such as iTunes, or easily approach high-profile buyers, like Netflix.
2. Distributors are able to put a film on far more platforms in the transactional world than the filmmaker.
3. Distributors have relationships with TV and SVOD (subscription video on demand) channels, and they have deal-making leverage due to representing multiple films.
4. Distributors are at the forefront of discovering and monetizing emerging delivery systems. It's often more lucrative to be first in the door with a new platform.

There's a good chance that if you get one offer, you will get multiple offers. How do you decide which to choose? Do the research. Some distributors are more friendly to certain types of films, whether documentary or narrative. Look at their track record. *Have they purchased similar product in the past? Were they successful? Was the release classy? Did they pay filmmakers on time?* Get references. Call filmmakers of films they have released, especially ones they don't give you as references. Because there are so many distribution company aspects to consider, make a grid and compare each company's terms. How do your suitors compare in each of these categories:

1. Type of company (distributor, steamer, middleman/sales company)
2. Who are the point persons? (What happens if they leave?)
3. Size of company (number of employees)
4. How are they financed (stability, longevity)?
5. Previous successes (in the right genres)
6. Trust factor (word of mouth)
7. Consider deal points (see below)

Negotiating a Distribution Deal

A good distribution deal results in an advance plus royalties, with a distributor paying release expenses. This process is where film reps earn their keep. Always counteroffer; nobody offers their best deal first. If you don't counter, they may assume they gave too much. It's the same as with any product: start high, the distributor goes low, and you meet in the middle. How high depends on the degree of interest the film has generated. You will not get all the terms and protections you need if you don't ask. It's not in the buyers' interest to present a contract written in your favor. When you are faced with only one or a handful of low offers, it goes more quickly. If you don't have the leverage to demand a much better deal, nibble around the edges and improve the boilerplate. Your lawyer and film rep will be on the lookout for onerous clauses to avoid and standard benefits you should get.

It's hard to remember every potential deal point. Prepare a list of what you want so you are ready. So that a crucial requirement does not slip through the cracks when choosing among companies, add each company's deal points to a comparison grid when considering multiple offers. You want the following:

1. **Short licensing term.** The typical range is three to twelve years. Some bigger companies want fifteen or more. But they have to pay more for that, especially if it's worldwide. Two to four years is fair. Try not to go above seven. Read the automatic-extension clause carefully to make sure you don't accidentally extend if you don't want to. You might even build in a performance clause, which gives you a right to terminate if minimum amounts of license fees are not paid by certain dates.

2. **Low distributor fee.** They will ask for a 35 percent commission. Try to get closer to 20 to 25 percent. If they are paying an advance, they will demand a higher commission. A typical theatrical deal results in a 25-to-30-percent fee off the top of the gross receipts. And then after they recoup their expenses, the balance goes to the filmmaker. A straight-to-digital distributor fee would be lower: 20 to 25 percent from the gross receipts.

3A. **High advance** (if it's a distributor). This is also called an MG (minimum guarantee). The advance will be deducted from the filmmaker's future share of net revenue. Make sure there is no interest charged on an advance. They may try to treat it like a loan; it isn't.

3B. **High license fee** (if it's a streamer). Streamers pay a fixed-sum license fee for a certain period of time for the film to be on their platform. It is usually prorated (distributed proportionately) quarterly over the license period. Some pay it in two or three installments. Try to get as much as soon as possible.

4. **Back-end profit participation.** In some no-advance deals, the filmmaker keeps 100 percent of net revenue after breakeven (which is after subtracting commission and expenses). But with a large MG and theatrical spend, distributors feel like they are also investors in the movie, so 60 percent of net revenue (after breakeven) to the filmmaker is common. How "net" is defined in the contract will determine if you see profit—so read that part closely. If you have substantial leverage, you might be able to demand a "gross corridor," which means you would get a percentage of every dollar of gross revenue before deducting fees and expenses. Closely check your rights to do an accounting of their books.

5. **Guaranteed marketing budget.** The more a distributor spends, the better chance a film has of being discovered. This is crucial for a streaming premiere because how else will anybody find out about the film? The downside is that marketing increases expenses deducted before seeing royalties.

6. **Capped distribution expenses.** "Rolling breakeven" is when uncapped expenses keep adding up. A distributor should not be able to exceed a negotiated cap without written approval from the filmmaker. Typical expenses are $8,000 to $30,000 for a straight-to-digital film. A theatrical release could cost seven figures. The highest expense is usually marketing.

7. **Theatrical release.** Will the distributor guarantee a certain number of markets? Which cities?

8. **Final cut.** Who will control artistic decisions? They may insist on reshoots, a new ending, or other changes, especially if they pay a high advance. Will a distributor's name be added to the credits?

9. **Approvals.** They will probably insist on having final say over artwork, publicity, and release details. If you can't get approval, get "meaningful consultation."

10. **Awards campaign.** Will they commit to promoting the film for awards?

11. **Reserved rights.** A filmmaker should retain all rights not specifically licensed. Rights to ask to retain include: outtake material, remakes, sequels, TV series, artwork, websites, underlying works, novels, speaking fees, private screenings, and so on.

Sometimes, the best offer you can get is a zero-dollar advance but with a marketing-spend guarantee that still gives the film a shot at breaking out. Even a no-advance release is better than nothing. You made the film to be seen, right? When Gravitas Ventures acquired *The Truth About Marriage* (2020), they went low with a small advance of $5,000. Since my mortgage payments were up to date, I didn't counter with a higher number; instead, I said keep the advance (which would be deducted against my royalties anyway) and instead increase their guaranteed marketing spend.

The Going Rates for Acquisitions

A few charmed films hit the million-dollar-advance payday, but most independent films (with no major festival wins and no big names) get a small straight-to-digital release with no up-front minimum guarantee. The negotiation is mainly over the size of distributor's fee, license term, and the cap on expenses.

Glen Reynolds said, "I had a film with no big names, but it just clicked with the right company. One offer came in at $50,000. So, I intimated to another company that I had a good five-figure offer, but we were looking for six, and they went to six, a hundred grand MG on the table for all rights worldwide. There are ways to talk it up without lying. I sold another film to HBO, and it was a happy number for the filmmakers, who had finished the film for $200,000. The sale didn't quite make them whole, but it was a prestigious placement, and it helped push up foreign rights that we were able to monetize afterward."

A good license fee from a streamer can be in the $80,000 to $400,000 range. Reynolds cautioned, "That's not every day. That's hard to get. Typically, it's either a big number, or they don't want it at all. Netflix wants originals, so they're paying a decent price." When streamers buy a film from a distributor, if it's not going to be an original or it's something that's been around, they might pay $5,000 to $20,000. Whatever the advance, Reynolds believes his job is to get the best possible placement for the filmmaker, then it's the distributor's job to monetize the film, and it's the filmmaker's job to help push it. After that, it's up to the cinema gods to decide if the film will catch on.

Making Delivery

Once you close a deal, you must provide acceptable delivery materials by a certain date. The distributor will include a checklist in the contract. If the files you provide do not meet their requirements and specifications, or if they do not receive all required materials and metadata, it could delay the launch or even terminate the deal. Below is a sample checklist:

Delivery Materials
+ Feature file (see complete specs below)
+ Trailer file (see complete specs below)
+ Feature screening link(s) and password(s)
+ Trailer screening link(s) and password(s)
+ Credits and billing block
+ Chain of Title and Copyright Information

- Title Search Report (Created by a company that provides an opinion as to whether your film's title infringes on, or is trading off, the fame of prior existing programming. Although titles cannot be copyrighted, if there is a likelihood of confusion with another famous work, you would be wise to change titles to something unique.)
- Feature closed caption files (.scc preferred; .mcc and .srt accepted)
- Feature English subtitle files (fcp.xml preferred; .mcc, .srt, and .stl accepted) [If primarily non-English dialogue.]
- Vertical key art; film poster as layered (.psd preferred, or Adobe InDesign, or Adobe Illustrator). If a layered .psd is unavailable, a clean vertical poster as a .jpg, .png, .tiff, or .pdf may be acceptable. It must contain no credit blocks, laurels, website callouts, company logos, and so on.
- Horizontal version of key art. Same specs.
- DVD/Blu-ray sleeve version of key art
- At least two (2) high-resolution (300 dpi) stills (.jpg, .png, .tiff, .pdf). Screen caps are not acceptable.
- Music cue sheet
- Crew and talent contracts, release forms, and archival footage and music licensing documentation
- Completed metadata spreadsheet with all the details about the film: year, country, language, runtime, genre, synopsis, crew, cast, production company, copyright info
- E&O Insurance. (I have sometimes delayed this expense by negotiating to provide it only after a distributor notifies me of the execution of a licensing agreement that requires it.)

Technical Specs
- Apple ProRes 422 (HQ) .mov file (or 444).
- HD: 1920×1080.
- SD: 720×480 or 720×486 or 640×480 encoded pixels.
- All encoded content must include a pixel aspect ratio that defines content as either 4:3 or 16:9.
- Native frame rate of original sources.
- Trailers must match the feature specs exactly (frame rate, resolution, aspect ratio), except that trailers may not always require 5.1 audio, and may not require closed caption files.
- The same specs apply to episodic television content.

- Closed captions must be delivered in .scc, .mcc, or .srt format and comply with FCC standards (a dialogue list is not a closed caption file).
- 29.97 frames per second can be delivered interlaced.
- 24/23.98 frames per second must be delivered progressive.
- Content must have stereo audio. Mono only accepted on a case-by-case basis.
- 5.1 audio can be accepted in addition to stereo tracks.

Theatrical Release

The number of movies released in theaters is declining. Going direct-to-streaming makes sense for many films, but theatrical is still usually the best way to launch a film product, and that includes documentaries. If your distributor agrees to give your film a theatrical release, it's time to celebrate, even if the film underperforms, because it's worth the risk. The potential profitability is so much higher for a theatrical release than a streaming premiere. Additionally, the value of your IP (especially if you held on to your remake, sequel, and series rights) will increase.

Paramount's strategy for the *Trekkies* theatrical was to double-book it at theaters showing *Star Wars: Episode I—The Phantom Menace* (1999). "They are only booking a maximum of two screens per cineplex," Paramount COO Rob Friedman told us. "George [Lucas] wants long lines. He wants to keep the number of screens down to 6,000." Our plan was when people couldn't get a ticket for *Star Wars*, they'd see *Trekkies* playing and check it out instead. Paramount first chose Portland and Indianapolis as test markets, followed by a wider release. Indianapolis is considered one of America's most "average" cities. As such, it's often used as a test market for movies, restaurants, and other new products.

We were overjoyed by our reviews but disheartened by the low box office. The *Entertainment Weekly* box office report wrote: "The documentary opened in a surprisingly hefty 339 theaters to nearly unanimous critical acclaim, but with hardly any promotional push, beamed into 34th place with $126,000." *Star Wars: Episode I—The Phantom Menace* opened to an announced $105 million for the week, finishing at $493,216,789 domestic. *Trekkies* finished with a box office of $318,246.[1,2]

Afterward, at a marketing meeting, Friedman said, "I know we all hoped for a bigger box office, but the gamble of putting it out with a minimum distribution expenditure worked in getting a huge awareness of the product with low expenses. I think we will do very well in video."

Not long after the *Trekkies* release, I had lunch with James G. Robinson, CEO of Morgan Creek Entertainment, to discuss the possibility of directing one of their projects. Robinson asked about *Trekkies*, and I mentioned the low box office figure. He said, "That's not the kind of film a wide audience will go see." He said the actual *Star Wars* box office figure for the first week was closer to $97 million, not the announced $105 million. "Lucas expected $150 million. He was disappointed. They would have been embarrassed if it didn't top a hundred million."

I asked, "How can they fudge the figures?"

"They take it from next week's numbers, and then they take it from the following week for the second weekend, and after five weeks, it doesn't matter."

Paramount's Rob Friedman was correct in that the financial silver lining for *Trekkies* was in the post-theatrical ancillaries: home video, cable, and foreign markets. Four years later, *Trekkies* had surpassed $5 million in gross revenues, most of which was profit due to the low $1.7 million theatrical and marketing distribution expenditure. By the end of Paramount's twenty-year license for *Trekkies*, the total gross reached $7 million, resulting in a net profit to me and my partners of $3.35 million. And the film continues collecting royalties today.

Sequels

Hold on to sequel, remake, and television series rights. It may be hard to top your first film with a sequel, but a second chance gives you an opportunity to do it better—and get paid twice. With my film *Suckers* (2001), we sold a pitch to HBO to write a series pilot. Although the pilot didn't get picked up, we were able to make this deal because we retained series rights. For *Trekkies*, we had given Paramount a "right of first negotiation and last refusal (i.e., a final matching right)" on sequel rights, so on November 5, 2001, I sent a letter to Rob Friedman announcing our intention to make

Trekkies *crew in front of Cologne Cathedral, in Köln, Germany; sound mixer Bill Martel, producer Michael Leahy, director of photography David Doyle, director Roger Nygard, producer/star Denise Crosby.*

Star Trek *fans in Haiger, Germany; sound mixer Bill Martel, director Roger Nygard, Christian Luft, Willi Wiegand, Ansgar Wehnge, Christoph Hees, director of photography David Doyle.*

a follow-up and gave Paramount fourteen days to reply. Michael Grizzi, in business affairs, responded with an offer to open negotiations: "Paramount welcomes the opportunity to further discuss the project with you."

This time, we did not demand a theatrical release, and they insisted any further sequel rights would have to be "frozen" so that no subsequent productions could be produced without mutual consent (they resented that we had been able to force them into the sequel negotiations). Unless they pay you a lot of money, don't let a distributor "freeze" your sequel and remake rights, but if they do, make sure the freeze ends with the expiration of the contract. As with the first film, we retained ownership, and they received a twenty-year license (twenty-five if unrecouped). We began filming on May 4, 2003, at a *Star Trek* convention in Bonn, Germany.

Bad Distributor Outcomes

Read distribution contracts carefully. Have a lawyer and your film agent review contracts *License* a film, don't *sell* it. I know a filmmaker who sold his film to a distributor in perpetuity. He has been kicking himself ever since. His movie is lost to him forever. When deal terms lapse or distribution companies go bankrupt, you need to be able to get your film back. When distributors are doing a decent job, and their statements and checks come on time, I gladly extend licenses. If they prove to be unstable or unreliable, I find another distribution route.

The first distributor for *The Nature of Existence* ran into financial difficulties and apparently comingled returns from my film with funds used to release other films, gambling he would be able to pay me what was owed out of other films' future returns. I discovered something was wrong when he began acting erratically and royalty statements were increasingly tardy. And then the publicist, Technicolor, and FotoKem contacted me, claiming the distributor was not paying their bills.

Make sure your contract gives you a recourse if a distributor does not live up to their commitments. Your first step is to do an accounting of the books. Contracts commonly allow a producer to audit a distributor's books once per year. If you find discrepancies, the next step is to send a letter and ask for payment. If none is forthcoming by your deadline, or if you can't work out a payment plan, have a lawyer send a letter listing the contractual breaches and making a demand for action/payment. If they are non-communicative or payments are not made current by your deadline, and if you decide legal action is the next step, how you proceed depends on the contract. Consult with a qualified legal expert early to ensure you get the protections you need and so that you recover whatever you can from any distributor bankruptcy judgment.

Most distribution deals prevent filmmakers from filing a lawsuit, instead requiring arbitration, which weakens your ability to pressure a distributor because a lawsuit is a stronger step than arbitration. But at least it gives you a forum to address grievances. Our contract had a clause that stated the following:

> In the event a dispute cannot be resolved by the parties themselves, such dispute shall be submitted to, determined and settled by formal arbitration at the joint equal cost to the parties in Los Angeles, CA, pursuant to the laws of the State of California and the rules of the Independent Film & Television Alliance (IFTA).

I filed for mediation under the rules of the Independent Film & Television Alliance. The distributor didn't show up, probably because he had no valid counterargument, and I won. The arbitration judge charged a total of $1,995 for his time reviewing the case. An arbitrator does not have the power to issue a Judgment; the Arbitral Award has to be filed in a court, and then, based upon that, a Judgment is issued. I had to hire an attorney to file a request for a Judgment Confirming Arbitration Award with the Superior Court of California for the County of Los Angeles. After getting the Judgment, my attorney filed a Declaration Re Affidavit of Interest After Judgment, which is a request that a Writ of Execution be issued against the Defendant. After obtaining this *original* Writ stamped by the Court, my lawyer engaged the Sheriff of the County of Los Angeles to enforce the judgment by going to the distributor's bank to levy the account. However, when the Sheriff arrived, the account had been emptied, perhaps a preemptive attempt to prevent collection. Ultimately, the distributor felt that an outstanding judgment against his company was not a good look, so he negotiated a payment plan where he paid back a reduced debt in monthly installments until it was paid off. Once he made the final payment, I filed an Acknowledgment of Satisfaction of Judgment with the Clerk of the Court.

When distribution companies release too many underperforming films and run out of cash, they sometimes file for bankruptcy and dissolve their current entity. They might start a new company, beginning again with no debt. At the point when a company you have an agreement with is dissolved, unpaid royalties are probably lost to you.

I always make sure I have a clause in my contract that states that all rights will immediately revert to me unencumbered in the case of bankruptcy or dissolution or if reports and remittances are delinquent more than 120 days. When making delivery, keep backup copies of all your masters, marketing, and deliverables so you won't have to worry about getting them back from a delinquent or intransigent distributor.

DIY (Do-It-Yourself) Distribution

If you're unable to grab the brass ring of a major streamer, or convert your film to an original on a cable network, or have a studio put it on 1,000 screens, most backup plans are either smaller distribution, hybrid distribution, or self-distribution. Releasing your own film can be as simple as putting it online (Amazon Prime Video Direct, Vimeo OTT, YouTube Studio, etc.).You can offer it for free, for sale and rental, or with ads. In that case, it's up to you to drive viewers to the film. If you do no substantial marketing and wait for people to find your gem until it goes viral, you may be waiting forever. There are a lot of competing videos. It's possible, without over-spending, through smart publicity, grassroots and Internet marketing, and niche advertising to help a film catch fire.

To release a film theatrically, anybody can rent a movie screen for a night, a week, or multiple weeks, which is called "four-walling." In this case, you are paying for the theater (and staff) and keeping 100 percent of ticket sales. Some theaters are thrilled, knowing you will fill the place with your friends, who will buy enormously marked-up popcorn and soda. If a theater costs $4,000 per week, you need 200 people at $20 a head to break even. Between you and the crew and the interviewees, you probably have 200 friends you can guilt into that theater. If you spend $10,000 on publicity and advertising, then you need 700 ticket buyers. That means you also have to convince 500 strangers it's worth the effort to drive to the theater. If you've got a strong hook and core audience, and you spend enough on marketing, it's possible. Sometimes, you can negotiate a deal with a theater where you don't have to pay a rental fee. Instead, you get the room for free and split the door, usually sixty-forty (60 percent to the theater). For one major city, with an inexpensive publicist, a small mar-keting budget, and a lower-priced theater, you're probably looking at a minimum spend of $15,000 to $20,000.You can also hire a company like Fathom Events to simultaneously broadcast your film to movie theaters throughout the United States.

There's a philosophy (similar to impact producers) that filmmaker Keith Ochwat has promoted for monetizing documentaries. If you have a film with a particular niche, he views traditional distributors as the last place you should go. His entity is called Show&Tell, a website where you can watch videos about how to release your film. Step one of his approach is to find groups that have common cause with your subject matter and then try to set up partnerships. Maybe you do free screenings for their membership, either virtually or live, and in return, they blast your URL to their audience with a pitch to sell your movie directly. Step two is selling your film's edu-cational rights. And then eventually it is to put your film on transactional VOD, AVOD, and the rest.[3]

Hybrid Distribution

It's probably not the encoding of a movie that excites you. It's not the ability to sell it to iNDEMAND that gets you revved up. It's finding an audience and having your film seen that brings you joy. For those considering self-distribution versus distributor offers, Glen Reynolds recommends a hybrid plan, where you let a distributor do what they do, making sales and getting the film on platforms. And then you do the marketing and publicity, treating it like a DIY release. You do everything you can to drive an audience to the film.

Some distributors operate primarily on the quantity method: acquire many films and throw them out there to see what gets traction. It's up to the filmmakers to create a spark, fan the flames, and keep throwing logs on the fire. One clear metric as to whether a film is picking up momentum is the number of presales. Gravitas Ventures emailed me this advice for their release of *The Truth About Marriage*: "Promote iTunes pre-order first and foremost. Our goal is to reach 300+ pre-orders by your release date. We've noticed that this is the minimum threshold that iTunes tends to favor when considering titles for premium placement. This would get your film off to a solid start upon its release."

Publicist Sylvia Desrochers said that when filmmakers ask publicists to help promote pre-orders, she has to explain that the media does not care about presales: "The press doesn't cover the film until it's actually available. A distributor is going to push filmmakers on presales. This is something you need to do with your friends and family because who else is buying your film on a presale? I have asked filmmakers, 'Have you ever bought a film on presale?' And they're always like, 'No, I guess I haven't.'" This is the time for the filmmaker to contact and cajole everybody on the mailing list they have been cultivating since they started shooting, and at every festival, and everybody sympathetic to their cause.

Service Deal

If you believe in your film and have saved money for distribution, you can negotiate a service deal with a distributor where you put up all or a percentage of the P&A (prints and advertising). In essence, you are paying this rent-a-distributor to work for you. They will take a fee and then split the profits after distribution expenses. Playing the film for a week in a theater in New York or Los Angeles has the added benefit of qualifying for Academy Awards consideration.

When we released *The Nature of Existence* in 2010, we made two 35mm prints (DCPs weren't yet pervasive) and chose a couple dozen cities. We hired a theatrical-booking and marketing consultant named Steve Fagan at Sky Island Films to pitch and book the film in theaters. It was worth paying this booker for his contacts. He got us into theaters in New York, Los Angeles, Irvine, San Diego, Austin, Dallas, Palm Springs, Houston, Portland, Eugene, Chicago, Santa Fe, Tempe, Honolulu, Denver, Boulder, and Minneapolis. Many cities passed: Boston, Seattle, Sacramento, San Francisco, San Antonio, Albuquerque, and Salt Lake City.

Once we had bookings lined up, we alternated cities to be able to work on publicity in the respective cities, each in turn, so we could move a print from one city to the next (called bicycling). DCPs and Blu-rays cost much less than a 35mm print, so it's cheaper now to do many cities at once. However, by spacing out each release, it allows you to focus your PR efforts on one regional campaign at a time.

The most critical element in marketing is the selection of the right publicists. They ideally need a three-month lead time to implement a national strategy, pitching your film to critics at major media outlets as well as pitching you and your cast and crew for feature stories in long-lead publications, web-based media, television programs, radio, podcasts, and freelance media outlets. We hired a publicist in New York and a separate publicist in Los Angeles. Publicists tend to know their turf best, and some have specialties such as digital releases or Academy campaigns. For different cities, it's good to hire somebody reliable in each region. We found it difficult to find affordable publicists in some cities, so we decided to have the New York publicist cover the regional cities. We also hired a media-buying and advertising firm, which specialized in handling ad placements nationwide.

The first markets (because they had the most media) were New York followed by Los Angeles. A month before those openings, we had press and tastemaker screenings and special-event screenings to secure local articles and reviews. For example, Professor Richard Brown's Movies 101 class at

New York University hosted a screening and Q&A. That was followed by a screening for the American Cinematheque at the Aero Theater in Los Angeles. Then we rolled out the film to other cities. If openings generate decent box office, it encourages other cities to book the film. If a movie catches on, you have to be ready to expand.

On opening weekends, I went on the road to do mini press junkets and be at the theater for opening-night Q&As. The film averaged $3,800 per theater overall. Some grossed $8,000, and some only grossed $1,000. Dallas and Tempe did exceptionally well, while Chicago and Honolulu did minimal business. The film grossed $65,000 by the time we were done. That may not seem like much, but putting the movie in theaters in several cities raised its cinematic profile and generated hundreds of reviews and articles, each of which was a free commercial. Afterward, this theatrical aura pushed up the price when it was licensed to Netflix.

Release Window

When working with a distributor, about thirty days out from a VOD release date, they usually provide the filmmaker with a "carriage letter," which lists the main digital platforms where a film will debut so the filmmaker knows exactly what to promote. If there's a theatrical release, there will probably be a ninety-day holdback before any ancillary market release is allowed. However, if you or the distributor are four-walling theaters, the theatrical release might be the same "day and date" as the digital release. If a pay TV or subscription platform pays a license fee for the premiere, they will require exclusivity against other rights, probably for two years or more. The typical order of digital release windows begins with transactional VOD (video on demand), probably simultaneous with DVD and Blu-ray. About ninety to 120 days later comes SVOD (subscription video on demand), PVOD (premium video on demand) where SVOD subscribers pay a fee on top of their subscription dues for early access to new content, AVOD (ad-supported video on demand), and non-premiere pay TV. Following or concurrent will be educational markets and other ancillaries (i.e., ships, hotels, airlines, etc.). If you have an international sales agent, they will also be making foreign sales.

Distribution Publicity

If your film is one of the lucky few to get picked up by a studio, they will take total control and tell you where to go and who to talk to. They will fly you to openings and set up publicity events, such as press junkets, where you (and your stars) sit in hotel rooms as dozens of representatives from various media cycle through. There are one-on-one interviews with writers in one room, a round table of press in another, and a video and lighting set-up in yet another. Each writer or interviewer gets only a few minutes to ask questions before being ushered out to make room for the next.

Once a film has a release date, a filmmaker needs a publicist, especially if the distributor will not pay for it. Glen Reynolds explained, "Many filmmakers go into the process thinking their film will work well enough that a distributor will take over the PR and marketing costs. The problem is that slots for that treatment are extremely limited." Every week, each film competes with ten or twenty or more releases. Three new movies on Netflix, two on Hulu, another series coming out on Amazon, and so on. At the same time, most media publications have downsized the number of reviewers. Those fewer critics may have thirty offerings to pick from every week. They're going to review two to five releases. A publicist's job is to convince them that you're as worthy of reviewing as a Marvel movie. Reynolds added, "A one-city theatrical gets you ahead in the publicity game over a straight-to-digital release. A two-city theatrical puts you a little ahead of the one-city release. If you're doing ten cities, then you're even higher up in the rankings in terms of critics paying attention."

Doing Your Own Publicity

Most distributors put a film out with minimal PR spending. The successful distributors who focus on straight-to-digital have discovered that it's better to concentrate on quality product, branding, selling to many platforms, and spending no more than $5,000 on social-media ads. They know that publicists have a hard time breaking a digital film. They love it when the filmmaker spends to supplement what they're doing, especially when filmmakers hire a media-buying specialist to target spending. According to Glen

Reynolds, "The filmmaker actually has more control if they're the ones spending on marketing and publicity. A big distributor can spend millions of dollars and still miss good opportunities. Set aside part of your film's budget for publicity and marketing to give yourself a chance. Most releases don't work without something pushing them."

Once a publicist is on board, they will work with a filmmaker to write press materials. Before you have a publicist, write your own drafts. Get examples of what others have used and emulate the format. Those materials will be the starting drafts for your publicist. A publicist will request copies (if they exist) of your press kit, press releases, logline, synopsis, tag lines, teaser and/or trailer, movie clips, title treatment, key art and poster, credits, cast and crew lists, cast and crew biographies, website, articles and reviews (so far), a written Q&A with the director, all your social media, and stills from the film, including BTS (behind-the-scenes) photos. Your photos should be high-resolution 300 DPI (dots per inch). Also, for emailing, create smaller versions of your photos; make the smaller versions close to but not over 1 MB each.

Don't hire a publicist and then sit back and wait. No matter how much help you have, work hard to promote your film. Nobody will work as hard as you because nobody has as much stake. And the harder you work and the more leads you provide to your publicists, the harder they will work. When your film finally lands online, start the reviews by priming the pump. Have trustworthy friends give it maximum stars and good, accurate reviews. Your mass emails or social-media pleas to friends for reviews will be ignored. Contact each person individually and specifically ask for the favor. It's much harder to ignore a direct request.

Ask your cast, profilees, crew, musicians, crowd-funders, investors, donors, and friends to mention and promote the film on social media. Don't expect them to do it unless you ask them directly. Tell them precisely what you want. Provide artwork, photos, text, ideas, announcements, awards, release dates, or reviewer quotes to give them a reason to crow on your behalf. If you know somebody who knows somebody famous, with a large number of followers, implore them to ask for a shout-out. Contact the nice folks at each of the film festivals where your film screened. Give them credit for your success; tell them you got distribution thanks to their help. Then, ask them to send an announcement to their mailing list that your film is now coming out. Make sure to keep your website and social media current, with links for all the places your film can be viewed. Join meetup sites to locate groups predisposed to your topic, invite them to make your screening a special meetup event, and offer to appear at the event. This is an excellent way to boost opening night numbers at a theater.

Write articles about making your film, the film's topic, or about your interviewees, and submit to publications on spec. Email and call publications or websites pre-sold on your subject matter to pitch a story. If you have a built-in core audience, there will be media outlets that cater to them and will see information about your film as bona fide news. I wrote an article called "On the Trekkie Trail," about the pivotal moments that led to the making and selling of *Trekkies* and pitched it to several newspapers; *The Los Angeles Times Magazine* picked it up.[4] For the release of *The Nature of Existence*, I wrote a spec article called "Conceptual Reality: It Doesn't Take Vulcan Logic to Fund Concept-Based Documentaries." *Documentary* magazine published it.[5]

Digital Promotion

Get creative with your social-media campaign. In addition to sharing requisite photos and updates on social media, come up with new angles, such as posting short videos leading up to the release of your film, in the hopes that one of your posts will find eyeballs virally and draw traffic to your movie. They could be new videos, separate from your film, or they could incorporate short clips from the film. Every video faces a new battle for views. You can toss them out on YouTube, TikTok, or Instagram and hope they catch on, but on each social-media platform, there is a way to boost videos.

To take one example, Sven Pape is a film editor with a YouTube channel called This Guy Edits. He interviewed me and created a video illustrating techniques from my book *Cut to the Monkey* (2020). When I asked how he promotes his videos using digital data points and analytics, he said he tweaks the title and image until a video starts to take off, as this video did, on its way to half a million views—and as a result, sales of my book and films increased.

To achieve breakthrough status, the first ingredient seems obvious: good, funny, or outrageous content. You will never catch up to "Baby Shark Dance," with over fifteen billion views, but if you come up with something memorable, you can ride a wave. The second crucial element is the thumbnail. Find an attention-getting visual. Advertising executives have known for ages that nothing sells better than babies, animals, breasts, or humor. The third component is a catchy title. Get one of these elements wrong and the algorithm that raises content in the rankings loses interest fast.

To increase views, ask (demand) that all your friends subscribe to your channel(s). Then, while testing and changing each of the three components, pay attention to the analytics that video-centric platforms share with creators. Click-through rates show how many people the thumbnail image persuades to try the video. Retention rates show how long viewers watch and when they drop off. Look at which parts of the video have above-average or below-average retention. After you post the video, you can still change the title, thumbnail, and even edit out parts with below-average retention numbers, to drive up stats. You are on the right track if rates go up with each change. If they go down, return to what worked. Most creators don't play with these factors; they dump a clip online and leave the outcome to chance. All the big creators watch, test, and tweak.

At the end of your video, include a brief plea to remind viewers to seek out your movie. Also, ask them to subscribe to your channel. If you build up a decent following, you might even meet the requirements that allow you to monetize videos, such as joining the YouTube Partner Program (4,000 watch hours over the last twelve months and at least 1,000 subscribers). The CPM (cost-per-mile, a.k.a. cost-per-thousand) metric is the going ad-rate for a specific video. The higher the rate, the more desirable the video is for advertisers, the more money YouTube (and you) make, and the more likely the algorithm will be to share the video. Sometimes, you can change the pay rate of a video by adding an extra spot for a mid-roll ad, which will drive up the revenue and re-trigger the algorithm.

Successfully releasing a movie requires creative brainstorming and exhaustive efforts on your part. Don't leave anything to chance. Actively manage your campaign. Work closely with your film rep, publicist, social-media specialist, marketing experts, the distributor's team, and everybody you can conscript into the war. Yes, you are an artist, but to be seen, you must also be a battlefield general, working harder than anybody, deploying all your resources in the fight. Victory and great rewards will follow your endeavor.

You have reached the end of my how-to-make-a-documentary portion of the book. The reality of selling a film is that it's a multi-stage process that can take months to get to a first offer and then longer to close a deal. Anywhere along the way, a misstep can lead to failure. So, in the following four chapters, I relate a case study: the grueling behind-the-scenes battles we experienced while attempting to sell our documentary *Trekkies*.

CHAPTER TEN

Screening Strategies

Be as prepared as NASA when launching your selling process.

As we approached the completion of *Trekkies* in April of 1997, Denise Crosby, the producers at Neo Motion Pictures, and I began trying to sell our film. The process today has changed slightly, with the convenience of screening links, which is how my latest documentary sold, but the process and psychology remain the same. There are four phases. Phase One is about getting buyers excited via simultaneous screenings. Phase Two begins with the first real offer, ideally leading to multiple offers, which launches Phase Three: the bidding war. Phase Four is accepting an offer and negotiating the rest of the deal points with the buyer's business affairs team.

Phase One: Screening Begins

As we approached completing a *Trekkies* final cut, we scheduled an open distributor screening for Wednesday, April 16, 1997. We planned to pack the house with Known Good Laughers. We invited studio acquisitions executives, as well as producers we knew, who might be able to help us get noticed. No top-level decision-makers RSVPed. If you are not personal friends with CEOs, the best you can hope for are underlings. The acquisition executive at Paramount, John Ferraro, blew us off, saying that Paramount wasn't looking to make or release smaller films. *Lassie* (1994) had been a disappointment; it cost $8 million and did only $9 million worldwide. But Ferraro said he would send his assistant Ben Pratt.

Roger Nygard, Denise Crosby, and Keith Border at a test screening for Trekkies *(1997) at Raleigh Studios.*

Neo Motion Pictures had a production deal with Miramax's horror label Dimension Films to produce films like *The Prophecy II* (1998), so the night before our big screening, Producer Keith Border arranged a secret pre-screening for Jeff Kurz of Miramax. This screening was plagued with troubles. The air-conditioning broke, during the first ten minutes the sound was low, there was time-code bleed through, and the last third of the film was out of sync due to a bad tape. When the screening ended, Kurz bolted like he was late to catch a plane back to Toluca Lake. Keith intercepted him and asked, "So how much are you going to pay for this, Jeff?" Kurz edged toward the door as he replied, "Well . . . I'll call you tomorrow." Which he didn't do.

Denise Crosby also invited an executive producer named Marc Abraham, co-founder of Beacon Pictures. Beacon started out strong with *The Commitments* (1991) and then stumbled with *The Road to Wellville* (1994) and *The Babysitters Club* (1995). They had recently formed an output deal with Universal Pictures, which would be releasing their $90-million-budget *Air Force One* (1997), starring Harrison Ford. After the screening, Abraham raved on and on about *Trekkies*, saying how impressed he was.

Because our secret screening served to iron out the bugs, our official screening went off without a hitch. The laughs came and never seemed to stop. As we confirmed who attended, we found that it was indeed only lower-echelon scouts.

The First Responses

The next day, Keith received calls from Sara Rose at Orion Pictures, Arianna Bocco at New Line Cinema, Carol Smithson at Trimark Pictures, and Matt Brodlie from Miramax. They all wanted tapes, but we refused because we had decided upon a "no tape policy" for two reasons: we preferred that buyers see the film with an audience, and we wanted to prevent bootlegs from circulating. Instead, we offered to set up private screenings anywhere.

Abraham said he would arrange a screening for Chris McGurk, the COO at Universal. At the time, Beacon and Universal were pursuing a joint purchase of October Films (later, it became USA Films and then Focus Features). Separately, Universal's acquisition executive Matt Wall called to say he had been at the screening and loved the film but didn't know what to do with it. Plus, he hadn't been able to get them to acquire anything. He had tried to pick up *Sling Blade* (1996), and they said no. I told him Abraham had already gone over his head to McGurk.

When Abraham called McGurk, McGurk responded, "It sounds wild, but what would you do with it?"

"A classy theatrical," Abraham said. "Nobody knows what works, but I know when something's entertaining."

Scott Anderson, a friend who was Senior Vice President of Production for Stuart Benjamin Productions, told me, "I feel like calling John Ferraro and telling him to see it."

I said, "You know John Ferraro?"

"I've known him a long time."

The whole point of the screening was to get connected execs to praise the film to buyers, so I said, "If you could tell him how much you liked the film, that would be great."

"I should probably not tell him I know you so it won't seem like I'm working on your behalf."

Ferraro took his call, and Anderson said, "John, you've been on my mind all morning, and I've been meaning to call you to congratulate you."

"For what?"

"I saw this wonderful film last night called *Trekkies*. It was terrific. I thought it had to be yours."

"No, it's not."

"Really. Oh, well then, never mind. I assumed it had to be yours since it's all about *Star Trek* fans."

"No, the producer won't let us see it without an audience. The producer is being so difficult."

"Oh, I think I saw him there, some guy named Brannon?"

"No, Keith Border."

"Oh, that's right, Brannon Braga was the Paramount producer who was *in* the movie."

Ferraro was shocked, "Brannon is in the movie?"

"Yeah, you guys should buy it. Then I'll call you later to congratulate you." Anderson was having so much fun, he tortured him a little more: "How can these people make this movie without you?"

Ferraro was a little fuzzy on that point, "I don't know. That's part of the controversy. I guess they can because they have."

Ferraro immediately tracked down Denise at home. "My assistant came back from the screening raving about the film. Everybody's calling me. I've got to see this. It's so difficult for me to set up a screening because I need a month to schedule something for Sheri Lansing or Rob Friedman."

Denise didn't fold. "If you need a month, give us a date, and we'll set it up."

After that first screening, there was lots of talk but no offers, and we were frustrated. Keith and I agreed that we needed to schedule another screening in a few weeks to keep the momentum going. In the meantime, the front-line scouts started arranging private screenings for middle-level executives, but still, there was nobody who could say yes to a deal.

Know the Deal Points You Want

Marc Abraham asked what we were looking for in a *Trekkies* deal. We didn't have any cohesive idea, so I put together a list, topped by an ask of a $2 million advance. Keith said he was thinking more along the lines of $10 million. I said ten is a nice round number but maybe a tad optimistic. At this point, *Roger & Me* (1989) held the documentary-advance record, selling for $3 million to Warner Bros. In second place was *When We Were Kings* (1996), which we heard garnered $1 million from PolyGram Filmed Entertainment (distributed through Gramercy Pictures). *Hoop Dreams* (1994) was rumored to have gotten $500,000 from New Line Cinema, who released it through Fine Line Features. And Miramax had paid $400,000 for *The Thin Blue Line*. That was the rarefied realm into which we were hoping to ascend.

Whoever Speaks First Loses

Arianna Bocco at New Line called Keith to ask, "What do you want for this film? Obviously, we're very interested."

Keith and I had been discussing our response, so he was ready. One of the earliest lessons in the art of negotiating was taught to me by the old-timer who owned Ed's Trading Post in Long Lake, Minnesota. Ed was a junk dealer with a store packed with odds and ends and a few antiques. Ed told me, "Never make the first offer. Always make the other guy go first because he might go a lot higher than you expect."

Keith talked around a price. "There are two ways you can approach this, Arianna. The first is a substantial advance, plus guaranteed bonuses tied to the film's performance. That will take a lot longer and a lot of negotiating. Meanwhile, we will continue to screen the film. The second way is a preemptive offer to take it off the market. It would have to be significant enough to withhold the film from further screenings. Roger, Denise, and I realize we probably will have to take this film to Telluride before we sell it. You have to decide if New Line wants to be there watching and bidding with everybody else. Or do you want to be watching the film with a New Line logo on the front?"

Cultivating Potential Offers

Trimark co-founder Barry Barnholtz screened the film on May 21. Carol Smithson said afterward they were "running the numbers" and planning to make an offer. The next day, Mitch Goldman, Mark Ordesky, and Sara Risher screened at New Line. They also went away to "crunch the numbers." I discovered that running the numbers meant coming up with the minimum revenue projected for a title, a can't-lose number they're virtually guaranteed to get back, then they base an offer on it.

Trimark wanted us to sit in a room and not leave until we made a deal. Matt Berenson at New Line asked, "Just what is your minimum deal?" We refused to go first, especially since we had another big screening scheduled the next day.

On June 11, we overbooked a 170-seat room with 220 people. The place filled up, and we grabbed chairs from the lobby to add another dozen seats. We had invited several of the interviewees. Walter Koenig was there, the first of the *Star Trek* cast to see the film. A few people arrived late and were turned away because there wasn't another inch of space.

Star Trek fan Gabriel Koerner was in attendance. After he tossed around mispronounced big words like "plethora" and "adamant" on screen, one of the Klingons in the audience behind him said to a friend, "Oh my gosh, he's only fifteen."

Koerner was sitting in front of her, and he turned around and said, "I'm fourteen."

Eyes wide, she whispered to her friend, "Oh no, shoot me. I didn't know he was here."

Anne Murphy, who called herself a "Spiner femme," said that seeing the film for the first time was surreal: "When I walked into the theater, nobody gave me a second glance. Then when the lights came up, people were pointing and saying, 'That's her!' I guess that's what celebrities feel like."

One woman said as she left, "My face hurts from laughing so hard." No Paramount executives showed up. Universal's Chris McGurk attended, but walked out after twenty-five minutes. Later, Marc Abraham said McGurk felt he had seen enough to make a determination.

The following morning, Brannon Braga called to say, "Wind is blowing through Paramount about your screening last night. I just spoke with Jody Zucker, head of Paramount legal affairs for *Star Trek*. I told him that if Paramount is smart, they'd buy the film. It's their franchise. Why let somebody else have it? I guarantee once he sees the film, he will love it and see there's nothing to worry about. And he's the guy who's gonna get it to the right people."

Braga invited me to a party at his house near Paramount. The guy definitely knew how to throw a Hollywood party. There were wall-to-wall playmates, an all-girl band with lingerie dancers, plenty of M&Ms, and lots of "but alsos." Being an actor is not enough in Hollywood: "I'm *also* a writer," "I'm *also* going to Cal State Northridge," "I *also* train horses."

Zero Down

Trimark's Peter Block, VP of Acquisitions and Business Affairs, the person who makes offers, called Keith Border to discuss the parameters of a potential offer: "What if we give no advance but make a $400,000 prints and ads commitment?" If they were willing to guarantee spending $400,000 on distribution expenses, that meant they were confident they would make back an amount beyond that, and the problem was that they would deduct those P&A expenses before they paid us any profit share.

Keith responded, "There would have to be a hell of a back-end deal." Keith emphasized that we would consider any realistic offer. Block said he would get back to us. We weren't excited by zero up front. I suppose they had to give it a shot. It was almost two months since our first screening, and we still had no cash offers and were anxious to field one. Strains of worry were creeping in that we were doing something wrong.

Alex Ryan, a creative executive at Paramount, heard about *Trekkies* from Dana Goldberg at Baltimore Pictures, and so Ryan stepped in and set up two screenings at Paramount. Defying the odds, John Ferraro showed up at the first showing of about thirty people. He chuckled all the way through but bolted at the end. The second screening had about seventy-five people. Don Granger, Senior Vice President of Production (who would soon be elevated to Executive Vice President), was the biggest fish. Afterward, Granger said, "I loved it. It really captured the right sentiment. I know the fans have felt ignored by Paramount, and that's why we should embrace this film, so we can embrace the fans. This film is going to be a huge success." He said he would call Paramount COO Rob Friedman and tell him to see it. Mary Kerr, who worked for the Sundance Institute, was at the Paramount screening. She enjoyed the film and suggested we submit to Sundance right away.

Andrew Rona and Jeff Kurz at Miramax asked to set up a screening. The reason they hadn't done so yet is because they were all afraid of putting themselves in the line of fire with the Weinsteins. Keith got on the subject of copyrights and trademarks with Kurz and asked him if Miramax was worried about Paramount's proprietary interest in the film due to *Star Trek*. Kurz replied, "Don't you think we have as many lawyers as Paramount?"

John Ferraro called Keith to say, "It's a nice film, but it's a little film. It's a documentary. What's the upside?" Ferraro sounded indifferent. "Rob Friedman is hearing about the film from several sources and has decided he needs to see it. It's impossible to schedule a screening for him. He's so busy. The best thing to do would be to give him a tape for the weekend." We refused the tape request but offered to screen the film any time.

On June 27, almost three months after our first screening, we still had no cash offers. Barbara Sintes called from Sony Pictures Classics in New York asking for a screening. Jim Middleton at United Artists wanted to re-screen for the head of video. He said, "What drives this theatrically are the video numbers." Jim Wilson and Brandi McDougall from Fox Searchlight Pictures screened the film. One of the lessons we learned is never underestimate the power of assistants. If our cause was picking up momentum, it was because the assistants who came to see the film in the first waves persuaded their busy bosses to see it.

Mark Amin, co-founder of Trimark, had snuck into the Paramount screening and told Carol Smithson that he loved the movie but, "Paramount is going to buy this. I'm not going to waste our time until they formally pass."

Marc Abraham set a meeting at Universal with Chris McGurk for the next day, June 30, apparently for us to hear an offer.

At Paramount, Rob Friedman set a date to screen *Trekkies* for Wednesday, July 2.

We were disappointed when we found out our meeting with McGurk was really only a meeting with Matt Wall, who had no decision-making authority. Denise called Abraham to find out what the agenda was.

Abraham said we should take the meeting. "I've got these guys where I think this deal can happen. They understand what you want, and Chris McGurk said, 'Let's do it.' Matt's enthusiasm is great. And I want Beacon to be involved, to initiate Beacon's foray into smaller films." Abraham's demeanor was so calm and reassuring it was impossible not to like him. Amongst ourselves, we agreed to listen to what Universal had to say but not to talk about any counteroffers until after we left.

CHAPTER ELEVEN

Getting the First Offer

*The advance is a measure of a distributor's belief
in a film.*

I dropped our film with an application at the Sundance Film Festival
office on my way to the meeting at Universal. If we wanted to get into
film festivals, there was no way to avoid giving out copies of the film. In
the waiting room at Universal, I asked Marc Abraham whose money we
would be dealing with, and he said it would be a combination of Beacon's
and Universal's. Keith, Denise, Abraham, and I met with Matt Wall (Acquisitions), Andrew Kairey (Executive Vice President), Greg Anderson (Director,
Business Affairs), and Jeffrey Korchek (Executive Vice President of Legal
and Business Affairs).

Phase Two: The First Cash Offer

Wall always wore a suit but looked seventeen years old. He welcomed and
congratulated us on producing *Trekkies*. Abraham took over and discussed
marketing and release strategies.

Kairey gave us his marketing approach: "Universal has a big distribution
apparatus. That works great for *Liar Liar*, but for *Trekkies*, whatever rules
exist, throw them out. It's a fun film that we can definitely make money
with. Keith's idea of a mega-premiere at the Chinese Theater is a good
one. We can make a circus out of it. And we can tie a release in with the
conventions."

Denise agreed, "The time is right for a new event. I've been at conventions all over the world, and I've sensed the fans are hungry for something new."

Abraham asked us what else we wanted in addition to the marketing plans that had been discussed. I said, "There are five or six topics we need to address: advance, back end, release guarantees, support for film festivals and publicity, and approvals of artwork and trailers. The bonus topic includes three-picture deals."

Kairey looked at me, Keith, and Denise and said, "So that's nine pictures total?"

"That's right."

More laughs.

Korchek said, "I spoke to Tom Bliss [COO of Beacon]. He was on a glacier—but we discussed the film, so we can make a deal. We're really enthusiastic about this film." Although Korchek had yet to see the film, he had ideas for it. "We see it as a theatrical, but it'll really make more out of video. The amount we put up for an advance affects the rest of the deal. The lower the advance, the more we have to spend on prints and ads. We can offer you $500,000. Universal will take a 25 percent distribution fee off the top, and after we recoup our costs, we'll split the balance fifty-fifty."

Two and a half months after our first screening, we finally had our first bona fide cash offer. Their advance was lower than we'd been hoping, but we held our poker faces.

I wanted to make sure we acknowledged Abraham since he'd been our strongest ally. "We'll consider your offer seriously because of Marc. We're here because of him; we like his approach, and we want to work with him. Keith and Denise may want to add to this, but we feel that *Trekkies* has a unique value. We know what the market has paid for other documentaries. We need to huddle with Marc, and we'll get back to you."

Offering half a million dollars meant that they were probably willing to go to seven hundred. We needed to get out of there so that we could find out if Abraham thought their offer was fair. We shook hands all around and promised to speak soon.

After the First Offer

We congratulated each other. Although we agreed $500,000 felt low, the amount was no insult. Why should they offer more than that? Maybe we would say yes.

The next day, July 1, Brandi McDougal at Fox Searchlight passed. She said that as an acquisition, *Trekkies* was not right for them. They're booked up for the next year and a half, and documentaries were not their mainstay. As far as marketing, they wouldn't know what to do with it. Fox Searchlight films are critically driven art-house releases. She acknowledged the home video potential and said they would likely still be interested in releasing on video for us. I told her that's not an option because whoever buys the film will want all rights.

I ran the Universal scenario by my attorney, Todd Stern. His reaction was, "That offer's way too low to be preemptive. If they want to prevent a bidding war, they need to offer you a bigger number."

The next morning, I delivered tapes for Rob Friedman's solo screening. I tweaked the room's sound and hung out in the projection booth. Friedman screened the film alone. He didn't even want the projectionist in the room to switch tapes for him. Halfway through the screening, he left. John Ferraro called Keith to say that Friedman was called out of the screening by Chairman and co-Chief Executive Officer Jonathan Dolgen for some kind of crisis. But he is interested and wants to know what we want for the film.

Craig Emanuel, Denise Crosby's attorney, weighed in on the Universal offer. "The television rights alone are worth $500,000. You guys have played everything right so far. It would be great to get Universal and Paramount into a bidding situation. It would send a bad message to the rest of the town if anything that had to do with *Star Trek* went to another studio."

Response to the First Offer

Denise, Keith, and I called Abraham to respond to the Universal offer. We said we couldn't counter because the advance wasn't in the ballpark.

Abraham said, "You can't ask Universal to negotiate against themselves."

191

We told him that to make a deal work, we needed a preemptive-sized number, plus a share of the gross and support for a theatrical release.

Abraham argued that there is no sure thing. But with a solid back-end participation, we'd see the kind of numbers we wanted. "Let me relay this conversation to Universal. I won't put any spin on it."

Producer Joel Soisson, at Neo Motion Pictures.

When he summarized our conversation to Universal, Jeff Korchek was incredulous: "What do you mean they don't want to respond to us?"

We discussed the situation, and Denise felt strongly that we should counter. Keith was against it. Executive producer Joel Soisson had a great idea. This was a break with tradition since Soisson freely admitted he had been dead wrong about everything up to this point. He suggested countering at $3 million. It's a legitimate offer, and you tell Universal, "It's good for you guys, too, because your advance says this is the best thing since *Roger & Me*. You go into Telluride and the marketplace with that hype working for you." I agreed because we needed to keep Universal in the game.

Abraham called back. I put him on the speaker and read him our manifesto: "Marc, you took us to the mat. You wanted a number, and we are now going to give you a specific number. And then we'll tell you why we think it's a brilliant number. First, of course, we want a real back end where we don't have to audit expenses. Maybe something with platforms."

Abraham said, "That's a very good way of approaching it."

I continued, "Second, we'll need to iron out various release strategy guarantees and approvals. Both of these points come after we get the advance up."

Abraham concurred again.

"And third, the magic number is four million." There was no shocked gasp, so I continued. "Why is that an excellent number for Universal and Beacon? Four reasons: first, the worst-case scenario is recouping in home video where *Roger & Me* delivered $4.5 million. *Truth or Dare* is actually a better comparison, and that brought in $7.8 million."

Abraham agreed that *Truth or Dare* was a more accurate barometer.

"Second, an advance that size makes a statement. It tells the industry (and us) that Universal is serious and believes in this movie. Third, it puts the film out into the marketplace as the biggest thing since *Roger & Me*. The publicity will be huge. Which leads me to number four, the P&A for *Roger & Me* was $6 million. *Trekkies* doesn't need a huge push because the core audience is pre-sold and already knows about the film. And, of course, our final point, the nine pictures in our three-picture deals—but that's negotiable."

Abraham laughed at that and thanked us for acknowledging and respecting the Universal offer. He added that he would reiterate our discussion to Universal in secrecy. He didn't come right out and ask us for confidentiality, but that was the implied request. Clearly, it would be to their advantage to keep this under wraps to avoid a bidding war. It would be to our advantage to leak the information.

When Abraham relayed our conversation to Universal, it was met with a pause, followed by a giant gulp, then, "We're going to have to re-think this." Abraham felt this was all very good because they didn't say absolutely no, and they wanted to screen the film on Friday for Casey Silver, the top executive at Universal. Their point of view was that no documentaries had made enough money to support that advance.

Denise's response to Abraham was, "Why are they interested then? Because there's thirty years of documentation about how much *Star Trek* products sell. We've got them hooked because they think we might be right."

He agreed. "You guys are in a great position. I asked you to counter, and you did. No matter what they do, I'm still going to be interested. And being in negotiations with them is a good thing."

Seeking Multiple Interest

New Line passed. They weren't willing to pay the size advance they assumed we were looking for. Arianna Bocco said they might be able to turn Mark Ordesky around if he sees it making a splash at a film festival.

Carol Smithson and Peter Block at Trimark bounced a couple of scenarios off Keith: a $200,000 to $400,000 advance; or no advance but a guarantee of $1 million to promote the film. Keith asked them to write down their best offer and send it over.

I dropped the *Trekkies* tapes off at a Universal screening room. It turned out that the projectionist, Bob Valasek, was a *Star Trek* fan who had an uncle who worked as an effects man on the original series, throwing foam rocks down onto Captain Kirk at Vasquez Rocks. Matt Wall, Chris McGurk, and a few others showed up. McGurk said he wanted to see it all this time. According to Valasek, the execs laughed all the way through. Be nice to projectionists. They are a source of invaluable intel.

Wall confirmed the screening was a hit. Unfortunately, Casey Silver didn't make it. "But that is not going to hold us up in any way. We're talking about it internally. I want to keep the enthusiasm going."

After a screening at the Samuel Goldwyn Company, Rosanne Korenberg, VP of Acquisitions, said everybody at the screening was enthusiastic, including President Meyer Gottlieb. After they discussed it amongst themselves, she pitched it to Samuel Goldwyn Jr., who didn't get it. Regardless of what his staff thought, he had no interest in the concept. She said the only way to get Goldwyn to screen it now would be after it got some kind of festival acclaim.

Film Festival Obstacles

A standard form letter from Marc McDonald at the Telluride Film Festival read: "We regret to inform you that your film was not selected for exhibition." This was a terrible blow to our chances for distribution and our first experience with festival rejection. Telluride is first in the fall festival lineup of top festivals. We needed to get into the next big ones, or our suitors could lose interest.

Slightly panicked, I called other festivals to see if I could get information. The Toronto International Film Festival receptionist looked through some papers and said, "The festival has passed on *Trekkies*. A letter of rejection is on the way."

I thought, *Oh no! How could Toronto pass? They have 200 slots available to program, more than twice as many as Telluride. This is not good.*

Sundance said they were still considering the film. They requested a second copy so Trevor Groth and Geoffrey Gilmore could look at it. The AFI Film Festival liked the film but hadn't made any decisions. The New York Film Festival wouldn't make final decisions for another month. When word gets around that we are striking out with top festivals, our leverage will start evaporating. A bit rattled, I hurriedly sent more submissions to festivals in Chicago, the Hamptons, Hollywood, London, San Jose, and São Paulo.

The next day, I received a voice message. "This is Zoe Elton at the Mill Valley Film Festival. My office has been taken over by Klingons! We have to show your film! Please call me back!" Mill Valley is not one of the top-tier festivals, but it is a well-respected regional festival. I called and thanked Elton and asked for time to discuss it with my partners.

On July 25, *Air Force One* opened at $37.1 million for the weekend, an all-time record for an R-rated film. Marc Abraham and Beacon should be able to really pull strings now.

On August 1, five Universal executives screened the film. Matt Wall said the screening went well. "Louis Viola, Eddy Egan, and Mark Crystal didn't think we were crazy for wanting this film." Casey Silver didn't show up again, but Wall said jokingly, "The official word is he hasn't seen it, but he really likes it."

On the negative side of the ledger, Barry Reardon at Warner Bros. Pictures passed on even screening the film, saying, "I don't think this film has feature potential."

Mary Kerr from Sundance called to say that four people had seen the film and loved it, but a couple others still needed to take a look. She said it would probably benefit us to do Mill Valley and then talk about other options at Sundance that don't require a world premiere, like the American Spectrum or the Midnight section.

Sweetening the Pot

Marc Abraham, Matt Wall, and Jeff Korchek phoned Keith Border to present their second offer of $750,000. Keith responded, "I'll talk this over with Roger and Denise, but since you are so far off from the advance that we want, the easiest thing would be for you to send over the back-end deal you have in mind."

Abraham said, "Since it's so beautifully simple, that'll be easy. Right, Jeff?" Korchek agreed to fax it to us.

Joel Soisson said, "If they're offering three-quarters of a million, they're certain they can make back at least 1.5 million."

I said, "If they'll go to 750, they'll go to a million."

Keith called Arianna Bocco at New Line to see if they could get into the million-dollar range. She said they wouldn't top Universal's bid because no matter what, everybody at New Line considers the "dreaded documentary" a category that doesn't make theatrical money. *Roger & Me* (1989), at $6.7 million in box office returns, was the top. In the years to come, they would be proven wrong when documentaries cracked not just seven figures, but nine figures at the box office, such as Michael Jackson's concert film *This is It* ($252 million worldwide, 2009) and Michael Moore's *Fahrenheit 9/11* ($221 million worldwide, 2004).

August 8, Universal faxed their formal counterproposal. Their back end was the same as their first offer: a fifty-fifty split of net revenues, which would be what remained after they deducted a 25 percent distribution fee off the top plus all distribution expenses. It contained all the standard deductions, with no caps on expenditures, and they cross-collateralized everything with home video, which could make sure we don't see a profit. It was Friday, and their offer was set to expire Monday. Neo Motion Pictures Attorney David Steinberg suggested we counter with $2.5 million and a back end we like. We decided to counter Monday with a $3 million advance and 12.5 percent of the gross receipts plus a fifty-fifty split after expenses.

I asked Zoe Elton at Mill Valley for an extension to Monday of their deadline to accept their invitation. I knew the AFI would be making decisions then. She said she had a lot of other films champing at the bit but agreed to wait.

Mary Kerr at Sundance called to say that John Cooper and Geoff Gilmore still had yet to watch the film and needed to do so before a decision could be made. She said if our film played AFI, that could count against us, as it's a higher-profile festival than Mill Valley.

On Monday, the AFI Film Festival invited *Trekkies* to participate in the documentary competition. They only accept world premieres, so Mill Valley would be out of the running. I called Elton to tell her about the AFI and that we were still going to have to wait on Sundance. She was disappointed that we wouldn't be coming to Mill Valley but was also supportive and sympathized with the difficulties filmmakers face in choosing festivals.

There was still nothing from Paramount. John Ferraro had not returned Keith's call for a week. Denise's attorney, Craig Emanuel, called Ferraro to shake him up, to make sure he knew we were countering Universal's second offer. Emanuel got Ferraro on the phone, and Ferraro emphatically stated that he had no idea that Universal had made an offer. Possibly because he hadn't bothered to call Keith back? Then Ferraro started complaining again about how difficult Keith had made it for him to see the movie—which was now irrelevant, as everybody had seen it. Ferraro ended by saying he'd talk to Rob Friedman.

We held a screening at Sony Pictures Imageworks for Michael Barker, co-founder of Sony Pictures Classics. We filled the room with 130 digital-effects personnel, which was the same as having a room full of Trekkies in the audience, and as a result, we had a gangbusters screening. Barker maintained a poker face, and afterward, he was out the door like a shot.

Offers Can Be Rescinded

On Wednesday, August 13, Marc Abraham called in an unofficial capacity to say that Universal will be officially withdrawing from negotiations because we were so far apart on the advance. I asked Abraham to look at our offer, not as some kind of savvy negotiating response, but to understand our concerns, and if they are interested in addressing them, we could work it out. I also said there was no way we could accept less than a seven-figure advance.

Craig Emanuel called Denise to say that we certainly lit a fire under Paramount. John Ferraro called him twice to say, "The numbers are coming. We're working on them." Emanuel speculated that Paramount would pay a premium to keep this in the family. Everybody will come up with the same numbers, but Paramount can push it a little higher because they know the *Star Trek* market better than anybody. He suggested making the same proposal to Paramount we had made to Universal. We decided to have Emanuel send over our $4 million letter to Paramount. (This later turned out to be a mistake because Neo Motion Pictures's attorney David Steinberg had been handling our counteroffers, and it's always best to negotiate via a single channel.)

The Vancouver International Film Festival faxed a rejection saying, "Our selection committee has not selected the film for inclusion in our programme this year even though it has many strengths." At least our film has strengths.

Four days later, on Tuesday, August 19, Michael Barker of Sony Pictures Classics called to say how much he enjoyed the movie. He had questions about rights issues, the festivals submitted, the critics' responses, and what sort of deal we were looking for. He also outlined some thoughts on distribution and pitched Sony Pictures Classics as the filmmaker-friendly distributor. He still wanted his partners, Tom Bernard and Marci Bloom, to see the film. I said we appreciated his company's classy track record, which would count strongly when we make a decision.

Ferraro called Emanuel to say that Sheri Lansing and Jonathan Dolgen needed to see *Trekkies*, and they needed a tape. With no prompting, Denise told Emanuel, "No tape. Everybody else has seen it under these conditions."

Keith called Ferraro and said, "I feel dreadful because I'm putting you in the middle of this. But we haven't given tapes to anybody. The first thing I do when somebody sends me a tape is say to my assistant, 'Make me a copy of this and send it back.'"

Ferraro responded, "Given the fact that you're asking so much money, you should be a little more facilitating."

"We will be happy to show up with a tape any time, any place, whatever is convenient. And four million is not a lot." Ferraro said he'd talk to Rob Friedman. Apparently, Jonathan Dolgen asked for a tape, and Friedman had said okay and then told Ferraro to get it.

Choosing a Premiere

One week later, on August 25, Steve Gallagher from the Hamptons International Film Festival left a message. Despite getting rejected by the first A-level festivals, the Hamptons and AFI are strong B+ festivals located near distributors in New York and Los Angles, so we hoped to be able to pull out of our festival tailspin. I first called Mary Kerr at Sundance to let her know. She said that Geoffrey Gilmore has the film and may have seen it, but she didn't know yet.

When I spoke to Gallagher, he said he wanted to schedule the film for Saturday, October 18, at noon. Gallagher said the reason the screenings are so early in the day is because "at the Hamptons Festival, our emphasis is on the parties." There would be ten international documentaries in competition. They were offering to fly Denise and me in for the weekend event. I asked them to include producer Keith Border.

On October 27, a letter arrived regretting to inform us that the New York Film Festival would not be including *Trekkies* in their series of thirty-five films (out of 900 submitted). The rejection was disappointing. I hoped the rejections were because our film was too commercial for high-brow festivals. Then The São Paulo International Film Festival faxed us a formal invitation. Keith was dying to go to Brazil, but Denise jumped on it first, and she was the star.

On Friday, August 29, Peter Block at Trimark Pictures faxed us a formal offer that read:

> I am pleased to be able to make you a formal offer for the North American rights for the Picture. . . . In the event that you decide to self-release the Picture, or are able to find a third-party theatrical distributor, Trimark is interested in distributing the Picture via all other media (i.e., television, home video, etc.). . . . Based upon your theatrical release of the Picture, Trimark is willing to handle all other rights on a "distribution fee" basis. . . . If you are interested in joining forces in this manner, please let me know.

We looked at each other like we were being pranked. We do all the hard work, give the film a theatrical release, and then pay Trimark a fee to take home video, the most lucrative ancillary market. We didn't bite.

John Fitzgerald at the AFI Festival really wanted the world premiere of *Trekkies*, but since the Hamptons Festival came a week earlier, we had to choose. Because the Hamptons was smaller and more select, and the AFI was under new leadership, and as such, was more of an unknown, our consensus was in favor of the Hamptons.

Mary Kerr at Sundance said Geoffrey Gilmore had now seen the film, and although *Trekkies* was being strongly considered, they couldn't give us a definite indication yet. "It's too soon for us to say for sure. It still depends on what else comes in." She said the Hamptons festival wouldn't hinder our chances, and the AFI and São Paulo festivals probably wouldn't either.

First, we called Gallagher at the Hamptons to make sure it was a lock. Next, we called Fitzgerald at the AFI Festival and told him that we were not going to pull out of the Hamptons. He was upset yet gracious in not taking us out of the AFI festival as a result. He felt that we had promised him the world premiere; however, the official Hamptons notification had preceded his.

Paramount creative executive Alex Ryan called to ask what was going on. I told her we were waiting for John Ferraro to set a Jonathan Dolgen screening.

At the Toronto International Film Festival that we were shut out of, Miramax bought Michael Moore's latest documentary, *The Big One* (1997), for $600,000.

On September 25, Marc Abraham told Denise we'd made a mistake. We were taking too long. We missed the good festivals. And Chris McGurk doesn't want to revisit this deal anymore.

Denise said, "We understood that was possible, but based on the low amount of Universal's offer, we had to wait for everybody else to weigh in."

Abraham said, "If you're waiting for Jonathan Dolgen, you're waiting for the biggest prick in the business."

"Aren't they all?"

"Dolgen's in a league of his own."

A Sony Pictures Classics screening went down as planned. Dylan Leiner, VP of Acquisitions, told me, "We all like the film, but we are not sure how to handle it. Its main audience is not theatrical. They're not the kind of people who go to movies. The challenge is how do you get the people who aren't interested in the TV show to see it?"

This sounded ridiculous. I said, "The same way non-fans of Crumb and Madonna went: word of mouth. *Trekkies* has a large core audience that will sustain the opening of the film while crossover word spreads."

"It's just not clear to us what to do with the film. It took us eight months from when we first saw *When the Cat's Away* (1996) until we bought it. We didn't know what to do with *In the Company of Men* (1997) until we realized that we needed to market it to women."

"You also didn't buy it until after it got a rave review at a festival. Specialized films are review-driven, and everybody wants to wait for the sure thing. The savvy distributor will pick up the film for much less before the hype takes off."

He kept repeating that they just didn't know what to do but wanted to stay in touch and keep talking about it.

Did We Wait Too Long?

As we arrived at the end of September, five-and-a-half months since our first screening, *Trekkies* Executive Producers Michael Leahy and Joel Soisson were worried we'd been "souped." The film *In the Soup* (1992) won the Grand Jury Prize at Sundance, and the producers walked away with several offers from independent distributors. But to increase the advance, they waited to screen for the big studios. By the time they finished the rounds, having gained no new offers, they were ready to sell, but the indie distributors had cooled off. The best they could get was a no-advance deal from Triton Pictures. This happens all too often. There will be a moment when interest in a film will peak and the price buyers are willing to pay will peak simultaneously. That's the time to sell, even if the price is not yet what you want, or need to break even. Recognizing that moment is difficult, and often, there's no way to be certain until the dust settles months later.

As they say on Wall Street: "Bulls make money, bears make money, pigs get slaughtered."

On October 1, Meredith Emanuel, Director of Acquisitions and Licensing at MVP Home Entertainment, faxed us an offer: $40,000 for a seven-year license to the home video market; plus, we would get 15 percent of the sell-through wholesale price and

Producer Michael Leahy, at Neo Motion Pictures.

201

25 percent of the rental wholesale price. They had made a ton of money licensing home-video rights to the television show *Cops* (1989–TBD) from Barbour/Langley Productions. They also came up with some offbeat ideas for promotional "themed gift kits," such as "The *Trekkies* Escape Kit," which could include: packaging shaped like a spaceship, the video, a space food-bar, a T-shirt, *Trekkies* playing cards, and some Band-Aids. Our greatest fear now was that this was the sort of deal we might be forced to take.

A Financial Disaster

A couple days later, Denise was devastated to discover that her talent agency, Ambrosio/Mortimer & Associates, was being investigated for nonpayment of their clients' money. They weren't answering Denise's calls. She feared they were going down the tubes and taking $19,000 of her money with them, part of her salary from acting in *Deep Impact* (1998).

I called Marc Abraham and told him that I was calling without the knowledge of my *Trekkies* partners, and I asked if we could speak confidentially.

Abraham said, "You can trust me. You'll find out I'm like a tomb."

I told him about Denise's agent's alleged sticky fingers and that I thought that we could close a deal now, that I could get Keith to come into line (I was using Keith as the "bad cop") if Universal came to the table right now with a million-dollar offer, and an invitation to meet to work out the back end. "This is also the last chance for a distributor to grab the film before we begin our film festival publicity buzz."

Abraham thanked me for coming to him and said he didn't know if he could get Chris McGurk to focus on this. Plus, they felt $750,000 was a solid number. But he said, "I will sniff around over there."

I called Alex Ryan to see if she had heard anything, and she said that the Paramount paralysis was because nobody around Dolgen had the balls to say anything. I promised to call her after the Hamptons Festival, which we were on our way to attend. While we were in Long Island, John Ferraro's office called the Neo Motion Pictures office. Jennifer Conroy, the receptionist, took the call.

Ferraro's assistant said, "This is Ben. We've got to see the movie right away."

It had been a while since they'd called, so Jennifer was confused, "Ben who? What movie?"

"Ben Pratt! At Paramount. John Ferraro's office."

"Ohhhhhh. They're at the Hamptons."

Typical studio modus operandi: no activity for weeks, then everything must happen *immediately*. Keith called Ferraro and told him we were in New York for a Miramax screening, then we've got the AFI and São Paulo festivals. Scheduling a screening now will be tough, but we'll do our best— as long as the print is available (we now had a 16mm film festival print). I called Dylan Leiner at Sony and made sure he knew about the latest developments. Keith also called Carol Smithson at Trimark and Arianna Bocco at New Line and gave them an opportunity to structure a strong back end to make up for their inability to put up a significant advance.

Ferraro finally set a screening for co-CEOs Jonathan Dolgen and Kerry McCluggage on Thursday, October 23. Keith dropped the *Trekkies* print at Paramount, leaving a runner to keep an eye on it. He reported back that the film had three viewers, including *Star Trek* actor Jonathan Frakes. They stayed all the way through to the end and exited looking upbeat.

The Reviews Come Out

On October 26, the first AFI Film Festival screening was standing room only. *Star Trek*-fan Gabriel Koerner was in attendance. Each time he came on screen, he shook his head or plugged his ears. I brought him up for the Q&A and asked, "What did you think, watching yourself in the film?"

He said, "I found myself grating and irritating." This got a big laugh. Koerner signed his first autographs afterward.

Leonard Klady's review came out in *Weekly Variety*.

> A largely affectionate look at the weird and wonderful subculture that's ensued and endured since the sci-fi series first beamed up in 1966. This nonjudgmental look at fans who boldly go where aficionados had not gone before should zap brisk TV exposure, lively cassette sales and some specialized theatrical play.

Frank Scheck's *Hollywood Reporter* review also came out, labeling many scenes as "positively priceless."

The next day, Ferraro told Keith that the Paramount screening went "exceedingly well." They wanted another screening, this time for their legal department. Denise Crosby's experience with Paramount has taught her to be cautious. She worried they may be looking for legal ways to chop our price down. They could complain that we filmed at a Carl's Jr. without permission from the corporate headquarters or something—groundless saber-rattling. Craig Emanuel suggested going back and saying we wanted an offer first to see if we're in the ballpark before we go to the trouble of arranging another screening.

Ferraro freaked out when Emanuel told him we wanted an offer first. He screamed, saying that Keith was so nice and easy to deal with this morning, but now Emanuel had poisoned Keith. Emanuel backed off and changed his recommendation, worried about ruffling feathers at Paramount. He suggested Keith set up the screening. He said Ferraro is extremely positive that there is a deal there.

After the festival premiere and good reviews, more calls from distributors rolled in. Film Forum, Soho Entertainment, Mandy Films, and 7th Arts Releasing wanted to screen the film. 7th Arts was even more of a bottom-feeder than Trimark. The best Orion could come up with was, "If it doesn't work out with the studios, let us know."

Keith was appalled and responded to them, "That's not the way to go about acquiring a film. The players don't say, 'Let us know.' They make a pitch."

Their response was, "Well, I'll fax you some information about our company. Then stop by if you want to talk." They want to buy the film, but we have to go talk to them about their company. I don't think so.

Alex Ryan called to get the *Trekkies* status. I told her that the Dolgen screening went "exceptionally well," but they want to screen it again.

Ryan said, "For whom?! The Dali Lama?" Even she was puzzled.

On October 30, Jason Blum, Senior VP of Acquisitions and Production at Miramax, called to say Harvey Weinstein wanted to take a print to his house in Connecticut. Keith explained that the print isn't available until next week and that we don't send it anywhere without a chaperone. Blum said they were willing to fly somebody to New York, as they had to have it this weekend, so why not send a tape? When Keith reiterated that just wasn't possible, Blum got annoyed and said, "Are you telling me you won't screen this film for us when you know Miramax will pay more than anybody else?!" Keith promised to accommodate them as soon as possible.

Denise Crosby carried the 16mm film canisters down to São Paulo while five months pregnant. She said the film played exceptionally well, although the Brazilians were a bit confused by the existence of the filk singer in a wig and lipstick. (Gabriel Koerner had explained his costume to me, "He was dressing as the *wife* of a character who was seen in an episode of *Star Trek: The Next Generation* only as a skeleton.") After her return from Brazil, Denise's resolve to hold out for a better deal was weakening. She and her husband, Ken Sylk, had picked up a touch of Montezuma's revenge, and things were looking a little bleak to her.

A film is only worth a decent advance if two or more buyers are interested. After six and a half months of pushing our film to distributors, we badly needed a second major company to put another cash offer on the table.

CHAPTER TWELVE

The Bidding War

Every negotiation ride reaches a climax, and that's when you need to get off. Don't miss that moment, or you won't.

T he *Trekkies* bidding war began Monday, November 3, 1997. Paramount business affairs called Craig Emanuel with an offer to purchase *Trekkies* for $250,000 plus a standard studio back end. We finally had the genuine cash offer we needed from a second company.

Phase Three: Exploiting Multiple Interest

When John Ferraro called Emanuel to follow up, Emanuel said, "They're not going to be happy with this deal."

Ferraro responded, "We don't expect them to be happy."

Joel Soisson's reaction was, "Any offer with 'in perpetuity' and only 'thousands' after the advance is a non-offer."

We understood that "a standard back end" meant zero. We told Emanuel to make it clear that the offer is so ludicrously low there was nothing for us to respond to because they know the size of offers we've already turned down.

At the same time, Trimark's Peter Block faxed over an updated offer that added a theatrical release but refrained from setting out specific fees and guarantees until we entered "a limited period of exclusive negotiations."

Tiffany Daniel at Amblin Entertainment called Jennifer Conroy, Neo receptionist, to say that Mark Johnson and Steven wanted to screen the movie.

Jennifer responded, "Steven who?"

Confused, Daniel stammered, "Steven Spielberg!"

Keith told Jennifer to call back and say we'd be happy to schedule something.

Once our non-counter message had been delivered to Paramount, Ferraro frantically called and asked why we weren't responding.

Keith replied, "How do you respond to offers inferior to the ones you turned down? We already told you the ballpark we're in. The $4 million is very real. We would at least like a reasonable offer before we consider countering."

Ferraro said, "I can't negotiate against myself."

Keith was now familiar with that tactic. "That is such a studio catch-phrase. You're not the first person to say that to us."

Ferraro's next approach was, "This project is starting to get stale."

"That's not exactly true. We just got a call that Steven Spielberg wants to screen it."

"Well, this is just our opening bid. We want to start negotiations." Ferraro went away saying he had to talk to his boss—similar to the car-buying characters in *Suckers*, which I had just begun shooting that week.

A salesperson always says he has to talk to the boss. "That number is low. I've never seen a deal go down like this before, but if I could do that for you, would we have a deal right now?" He nods at you, subconsciously prompting you to nod. Then he says, "I'm going to try for you, but my boss is going to kill me."

Denise told us that the screening request from Amblin Entertainment was not about Mark Johnson and Steven Spielberg wanting to screen the film. It turned out that Tiffany Daniel and Denise were friends, and when writers were brought on to do a rewrite on *Galaxy Quest* (1999), Daniel had reached out to Denise. The writers asked if they could attend a *Trekkies* screening to do research for their script.

The Second Suitor Sweetens the Pot

Eight days later, on Tuesday, November 11, Paramount upped their offer to $500,000. I told Keith, "As far as I'm concerned, we can tell Paramount to stop bothering us if they aren't interested in making a real offer. Tell them we're busy shooting *Suckers*, and we don't have time to consider non-viable offers."

On the *Suckers* set, a rainstorm soaked through the roof of the abandoned car dealership we were shooting in and a fluorescent light fixture fell onto a row of chairs, nearly hitting two actors. We dealt with the leaks by duct-taping super-absorbent diapers to the ceiling.

After everything had settled down, Antoinette Squeo, the wardrobe supervisor, asked me, "How do you stay so calm?"

I said, "It's not *my* money." To function, while in the middle of a stressful negotiation with multiple studios, while at the same time directing a movie I co-wrote, I had to keep things in perspective. It's helpful to have a hard shell. When I was young, I was the smallest in my class. I didn't catch up until I had a growth spurt in my teens. Being an easy target for bullies forced me to develop survival strategies, like staying calm no matter what.

Denise told Quentin Tarantino, for whom she had just filmed a role in *Jackie Brown* (1997), about the offers we had received. Tarantino offered his advice. "Stay grounded. I've seen so many people blow it because of greed or naiveté. You don't set out to sell a phenomenon. A phenomenon just happens. A million-dollar advance is a huge profit. Just as important is how the film will be handled. Miramax will do a better job than Paramount. Using *Roger & Me* as an example is like using the most unusual example as a goal. A $250,000 offer from Paramount is insulting, but the same offer from Trimark isn't."

On November 13, Jonathan Frakes called Denise and said, "I can't believe a deal hasn't been done. Kerry McCluggage turned to Jonathan Dolgen during the screening and said, 'We've gotta have this.' Dolgen asked me afterward, 'Are they really like this?' I said, 'Yes.' Then he said, 'It's like owning a fucking religion. I've gotta have four more of these.'"

It pays to have moles. Obviously, Paramount was very interested. Keith wanted to simultaneously counteroffer Universal at $1.5 million, stick at $4 million with Paramount, meet with Trimark, and put out a last call to Sony, New Line, MVP, Miramax, and the others.

On November 15, Jeffrey Freedman, Executive Vice President, Business Affairs and Operations, Paramount's senior attorney, faxed a letter via Craig Emanuel saying:

I understand that your client is in production on another film and is currently unable to devote any time to addressing the sale of Trekies [sic]. Although I must formally withdraw my offer of November 6, 1997, Paramount remains interested in acquiring distribution rights in Trekies [sic] and we look forward to revisiting our negotiation in a few weeks' time.

The New Strategy

We hatched a plan to hit everybody at once with a $1.5 million counter-offer. Neo Motion Pictures's attorney David Steinberg began composing the letter.

On November 18, Jason Blum screened *Trekkies*. He called Keith Border and said he liked the film but found the people scary. Keith countered with the positive fans aspect versus the negative/downer aspect of films like *Crumb* (1994).

On November 26, an offer inviting *Trekkies* came in from the Cinequest Film Festival, but we got bad news from Mary Kerr, who said *Trekkies* didn't make the cut at Sundance. They loved the film and offered to write a letter or help us any way they could with other festivals. I thanked her and said they could save the ink; we were doing fine with other festivals.

Trimark set a meeting to discuss a deal. Carol Smithson said, "You're not going to be mean to us because Paramount was mean to you, are you?"

On December 1, we put the final touches on our counteroffer: $1.5 million advance, 10 percent gross participation, and fifty-fifty split of the net. David Steinberg said, "You realize this is somewhat unorthodox, and everybody may pass." Michael Leahy was against sending letters to New Line, Sony, or Miramax since they had not made offers, but we decided there was nothing to lose by including them.

On Tuesday, December 2, we sent all the letters at the end of the day to Universal/October/Beacon, Paramount, Trimark, New Line, Sony Pictures Classics, and Miramax. To be sure that nobody could say they didn't know what was going on, we CCed every executive who had been involved so far.

Fallout from the All-Purpose Counteroffer

The first call the following morning was from Smithson, who canceled the Trimark meeting. Our letter scared them.

John Ferraro called to complain. "The CCs were a real faux pas because Sheri and Jonathan will now be calling us and saying, 'What's going on?'"

Keith said, "It was necessary because I am getting skeptical that Paramount will be distributing this film."

"The only reason we don't have a deal yet is because you weren't available to negotiate."

Keith reminded, "Paramount took four months to make an offer in the first place."

"But I don't understand why you would CC people like John Goldwyn and Don Granger."

"Because they keep asking us what's going on."

"It's none of their fucking business!"

Keith said it was the only time he had seen Ferraro get so upset.

Peter Block told David Steinberg, "Trimark wants nothing to do with you. We found the offer insulting. And it was appalling that you CCed everybody. We told you Trimark is not in a position to pay any kind of advance."

John Freedman at Paramount told Steinberg he was confused. "Before, we were dealing with Craig Emanuel, and now we got this letter from you. Who are we dealing with?"

Steinberg said, "You're dealing with me." Freedman wasn't happy about that. Emanuel had recently revealed that Freedman used to work for Emanuel.

Marc Abraham called to say, "I'm trying to get the guys at Universal motivated to make a deal. October isn't as fired up about this as I'd like, so I'm going about it through McGurk and Gumpert." Abraham analyzed our gross and net deals, pointing out that we'd actually be into our 50 percent net participation before our 10 percent gross participation.

I said, "That may be true in a perfect world, but at least with a gross deal chipping away at the start, it doesn't matter what expenses the studio charges against us."

"Nobody goes into a deal expecting to screw the filmmakers."

"I'd like to believe that, but how do we structure a net deal so we don't have to worry about studio accounting practices?"

Abraham said he'd get back to us with something.

Arianna Bocco said they were discussing a deal at New Line.

Michael Barker at Sony Pictures Classics said, "You should go for Paramount. Nobody else is going to be able to make your film a success as well as Paramount."

I agreed that nobody knows the *Trek*-fan market better, but our main concern was their ability to handle the specialized film market.

Barker said, "Paramount opened *Kiss Me, Guido* well, and then dropped the ball. I'll give you some advice that the *Guido* producers didn't have. First, ask Paramount to guarantee an opening in twenty-five of the top fifty markets. That will give you what you want, and they won't consider it a big concession. Then meet Wayne Lewellen. Ingratiate yourself with that guy. After a film is acquired, the Ferraros have very little to do with the release, but Wayne is the guy who books all the theaters. He'll take care of you if you foster a relationship with him." Barker also predicted mixed reviews. "Your film is pretty even-handed, and the critics like films that are more biting, snide, or satiric."

Jason Blum from Miramax said he wanted to take the film to Harvey, but he wanted to be sure they could make a deal. He said, "Your expectations for what the film can do far exceed what we think it can do. There is no way we'd pay a $1.5 million advance or a dollar-one share of the gross."

Keith responded, "Nobody is more creative than Miramax. You should be able to come up with something that works. We should at least get our negative costs covered, so a $250,000 advance with a gross participation could be the way to go. And maybe Miramax gives up foreign." Keith told Jason Blum anything he wanted to hear so that Harvey would see the film because there's no deal until Harvey sees it, and so we'd be able to tell Universal and Paramount that Miramax made an offer.

The letters stirred up a lot of activity in waters that were becoming stagnant. We anxiously hoped we could finally close a deal.

Bidding Commences

The next day, Jeffrey Goore at Universal called David Steinberg with their counteroffer:

1. All rights worldwide in perpetuity.
2. Advance: $850,000, payable $100,000 on signature and approval of chain of title and the balance on delivery.
3. 5 percent of first-dollar gross corridor to a cap of $150,000.
4. Flat distribution fee of 25 percent, with video on a 25 percent royalty basis.
5. After recoupment (fee, expenses, advance, gross corridor), revenues split fifty-fifty.
6. Merchandising: 25 percent administration fee, costs, then fifty-fifty.
7. Soundtrack: 2 percent royalty subject to reduction if they are below 3 percent.
8. Remake and sequel rights frozen.

I suggested we counter with the following: Fifteen-year license, $1 million advance, 5 percent gross corridor to a cap of $650,000 (a gross corridor is a share of gross revenue, deducted from back-end net participation), video not cross-collateralized with other expenses, we keep a right of negotiation for sequels/remakes.

Marc Abraham revealed to Denise Crosby that John Ferraro had called Universal several months ago and asked, "Is it true? Did you make an offer for *Trekkies*? How interested are you guys in this movie?" That's how he found out the size of Universal's offer. They all also knew what festivals the film had and had not gotten into. Clearly, Ferraro was tracking the film closely.

Craig Emanuel told Denise he agreed that it was wrong of us to copy Sheri Lansing and Jonathan Dolgen on our letter. Keith and I disagreed. As Keith put it, "We kicked the anthill." And if Emanuel was worried about ruffling Paramount's feathers, whose feathers would be ruffled if we sold the film to Universal? At least we were aboveboard with all interested parties. Universal was now looking better and better, especially since we would have Abraham behind us. Who would protect us at Paramount?

Keith called Arianna Bocco and told her that since New Line claimed they would never go above $1 million, they should get creative on the back end—and use the words "filmmaker-friendly" a lot. She asked about Universal's back end, and Keith told her about their $150,000 gross corridor that was a way to delay paying part of their advance up front. She laughed knowingly.

Jeff Freedman at Paramount told David Steinberg, "We can agree to many of your points, so we'd like you to take the film off the market for ten days so we can negotiate with you."

When Steinberg relayed that information it was my turn to laugh. "Why would we take the film off the market and shut down all other potential buyers when we don't even know what Paramount's offer is? Let's tell them they have until tomorrow to make us their best offer, or we'll enter exclusive negotiations with Universal."

On Friday, December 5, we wrapped shooting on *Suckers*, and Paramount phoned an offer to Steinberg:

1. All rights worldwide in perpetuity.
2. Advance: $650,000 subject to approval of chain of title. (Payment schedule not specified.)
3. Flat distribution fee of 25 percent, with video on a 20 percent royalty basis (and no fee on top of the video royalty, which Steinberg said was a big give for Paramount).
4. After recoupment (fee, expenses, advance), revenues split fifty-fifty with producers bearing any third parties.

We were astonished. Why would we take an offer that was $200,000 less than Universal's offer?

Keith wanted to have Steinberg call Universal and say our two biggest concerns were the words "in perpetuity" and that the video royalty was being cross-collateralized.

I suggested saying, "We have received a 'comparable' offer from Paramount. We are prepared to enter into exclusive negotiations with Universal if you can address our concerns about your offer." Then we would call Paramount back and thank them kindly for their offer and tell them we were going to negotiate with Universal. Paramount would freak out and jump to a million, and we could use that leverage in our negotiations with Universal.

Steinberg said calling about only two points was unorthodox and suggested countering all Universal's points and then telling Paramount that we have done so and will respond formally to them next week.

More Counteroffers

I called Marc Abraham and said, "I want you to be the first to know that we will be countering Universal today or Monday. Paramount has made us a comparable offer, but I'll tell you the one thing Universal has that Paramount doesn't is Marc Abraham. Whereas Paramount is arrogant in their approach, we feel like somebody is on our side at Universal."

Abraham was happy to hear that we would be advancing the negotiations, and he appreciated our faith in him. He asked, when the time came, to make sure we told Universal we wanted him to continue to spearhead the release so that he wouldn't be left hanging out in the wind if he went to bat for us. I agreed that we needed to be unified.

I relayed this conversation to Keith and Denise, who agreed that Abraham was Universal's high card. I cautioned that even though he was our best ally there, he had his feet in both camps.

Steinberg faxed over a summary of our proposed Universal counter:

1. 15-year term
2. Advance of $1 million payable $100,000 on signature and approval of chain of title and balance on delivery
3. 5 percent of first-dollar gross to a cap of $500,000
4. Flat distribution fee of 25 percent, video on 25 percent royalty, video uncrossed
5. After recoupment: fifty-fifty
6. Merchandising: 25 percent administration fee, costs, then fifty-fifty
7. Soundtrack reserved
8. First negotiation and last matching right on sequels and remakes

After speaking to Universal, Steinberg said he would call Paramount and say we are countering Universal and will get back to Paramount next week.

A problem arose: Denise wasn't able to track down Craig Emanuel so that she could sign off on our new counterproposal. We couldn't send it until she did. She was especially concerned about doing so after the "CC incident." She said that Abraham also mentioned to her that he thought it was a wrong move on our part.

Everybody may not have loved our CC-strategy, but it got Universal back to the table, and with a better offer. In a negotiation, any advantage you perceive over your foe, you use it. I warned that if they see a weak link on our side—that we are more worried about everybody's feelings than getting the best deal—they will keep hitting us there. This little skirmish would be nothing compared to the storms to come, especially if Paramount doesn't get the film. They'll probably try to ruin the party for everybody if they aren't invited.

Keith said at the beginning of the week he thought Trimark was probably our best deal, but when their offer imploded, it looked like Paramount was the best. "Now," he said, "Denise, you have convinced me that Universal is the right home. Even if we got what we wanted from Paramount, they will be angry and vindictive every step of the way."

Denise agreed: "Paramount is not interested in the film. They are interested in acquiring anything *Star Trek*-related. It's been the same with their attitude toward the actors. They don't care about the people. All they see are dollars and cents. I can already see the headline: 'Universal Scoops *Star Trek* Movie.' They'll even call it a *Star Trek* movie."

I believed we had the high ground. They all ran the numbers and attached a value to our product, which won't change no matter what we say. However, what we said affected how close we could get to that number. Obviously, a balance needed to be struck. We needed to remain humble and refrain from advancing too aggressively, or we could risk blowing a deal over a CEO's wounded ego. I didn't worry as much about the scouts and the VPs; they were pawns to be outmaneuvered or circumvented.

After the weekend, on Monday morning, December 8, Craig Emanuel finally got back to us and said, of our proposed counter to Universal, "This is a very good beginning and a good progression of the points." His one note was definitional: to ensure that our back-end recoupment was out of 100 percent of all receipts. He also asked Denise, "What do we want to do about Paramount? Because if you respond to Universal, you would be entering into negotiations in good faith. If they agree to this counter, you have a deal."

Keith, Denise, and I discussed Emanuel's suggestions. Emanuel wanted to call Paramount and give them until the end of the day to make us a new, better offer than $650,000. Keith and I felt that since we'd had Universal's offer since Friday, it was essential to capitalize on our momentum and counter Universal that day, as soon as possible, with a $1 million ask. Keith was worried that Paramount would try to drag this out another day.

I concurred, "What if Craig Emanuel disappears again at the end of the day?"

Denise said, "He won't disappear. We told everybody I needed until Monday. That gives us the rest of the day."

I suggested we make 5:00 p.m. the end of the day for Paramount to make their offer. Otherwise, we'd counter Universal. We all agreed. Denise would have Emanuel call Steinberg first to coordinate Emanuel's call to Paramount.

Around noon, I checked in with Keith and Steinberg, who had yet to hear from Emanuel. Precious time was slipping by, so I called Denise, and she said she had called Emanuel again, and he had not called her back yet. I said I was worried that we were losing time and that we didn't want Emanuel to be taking offers to Paramount unilaterally. We didn't want to confuse Paramount with multiple point men.

The frustration was catching up with Denise. "I've called Craig. What else can I do? I don't want to talk about this anymore."

Denise also spoke to Keith, then he sighed and said to me, "Don't call Denise about this anymore. It's got her upset."

I worried that I had gone too far and harmed an important relationship.

Just after lunch, Emanuel finally called Steinberg, who confirmed to Emanuel that he can call Paramount as a friend, but any offers had to come through Steinberg. Emanuel was not to call as the official representative of the film.

Carol Smithson told Keith that when Mark Amin received our overall counteroffer, he ranted and raved to Peter Block about how there was no way Trimark was going to pay a $1.5 million advance. Keith reminded her that he had told her to ignore the advance and make up for it with a killer back end. Smithson said she didn't remember Keith telling her that.

I asked Keith, "She denied to your face that you ever said that to her?"

Keith said, "What could I do? I can't get mad at her. I like her. She's going back to Peter Block to say this is not dead. We'll see what they come up with."

Steinberg called at 3:00 p.m. to say Emanuel had spoken to Paramount and things were getting confused. Emanuel had revealed details about our proposed Universal counter to Jeff Freedman and John Ferraro. They claimed they didn't know about Universal's previous offer of $750,000. That's why they offered $650,000. They may not have known the exact amount, but when Keith called Ferraro from the *Suckers* set, he said clearly that Universal's offer was "nearly a million."

Emanuel told Steinberg that Paramount didn't blink at $1.5 million but said they'd never give a 25 percent video royalty, and it would *never* be uncrossed.

I asked Steinberg, "Did Craig just make a counteroffer to Paramount? The same thing he told Denise we shouldn't do to Universal yet."

Steinberg said that he told Emanuel that if he was going to represent us to Paramount, then Steinberg should withdraw and handle only Neo's interests. Keith and I said we didn't want to have multiple people representing the film. We said we'd call Denise to see if we could straighten this out.

Keith and I called Denise. I said, "Craig told David that he is talking numbers with Paramount, and now they're wondering again about who's representing the film."

Keith said, "There needs to be just one person representing the film. This looks very bad."

Denise responded, "I agree that it looks bad. That's why we agreed to have Craig call Paramount."

I said, "He was only supposed to call Paramount as a friend to wake them up and tell them that we plan to counter Universal so they should get another offer in by 5:00 p.m. under the wire."

Denise said, "Well, Craig is the only one pushing at Paramount and getting us offers."

I was getting frustrated too, and said, "Yeah, $250,000 offers."

That was the last straw for Denise. "You know what, I don't want to talk to you guys anymore. You can call my attorney."

Keith said, "Okay, goodbye." But she had already hung up.

Solidarity Crumbles

Sun Tzu's third rule of engagement, "ruin their alliances," had been successfully played against us. We weren't doing well at holding our partnership
together.

At 5:05 p.m., David Steinberg had heard nothing from Craig Emanuel.
Keith said that since 5:00 p.m. was our agreed deadline, Steinberg should
call Universal and have the same friendly conversation that Emanuel had
had with Paramount. Steinberg said he would make the call.

A few minutes later, John Ferraro called Keith and said he was confused
about who he should be talking to.

Keith said, "David Steinberg is representing us. But there are three partners, and Craig Emanuel represents Denise."

Ferraro switched subjects, "Why didn't you tell me you were in negotiations with Universal?"

Keith got out the original letter and reread the first sentence: "'As multiple offers are currently being considered. . . .' I don't think we could have
been any more clear." Keith also told Ferraro that Miramax, Trimark, and
New Line were still in the game.

When Steinberg relayed our proposal to Jeffrey Goore at Universal, the
only thing Goore scoffed at was uncrossed video, but everything else was
no big deal.

Right then, a call came in from Paramount COO Rob Friedman. Ferraro was sitting in Friedman's office, and Friedman was angry. He accused
Keith of trying to jerk Paramount around.

Keith said, "We have always thought Paramount was the logical home
for this film. You're not being intentionally jerked around. I apologize for
the confusion, but we are trying to address this."

Friedman made his pitch, "Let me give you some food for thought. I
have been informed that you are concerned about your back end. There
is no real back end unless this film can be properly merchandised. And
nobody can do that as well with a *Star Trek* product than Paramount."

After that call, Steinberg rang in again. "Craig Emanuel is horribly upset
that we countered Universal. Craig also said Paramount is running more
numbers and wants to make us an offer tomorrow."

I suggested conferencing with Emanuel so we could clear this up. Emanuel joined and launched into a tirade, screaming that we had no authorization to put in an offer to Universal, and he was putting us on notice that we were in breach of our agreement with Denise.

I said, "Keith, Denise, and I spoke this morning and agreed to put in the counter if we had not heard from you or Paramount by 5:00 p.m. That's what we did."

"That's not what my client is informing me, and I have to protect my client's interests. I can't have Jonathan Dolgen and Sheri Lansing calling me and saying they had a chance to make an offer, and now we've revoked it."

Keith interjected, "Do you think Universal is going to accept our offer outright?"

"No, but that's irrelevant. I am obligated to call Universal and tell them that the offer is not valid because it does not have the support of my client. Paramount can't make an offer because Universal could call you back and say they accept every point, and then you'd have a deal."

Keith said, "Craig, if we can be faulted, it's for being too honest with everybody. We have told everybody what we are doing every step of the way. I just spoke with John Ferraro, and he asked me why we were giving them deadlines, and I told him we had countered Universal and that I'm still waiting for Miramax's offer."

I said, "Do you think the Universal counteroffer is a good deal?"

Emanuel said, "Yes, but you can't go to them without the authorization of my client. It's improper, and I have to consider my reputation and the reputation of my client."

I felt like saying, *Your reputation?! If you want a reputation, become a monk or a rabbi or a Cub Scout leader,* but I said instead, "Craig, if you feel you have to call Universal to save your reputation, then go ahead, but are you more interested in saving your reputation than getting the best possible deal for your client?"

Long pause. Then, "I have to go. I have Jeffrey Korchek on the other line. And Jeffrey Freedman, too." I suggested he call them back, but he refused, saying he had to talk to Paramount.

It was now 6:30 p.m. After Emanuel hung up, Steinberg, Keith, Michael Leahy, Joel Soisson, and I speculated on Emanuel's motivations. We wondered if Emanuel was trying to cover his ass with Paramount and torpedo a potential Universal deal to force the film to go to Paramount. He had Denise worked up and was most concerned about giving Paramount every courtesy instead of trying to help us work together and play the studios against each other.

I called Denise to see if we could kiss and make up and unify our team. She answered and said, "I don't want to talk to you, and I'm on the other line."

It seemed like the first reason was enough. I said, "I think it's really important that you and I and Keith talk."

She said, "I am just flabbergasted."

I said, "I totally understand why you might be."

"I have to talk to Craig on the other line. Where are you? I'll call back."

Not long after, Emanuel asked if Steinberg would be available for a conference call in ten minutes with a guy named Bill Bernstein. "There's a chance we'd need to close this deal tonight."

I asked what happened to Jeff Freedman?

Steinberg said he didn't know.

I speculated, "Maybe this Bill Bernstein is the night-shift business-affairs guy."

Crossing the Million-Dollar Mark

At 7:35 p.m., Steinberg told us that Paramount made a new offer, and we had until 8:00 p.m. to respond, all of twenty-five minutes. The offer was: $1 million advance, all rights in perpetuity, a 20 percent video royalty (cross collateralized), and a 60/40 back-end split (60 percent to us).

Emanuel had gotten the cash advance up to a million, but Keith said "in perpetuity" was a deal breaker.

I asked Steinberg if he thought Emanuel had saved enough face that he could now gracefully extract himself from the negotiations so that when the film went to Universal, his buddies at Paramount would still like him?

He said, "Maybe. I'll suss it out."

Joel Soisson, ever the pragmatist, suggested we tell Paramount we appreciate their offer, but due to the short deadline, we can't respond by 8:00 p.m., and we will get back to them tomorrow.

With Denise on the line, Emanuel called Steinberg's office and conferenced us all. A more subdued Emanuel related Paramount's deal points again.

I said, "Would you consider this a superior deal to the most recent Universal offer?"

He said he was happy about the 60/40 split.

Steinberg suggested that Paramount's extra 10 percent of the net and Universal's 5 percent more from home video probably equaled out.

I said that with Universal's offer of 5 percent of the gross, capped at $150,000, we were essentially at a million dollars there too. Nobody disagreed, so I continued, "If these two offers are roughly equivalent, I think the one thing we've always agreed upon is that we like Marc Abraham. Paramount has never once told us they like our film; they are clearly interested in acquiring it for its profit potential. But at least Marc believes in the film on a creative level."

Denise spoke up, "That's true. Universal is a much better place for us."

There was a long silence. You could almost hear the wind leaking out of Emanuel's sails. He could not recommend Paramount's offer to his client now.

He said, "I guess I'll call Paramount and tell them that, given the current deadline, we can't accept their offer by 8 o'clock."

The first thing Leahy said after we hung up was, "We just turned down a million dollars."

Soisson added, "Yeah, but for twenty minutes, we had a million dollars."

It was getting late. Keith wanted to go home and collapse. Steinberg used to work for Miramax, and he said, "This is nothing. Harvey once kept me up all night working a deal. He said, 'You can't go to bed until I own this movie!' They love to be spoilers, to come in at the last minute before you are about to sign a deal with somebody else and offer you more money."

When Emanuel relayed our rebuff to Paramount, Bernstein told him, "You realize we have to revoke our offer."

Emanuel said, "Yes."

Bernstein, "Well, I hope you've got a better deal at Universal."

"Does that mean you don't want me to call you if we are about to accept a Universal deal?"

Bernstein responded quickly, "No, no, no, call us."

We had been forced to fight a battle uphill, but we survived the day, albeit bloodied. It felt like we were approaching ceilings on the deals. The time to sell was approaching fast. I hoped we were doing the right thing. It seems like every successful negotiation reaches a crisis point where everybody thinks it's going to fail—and then that's when the deal is made. Car salespeople don't stop negotiating until you physically get up to walk out of the dealership, the signal that you really are done.

The next morning, Tuesday, December 9, I called Abraham. I relayed yesterday's drama and that even though Paramount had come up to a million, we were all in agreement that, with everything being equal, we would prefer to go with Marc and Universal. He thanked me and said he'd make the calls and see if he could get the Universal money up. He also said of the back end, "The most important thing you should consider are your definitions. If you've got the language, you get paid. If your definition is good, you get the money."

And with Denise feeling distraught by the process, I invited Abraham to call her if he was so inclined. I also predicted that Paramount was not done and that we'd have another offer soon.

Emanual relayed that Paramount would weigh in with another, higher offer. Their reason: "We were only running the numbers for theatrical and home video. We forgot to calculate TV into it."

We also learned that Bernstein is Paramount's head negotiator. Before coming to Paramount in 1992, he had been President and one of the founding partners at Orion Pictures.

Another Million-Dollar Round

A little later that afternoon, Universal's new counter came to David Steinberg. It was somewhat disappointing—exactly the same as their last offer, except they had taken away the $150,000 gross corridor and added it to the $850,000 bringing their total advance to $1 million.

Craig Emanuel called Steinberg and said, "If Paramount offered $1.25 million and gave a 20-year term, with a five-year extension if they are unrecouped, would we have a deal?"

I recognized this as a car sales come-on. "If I could get you that price, would we have a deal *today*?" If we said yes, Emanuel would call Paramount and say we had a deal and would negotiate the other deal points "in good faith"—which, of course, would take months, and we'd no longer have leverage because our other suitors would go away. We told Steinberg to have Emanuel tell Paramount to address the rest of the deal points and then come back to us with an offer. Emanuel refused to call Paramount and bring up these points, so Steinberg arranged a conference call with Emanuel.

I began by saying, "Craig, these potential deal points from Paramount are terrific, and we should definitely try to get an offer. But I have one statement and three questions." I had preplanned the conversation, which is something I do when I know I have a difficult discussion ahead. I wrote down what I wanted to say, along with my best guesses as to his responses. After playing out a conversation in advance, I felt better prepared and less likely to forget one of my points. I continued, "My statement is that these are not new points. They were either covered in our recent counter to Universal or points we would bring up while advancing negotiations." Emanuel started to interrupt, but I asked him to let me finish. Interrupting your opponent's train of thought, or trying to confuse the issue, is a common parry. "My first question is, why not ask Paramount to address these points?"

Emanuel answered, "Because I'm sick of dealing with these points."

"You're personally sick of it?"

He stumbled a little, then said, "Yes."

"Okay, my second question is, what's the worst that could happen from asking for these points?"

Emanuel was starting to sound like a broken record, "I'm personally not interested in going through all these points when we can close a deal now."

I said, "You're *personally* not interested? Okay, I have one final question: Who's side are you on?"

This got him riled up. "I am on my client's side!"

"Great, then why not talk about how we can make the best possible deal?"

Emanuel's Australian accent really starts coming out when he's angry. "This is ridiculous. Paramount will never give these things. It's a waste of time to bring them up."

I said, "That's the same conversation you were having when Paramount's offer was at $500,000, and they've come a long way since then."

"That's just on the advance!"

I kept at him because I'd dealt with enough bullies to know that the only course of action is to stand up to them. "Craig, if you're sick of being involved in these protracted negotiations, perhaps you should simply remove yourself from them?"

"I'm the only one who's getting Paramount to make these offers! Paramount is very angry with you for sending your original letter."

I asked, "Who's angry?"

"Paramount! I got three calls the next day!"

"From whom?"

"From Paramount!"

You don't want to spend hundreds of thousands of dollars and years of your life creating something so special and important to you, but you blow the whole thing because, in a moment of exhaustion and frustration, you infuriate a studio chief.

I asked, "Who specifically is angry? You can't tell us people are angry at us and not tell us who it is."

Emanuel reluctantly revealed three names. "Sheri Lansing, John Ferraro, and Rob Friedman."

I said, "We just spoke to John Ferraro, and he was not at all angry. In fact, he told us he would prefer to be dealing with David Steinberg."

Emanuel said petulantly, "Well, then I'm going to call John Ferraro." And then he hung up.

Ferraro called a few minutes later to say, "Craig called and claimed you said I didn't want to negotiate with him anymore."

Keith apologized for putting Ferraro in an awkward position.

Ferraro said he wasn't upset. He was just confused by Emanuel's theatrics.

Keith said, "I don't know what you've offered. It goes through the Craig filter. I know exactly what Universal is saying."

Ferraro was dumbfounded that Emanuel was unwilling to come back to Paramount with all the rest of our points. He said, "All we're hearing from Craig is that Roger and Keith are being ridiculous." Ferraro said he'd talk to Bill Bernstein the next morning about going directly to David Steinberg.

Our Alliance Reunifies

The following morning, December 10, the first call was from Denise. She said, "We need to move on from this degenerating place we're heading toward. We need to be bigger than this."

I said, "I'm so glad you called. What would you like to do?"

"Kill you."

I laughed and said, "Let's make a deal first, then you can kill me."

She laughed too, and continued, "Let's not become another typical Hollywood story where greed causes everybody to self-destruct. This whole thing is making me sick. Plus, I'm pregnant, and I don't want to give birth to a studio executive."

It was good to be laughing again. We made up, saying we still loved each other.

Then Denise continued, "There's obviously some confusion here. Some miscommunications. I'll be the first to admit I don't have all the answers. I'm certainly not trying to screw this up. I think we all believe Universal is the place for this. But according to Craig Emanuel, Bill Bernstein told him Paramount has more money to throw at this. Craig thinks he can close it at $1.3 million." She also said she had called Marc Abraham since nobody was telling her what was going on. I had to credit Abraham for helping patch things up.

Abraham told her, "I don't think McGurk will budge on the perpetuity issue, but you can ask." Overall, he said he didn't think there was anything more he could do. We had to go to the source now: Jeffrey Goore.

At 1:10 p.m., Ferraro called and told Keith to speak directly to Bill Bernstein.

Keith was reluctant. "I'm comfortable with you, John. I can rant and rave, or complain, and say anything because I know it's informal. But calling Bill Bernstein is a very official call. David Steinberg should do it."

Ferraro finally convinced Keith to make the call.

At 1:25 p.m., Jason Blum called Keith and said, "Harvey sat through the entire screening, which is an amazing accomplishment. He really likes it. He knows about the Paramount and Universal offers, and there's no way he will enter an arena of those sorts of deals. If you don't sell the film to them, Harvey's your guy."

Steinberg told us it takes even longer to get to profit with Miramax. "On one film, Miramax was near break-even, so they ran national ads. They'd rather spend the money promoting the video release than paying the producers profits.

Cutting Out the Middlemen

At 2:30 p.m., Keith called Bill Bernstein. The first and most shocking news was that Paramount had made an official offer of $1.25 million and caved on "in perpetuity." Bernstein was appalled that the offer had not been presented to us as such.

The conversation had begun with Bernstein saying, "Hello, how are you?"

To which Keith laughed, and Bernstein said, "That's the first laugh I've heard in all these negotiations."

Off to a good start, Keith worked through the list. "We would like a theatrical guarantee."

"We can't give you a comprehensive release plan in twenty-four hours."

"I don't expect you to close a deal in twenty-four hours. But if you open the film in several major markets and it tanks, we don't expect you to keep going. We want to know that you'll give it a chance if it does take off. Also, we don't want you to open it in Sacramento, Omaha, and Duluth and call that the release. And as for sequels, everybody keeps asking us, 'When are you going to do the documentary about foreign fans and conventions?' We'd like to be in a position to be able to make that film. On final cut, we have a director that wants to know that you'll release his version of the film. If you have problems with it, tell us now. Most importantly, and this all ties in to needing to have a comfort level with the company you're about to trust with your film, nobody of any authority at Paramount has ever told us they like the movie."

Bernstein agreed, "That's a real problem."

Satisfied, Keith continued, "I know you don't give away final approvals on posters and art, but we want to be consulted." Keith finished on what would ultimately be the most important point: "We want to know how we will participate in the back end. Everybody says the video will be gigantic.

We want to know what the caps and floors will be. This is really a concern, especially when you hear studios say things like, 'Forrest Gump, Paramount's biggest film, is yet to turn a profit.'"

Bernstein said, "The reason *Forrest Gump* never hits profit is because both Zemeckis and Hanks are in for gross participation."

They discussed theories of back-end participations some more, and then Bernstein ended with, "I'm so glad you called. This is the first time I think I finally have a clear idea of what you want." He said he'd talk to Rob Friedman and get back to us.

When it was over, Keith said, "Bill Bernstein is so good and so slick. I hung up thinking I should send this guy a Christmas card or invite him to my house. It's no wonder he's their chief negotiator. He makes you feel like he understands all your problems." Closing deals is a special talent, and Bernstein was their closer.

At 3:30 p.m., we updated David Steinberg and Denise, who still hadn't heard from her attorney. I suggested that Keith call Jeffery Goore at Universal and have the same friendly conversation about their disappointing counter and our concerns about the various points.

Keith was a little reluctant, "My new best friend Bill Bernstein won't be pleased if we do that."

I said, "Universal has an official offer on the table. We can't ignore that."

Keith suggested waiting a couple hours to see if we get a Paramount offer on the table first.

At 5:05 p.m., Steinberg said, "Craig Emanuel has called several times to find out what's going on. What do I tell him?"

We said tell him that Keith Border had spoken to Bill Bernstein—at John Ferraro's insistence—and had laid out all our concerns. Bernstein had confirmed a $1.25 million offer and said he would now speak to Rob Friedman and get back to *us*. Implying, not Emanuel.

Michael Leahy noted, "Paramount must be looking at this negotiation thinking, 'The more the other side bickers, the more the price goes up. Something's wrong here.'"

Then at 5:30 p.m., Steinberg conferenced Keith and me with Denise and Emanuel. Denise asked if Paramount had made another offer.

Emanuel said, "Not formally. Now we have to decide how to respond to Paramount."

Keith said, "After my conversation with Bill, the ball is in their court."

Emanuel started complaining, "Why did you call Bill Bernstein? I thought we were all going to act together in concert and not make calls alone."

Steinberg interjected, "That's not the case. This was a decision decided between principals."

Emanuel asked Denise, "Did you authorize this?"

Denise confirmed, "Yes. It seemed like the right thing to do. It made sense, like they were making a gesture to the filmmakers."

Emanuel was stuck but persisted. "Bill Bernstein called me next and said he had no idea why Keith called him, and he felt very uncomfortable about it."

Keith was shocked. "Why would John Ferraro insist I call Bill Bernstein and then give me his phone number if they weren't expecting it?"

Denise supported Keith, "And Bill Bernstein told Keith he was very happy about this call. He was finally finding out what the filmmakers wanted."

Emanuel began interrogating his own client. "Did you hear him say that?"

I interjected, "Denise is accurately summarizing what Keith heard. I was there when Ferraro specifically asked Keith to call Bill Bernstein."

Emanuel said he was going to call Ferraro and conference him in. When he called Ferraro, he declined to be included in our call. Emanuel returned and acted like that was no big deal.

I asked, "Did Ferraro say that he told Keith to call Bill?"

Long pause. "Well, not in the terms you have described."

"Then, in exactly what terms did he say he authorized the call?"

"He said Keith asked him about the clarification of some points, and then he suggested calling Bill Bernstein." Emanuel hurried back to his initial point, "We need to respond to Paramount."

Keith said, "I am appalled at what you are telling me, Craig, that Paramount is telling me one thing and you another."

I agreed. "We just went from one hour ago being very high on Paramount to now being very unlikely to make a deal there. Since both Paramount and Universal are at seven figures, more important now is the lack of a comfort level of going with a company that's saying two different things."

Denise agreed.

I suggested that we counter Universal on all of our points, and if Paramount wanted to make an offer that included all those points, we would be glad to consider it. Emanuel wanted to know what those points were (unlike yesterday when he was too "sick of it" to be interested), so I went down the list. We also agreed that David Steinberg would draft a new counterproposal to send the next day to Universal.

Afterward, Denise called us back and asked, "What the hell just happened? Who's lying to who? I just got a call from my attorney, who balled me out. I felt like I was in grade school. He said, 'I'm really frustrated with this whole process. I've spent at least $10,000 of my time on this.'"

I said, "That's not appropriate for your attorney to try to lay a $10,000 guilt trip on you because he's on a percentage and he's frustrated."

"I know. I'm starting to think maybe he said to Paramount, 'Don't worry, you'll get this film.' But I have to say, my faith in Paramount is shaken."

We reviewed our new counterproposal for Universal: $1 million advance, $250,000 deferred as a gross participation, 20 year (plus 5) term, fifty-fifty split of the net, we reserve soundtrack and all outtakes and sequels/remakes, final cut, meaningful consultation on release, advertising, and trailers, and a US theatrical release guarantee with a minimum P&A commitment.

The next morning, Thursday, December 11, at 10:00 a.m., John Ferraro called Keith and said Craig Emanuel is turning everything around. "He's screwing this deal up. There have been very few deals handled as unprofessionally as this."

Keith said, "I apologize for even having to discuss this with you because I know you probably do a lot of business with Craig Emanuel, and you don't want to harm your relationship with him —"

Ferraro interrupted, "This is the most business I've done with Craig, and it hasn't been very pleasant." Ferraro said about the terms of the deal, "We've heard all of your other points, and nothing is outrageous. If you will agree to accept the advance, the term, and the back-end split, we can go further to the other points."

Keith said, "The priority for us now *are* the other points."

After that call, David Steinberg asked us what we wanted to do about Emanuel.

I suggested that since Emanuel was trying to keep everything verbal to maintain control, we draft a letter to Paramount comparable to the letter we sent to Universal and send it to Denise and Emanuel for approval.

The Deal

Craig Emanuel called to say what we already knew, that Paramount's $1.25 million offer was now "formal."

Keith said, "It's not about the advance anymore."

I concurred, "The other points are now the priority."

Emanuel said, "My only comment before sending this to Paramount is that we increase our asking price to $1.35 million."

David Steinberg said, "I know Keith and Roger would forgo asking for more of an advance if it eats up goodwill toward the other points."

Emanuel responded, "It won't."

I said, "I don't mind asking for more, but what indication has Paramount given on our other points?"

"They said that it should be no problem to resolve the other points, but we need a meeting of the minds with respect to the dollars and cents."

I made one additional change to add a request for a theatrical release and said, "Then I think we're agreed that David Steinberg will send out this letter as written with the two changes."

All agreed.

Bill Bernstein called Steinberg and Emanuel one hour after receiving our proposal: they stuck at $1.25 million (Craig was miffed at not getting $1.35 million), 20/5 term, we keep soundtrack and final cut, first and last negotiation on sequels and remakes, meaningful consultation on release pattern, advertising, and trailers. They balked on capping distribution expenses, or allowing us to control film festival and convention screenings, and merchandising—which they wanted to freeze, believing there was no merchandising that could exist separately from the *Star Trek* merchandising.

We decided to counter with caps on overhead and soft costs (and possibly prints and advertising), mutual approvals on film festivals and convention screenings after the theatrical distribution window, and a necessity for a merchandising deal. On the theatrical guarantee, Bernstein said we would have to call Rob Friedman to work it out. We decided to ask for the top fifty markets. We also decided that Steinberg should call Universal and ask them to respond by 11:00 a.m. the next day. As we finished the call, I signed off with, "Nice job, everybody, good work." It was the smoothest, most cooperative effort yet.

Steinberg placed the call and got an immediate answer from Jeffrey Goore: "We aren't going above a million, so we aren't going to address these other points until that's accepted."

Steinberg suggested to us, "Since Paramount is addressing your points satisfactorily, so far, at a million and a quarter, is there any reason to push Universal to do so at only a million?"

We agreed there wasn't.

I said, "But we're in a perfect position. Universal is still alive, and we can use that to close with Paramount."

Friday, December 12, 1997. Denise said she wanted to give Universal another chance to step up on the other points. Mainly because of our loyalty to Marc Abraham and because Universal had acted very honorably—and because her past experience with Paramount had led her to be distrustful.

Steinberg said we should be wary of doing this because it may negatively impact the Paramount negotiations, and it implied a weak bargaining position on our part with Universal to go back and say, "Do you really mean it?"

Denise said, "I wish I could be joyful. I just don't have a lot of faith in that studio."

I said, "I'd like to look at this as Denise's triumphant return to Paramount."

Steinberg said, "I've closed a lot of these deals, and when it's finally all over, the only thing everybody feels is exhaustion. You lose a lot of control in that moment when you sell the film. You have to let it go."

I gave Steinberg the updated list of deal points. He was skeptical of asking about some of them, like paying for all the delivery elements. "That's why you're getting $1.25 million, to pay for your film."

Keith responded, "For us, it's a matter of necessity. 10 percent down won't be enough to pay for these things and keep the doors open at Neo."

I seconded, "What does it hurt to ask?"

Bill Bernstein's response was yes almost across the board. They would give us a "good rider," which translated into capping expenses, no overhead charged on advertising, and no extra fees on foreign. They keep merchandising but asked us to come up with a list of ideas for them to exploit—the revenues all going into our general film revenues pot. They were only worried about us infringing on any of their *Star Trek* merchandise. They would allow us to screen the film at conventions one year after the theatrical and home video windows. They would guarantee that domestic theatrical and home video would be distributed through Paramount, not a third party. We could keep outtake material as long as we told them what we'd use it for. He agreed conceptually to picking up the costs for delivery items (35mm blow-up, telecine transfer, music and effects tracks, etc.). The only open issue was that they would have to examine the quality of the elements (film negative, Dolby sound master, etc.).

Regarding the final and most significant remaining point, the theatrical release, we (Roger, Keith, and Denise) would have to speak to Rob Friedman personally.

Steinberg finished with, "You guys have hit a home run. Congratulations."

Denise called Marc Abraham to say that it looks like the film is going to Paramount because, unlike Universal, they are addressing all our deal points.

I also called Abraham to thank him. He warned about Paramount, "Leopards don't change their spots." He also said that he was glad we were a happy family again. He added, "At seminars, I always describe making films being like *The Treasure of the Sierra Madre*. The team starts off happy, but then when they see the money, everybody goes crazy." John Houston's 1948 film is about gold prospectors whose insecurities cause them to distrust their partners when they strike it big. Greed consumes them, making them paranoid until they end up with nothing. Instant riches tests people.

After eight months, we finally made it to the finish line without stumbling. $1.25 million was the second-highest advance in documentary history at that point. Now that we had a deal, the real wrangling was about to begin. The business affairs sharks were about to take over and start grinding us down.

Tim Holt, Walter Huston, and Humphrey Bogart in The Treasure of the Sierra Madre *(1948).*

233

CHAPTER THIRTEEN

Closing the Deal

Negotiating does not end until the contract is signed.

When you buy a car, once they accept your price, you relax because you have closed the deal—or so you think. Next, they send you into finance, where your guard is down, and they make even more money from add-ons and finance rates. Re-trading is a practice that commences after you make a deal and the other side begins renegotiating and modifying previously agreed-upon positions, clawing back as much turf as possible or holding back anything that had not been specified clearly before shaking hands.

Phase Four: Getting to a Signed Contract

On Monday, December 15, I called Dylan Leiner at Sony Pictures Classics for advice for our upcoming theatrical-distribution meeting with Rob Friedman. Leiner amplified Michael Barker's advice. "You want twenty-five of the top fifty media markets, including Los Angeles, New York, and you can add five to eight other cities that you feel are important. Get a P&A commitment of $750,000 and a cap of $1.5 million to $2 million, with incremental increases based on box office performance. Try to protect yourself against what Miramax does. For instance, they sometimes buy a block, a full-page ad, in the 'Sunday Arts & Leisure' section. The top of the ad will be for one big film, and the bottom will be divided among the other five films. If all are unrecouped but one is well into profit, they bill the whole block against the profit leader. Later, it's almost impossible to determine that was done. You can also ask for a $100,000 bonus if the film is nominated for an Oscar and another bonus if it wins."

Rob Friedman called wanting to talk to one of us, so I picked up.

Friedman said, "So we're done?"

I said, "It looks good. As I understand it, we just need to meet to discuss release strategies."

"I'm going to New York until Thursday. Do you want to arrange a conference call?"

I said, "I think it's worth waiting until Thursday."

"Okay, good, so you can see the whites of my eyes."

"Yeah. Just between you and me. . . ."

"Sure, go ahead."

"I'd like to see this happen."

"So would I."

"I'm sure you know this, and you're going to say this anyway, but I'll tell you what you need to say to close this. Denise was on the *Star Trek* series, and she's had some up-and-down experiences with Paramount. She needs to hear you say you like the film and you're going to take care of us."

"Okay, let me have Celia check my schedule and call you back."

Celia set the meeting for 5:30 p.m. on Thursday.

Meeting with the Boss

On Thursday, the Robert G. Friedman meeting finally arrived. As we pulled up to the Paramount gates, Denise said, "Here I go again. I'm back at Paramount. It's a weird feeling."

Friedman didn't keep us waiting more than two minutes before bringing us into his office. Then he had to take two important phone calls while we admired the art and photography on his walls. Friedman is 100 percent the film executive, from his carefully trimmed salt-and-pepper beard to his casual blue shirt and khakis. He started the meeting by showing us a copy of the trailer for *Armageddon* (1998), Disney's competition for Paramount's *Deep Impact* (1998). He was keeping tabs on the enemy.

He started with, "We're finally here. It sure has taken us a long time to get to this point."

We agreed.

He admitted he was confused as to why we would have ever entertained the thought of going anywhere else. Then he took care of business right away. "I loved the film, and everybody here is passionate about it." He took a shot at wrapping up the meeting quickly by saying in very general terms, "I haven't been able to formulate a release plan yet. What I need to do, the first part of January, is sit my group down—most of them haven't seen the film yet—and strategize the best way to release this film."

Keith said, "We would really like to stay involved with the release and the promotion, stumping at conventions, whatever is needed."

He said, "Great. I'd be angry if you didn't!"

Keith laughed, then pressed a little, "I don't want to put you on the spot, but do you have any general ideas as far as the P&A or the number of markets?"

"I will go back over the *Star Trek* features and see where the strengths are, city-wise. I would try to get an education from the people here." He explained that he had only been at Paramount two years and, unlike Dolgen, he was not a *Trek* expert. "Maybe we should platform it around the conventions."

We discussed Trekkie strongholds, like Atlanta and Silicon Valley, as well as Brazil, Germany, and England. He continued with his strategy: "I wouldn't release it wide, not right away. More exclusive situations—underground, below the radar. So we don't quit if it doesn't take off right away. My fear is of getting too brave too fast. Then when the time is right, we take our shot."

Keith asked who would handle the release.

"Marketing, advertising, and publicity people will be assigned. Arthur Cohen is the one who runs the department. Keep talking to John Ferraro until then."

I brought up film festivals.

Rob didn't leave any doubt about where he stood. "No festivals. I don't want to use up those opportunities before we release the film. Any publicity the film gets goes cold in a few months."

I told him that we were already committed to San Jose and that it would be bad form to pull out on them.

Keith interjected, "Especially since they're making us the opening event."

Friedman said, "Well, at least make the call, and if they haven't made the announcement yet, you can use us as the bad guys."

We said we'd call, but it would be wrong to break a commitment. With the other festivals, we could play it by ear.

The big point still hadn't been addressed satisfactorily, so I steered the conversation back to the theatrical release. "How many markets can you guarantee for a theatrical release?"

"I can't give you a guarantee. I said we'd open it in a few markets, test it, and go from there."

"Why can't you guarantee what you just told us?"

"I don't want to be in a position of guaranteeing anything. I can't violate precedent. I've told you that we'll release it. Check me out. Everybody knows me. There are three people in the room. When I lie, I only do it when there's one other person in the room. Then I can say, 'Well, you don't remember the conversation correctly.'"

We laughed, which dispelled some of the tension. Then I pressed further, "This is nothing personal, we've just met, and I hope we'll work together on many projects, but just so we're on the same page, you are personally guaranteeing us a theatrical release?"

He answered obliquely, "You are profit participants, so we're all partners. We believe in the commerciality of this film. You wouldn't want us spending money unnecessarily, cutting into the profits."

"Will you open in New York and LA?"

"New York is one of the worst markets. It's almost impossible to make money there. I'd like to see this in every city in the country. And that's what we'll do if it takes off." And then, almost with a visible twinkle in his eye, "Don't worry, trust me."

We laughed, and then so did he, as he realized how inherently funny it was to hear somebody in Hollywood saying sincerely, "Trust me." Underneath the sincere plea, I had no doubt this guy would chop you in half if you were against him, if he had the leverage and felt it necessary.

I wasn't entirely done. "Obviously, we have to go away and discuss this."

He nodded, "Of course."

"The commerciality of the project is important to us also, maybe the most important thing, but the artistic aspect is also important. There is a value to us, a prestige factor, of having our film open in New York and Los Angeles, as opposed to Atlanta and Sacramento. We've put a lot into this film. We've spent a lot of nights in cheap hotels—"

He jumped in, "Don't get used to the expensive hotels yet."

Keith added, "You don't understand, he had to endure the DP and the producer snoring."

"Okay, we'll get you your own room from now on."

Denise said, "Can you guarantee that?"

More laughter.

Friedman said, "Los Angeles I think is a given. Maybe we'll open in New York. The artistic aspect is important. We won't ignore that."

Denise addressed one of the first things he said: "I just want you to know the reason that it took so long for us to get here today is not for lack of trying. We've always believed that Paramount was the best place for the film. We've been calling and faxing since the beginning."

He said, "I know. I apologize for our delays. This just got bogged down in places like business affairs for a while."

We finished the hour-long meeting with a screening of Paramount's *Deep Impact* trailer. Friedman didn't even know that Denise was in the movie. We shook hands and thanked him for squeezing us into his schedule. He emphasized he was looking forward to meeting again in January to discuss release specifics. He also said that he was leaving for Sun Valley for the Christmas holiday, where curiously, he'd be palling around with, among others, Marc Abraham.

After the Big Meeting

Denise said that she came away feeling positive, that Friedman was committed to a theatrical. Keith was also upbeat and in favor of moving forward. I proposed calling back and saying we were pleased with his approach and would move forward—pending a satisfactory deal memo. If we tell him we're interested because we trust him, that will subtly put him and the reputation he brandished on notice.

The next day, we called and said, "We enjoyed the meeting, and we felt that you are sincerely committed to a successful theatrical release. So we're taking you at your word. And we are looking forward to receiving a deal memo so we can make this final."

He said he was thrilled and would call Bill Bernstein and have him send over the paperwork.

Another film festival rejection letter arrived that same day from the Slamdance Film Festival. It was moot at that point. "You can't reject us! We quit!" Slamdance's letter was the most unpretentious. It ended with, "As filmmakers ourselves, we know the sting of a rejection letter, and we hope this didn't hurt too much."

On January 6, 1998, an official invitation from the Santa Barbara International Film Festival came in, and I referred it to Blaise Noto, Executive Vice President of Worldwide Publicity at Paramount. Noto told them they couldn't have the film, and we wouldn't be doing any festivals until we had a release date. As more invitations came in (The Taos Talking Pictures Festival, Sedona International Film Festival, and South by Southwest), they got the same response.

Marc Abraham ran into Friedman in Tahoe. Abraham told Denise, "You guys must have been saying nice things about me." He said that Friedman was gloating that Paramount was making a deal for *Trekkies*. Abraham said he responded, "Just be good to them. I fell in love with that movie. I'd really like to do it, but it makes a lot of sense for you guys."

Friedman also told Abraham that there was to be no theatrical promise in the contract.

Denise explained that wasn't entirely accurate. We definitely required a theatrical guarantee, but we were relying on Friedman's word as to how it would be effectuated.

Abraham said, "Rob's a tough guy. He's gruff. He didn't get to where he is on charm. But if Rob Friedman gives you a personal guarantee, he'll live up to it. He's not a dishonorable guy."

More Than a Memo

On January 14, Paramount's "deal memo" came in at a whopping sixty-seven pages, from Alexandra Denman, the attorney drafting the deal for Paramount. They had jumped right to a long-form agreement. The first mistake I noticed was that they were paying us $125 million. I was pretty sure they would catch that decimal point error. I also discovered they left out any mention of a theatrical release, our right to keep outtakes and trims, and there were no caps on their overhead and soft costs and distribution expenses.

Keith's reaction was that we needed to clearly state that they aren't acquiring the underlying rights to anything. They are licensing only what's contained in this eighty-six-minute film.

David Steinberg also had his notes, such as their clause about packaging *Trekkies* with other films. He said he could call them and say, "Here are the material points not addressed in your contract. What are your intentions concerning these points?" Or we could send back their contract with all our notes and wait for their response. We decided upon responding to all points because that way we weren't tipping our hand as to which points were most important to us. Many of our important points might slip through without fanfare, and their response would tell us what they considered to be important. Then we could pick which battles to fight. Ever the loose cannon, Craig Emanuel planned to submit his own separate redefinition of gross receipts.

The Last Film Festival

We kept our promise to Cinequest to allow them to screen the film. On January 29, Keith, Denise, and I flew to San Jose. This festival rolled out the red carpet—literally. After flying us in first class, the limo driver dropped a three-foot red carpet on the ground in front of the limo door.

During a *Trekkies* Q&A, somebody asked about the status of profilee Gabriel Koerner and his film project. Richard and Gabriel Koerner had driven up from Bakersfield and were sitting in the audience, so I said, "Gabriel's here. Why don't you answer that question." There was a collective gasp as the audience realized the kid they had been watching (and laughing at) was in the audience.

Upon hearing my invitation, Gabriel leaped out of the audience like a contestant on *The Price Is Right*. He ran to the front and grabbed the microphone like a pro. He said he had been commissioned to do graphics work for a *Babylon 5* (1994–1998) movie trailer. Then Gabriel asked if there were more questions. The kid was ready to take over the show. This had everybody rolling in the aisles, and Gabriel soaked it up.

241

As February began, rejections came in from Cinéma du Réel, The Rotterdam Film Festival, and The San Francisco International Film Festival. However, The Cleveland International Film Festival, The Singapore International Film Festival, and The Hot Springs Documentary Film Festival were interested. John Ferraro said to keep sending the inquiries to Blaise Noto "so they'll think there's a lot of interest in the film and get moving on it."

Hashing Out Boilerplate

It took Paramount's attorney Alexandra Denman three weeks to just write "yes" or "no" in the margin to all of our points. And the most concerning thing was she said no to many of our major points—all agreed to orally—such as outtakes and trims, sequels and remakes, 10 percent of the advance payable on signing, final cut, and so on. Not entirely unexpected but annoying, nonetheless. We told David Steinberg to take a hard line. When he did, Denman folded immediately on several points and said she'd check with Paramount on the others. Her excuse was that she was "out of the loop."

Cece Karz, a ten-year PR veteran, told us she couldn't tell us anything about the publicity strategy until they got a release date from Rob Friedman. "One thing we do have on our side is that *Star Trek* sells magazines." She said they also knew who all the *Trek*-fan journalists were.

On February 26, as the back-and-forth seemed to slow down, Denise asked Craig Emanuel to call Paramount to help move things along. He said he would. Then he faxed a letter to Bill Bernstein without allowing me, Keith, or Denise to approve it. His letter read:

> There are two matters which greatly trouble me for which I would like to enlist your help:
>
> 1. It had originally been the intention of the parties that an initial payment would be made on execution of a short form agreement. While I appreciate that there may be merit in going straight to a long form, my clients are under some financial pressure and I would like to see if there is a way that we can address at least them receiving some partial payment now.

2. A more fundamental problem has arisen in connection with Paramount's ongoing refusal to commit to a theatrical release of the film. The producer's decision to accept Paramount's offer instead of another studio was premised on discussions that took place with various Paramount executives in which an assurance was given that the picture would receive a theatrical release. While we understand the difficulty in committing to a minimum number of screens, at least some affirmative obligation to theatrically release the picture is of critical importance.

If Craig Emanuel had shown us this letter, I would have struck the part about "financial pressures." That made our side seem weak. He also referred to his "clients," erroneously implying that he represented Keith and me. But he was correct about the theatrical release obligation. His phrase "two matters which greatly trouble me" implies that these are the only two outstanding points. I asked Denise to please instruct Emanuel to refrain from sending notes before we review or approve them. She was surprised that he had done so and said she would talk to him.

March arrived, and we still had yet to receive a revised contract. We were frustrated and nervous about Paramount's lethargic pace. Keith wanted to bring negotiations to a head with Paramount, even if that meant walking away from the table.

I agreed. "We need to call Rob Friedman and say we're not getting what we need."

A Theatrical Guarantee

David Steinberg ran into John Ferraro at the American Film Market. Ferraro told him, "We're trying to work it out. This is all new territory for us. Giving any kind of theatrical guarantee opens us up to being sued. You can say we botched the release, or we deliberately sabotaged the release. We understand your concern over *Trekkies* being packaged with other product, but how do we alleviate your concern without setting new precedents?" His message was basically, "We're working on it. Hang in there."

Bill Bernstein said they would be addressing our points. We realized that the biggest problem with Rob Friedman's personal guarantee of a theatrical release was that it was possible he would not be there a week after we signed our deal. Executives often move around between companies. We agreed to wait for Bernstein's conversation with Friedman. I also reminded our team that, courtesy of our inside information from Jonathan Frakes, Paramount would likely cave on any point on which we held firm. Jonathan Dolgen had said, "Acquire this film." His minions would look like idiots if they let us get away. Emanuel claimed that Paramount was going to give us our theatrical guarantee but would do so in a separate rider to the contract, an approach that allowed them to not violate precedent in the contract proper.

Keith told Ferraro about Emanuel's information about some kind of rider to the contract. Ferraro said he had heard nothing about that except that Friedman wouldn't be giving any guarantees. Ferraro called Alexandra Denman, who had also heard nothing about a rider. By mid-March, there was still no redraft from Denman.

I told Keith, "We need to speak with Bill Bernstein directly. By the time second-hand and third-hand information gets to us, it's almost worthless."

On March 20, Bernstein called Keith back with a lengthy apology about how long it had taken. Then he explained what the issues were. "Only Rob can resolve this theatrical issue by meeting with Jonathan Dolgen. He's got to ask Dolgen: 'How badly do you want this movie?'"

Keith said, "We would like to know now, not a month from now if this can't be resolved. Because as horrific as it is, we have to acknowledge the possibility that may be what will happen."

Bernstein said, "Because it's up to Friedman and Dolgen, I can't give you a time frame for an answer." The crucial strategic aspect of the call was that Keith told Bernstein we were entertaining the thought of walking away. Steinberg felt that the packaging language was our biggest concern. Their ability to package the video with other product was a loophole to divert revenue away from us.

Defining the Back End

On March 25, Steinberg faxed a memo to everybody on our team outlining his conversation with Alexandra Denman. Paramount responded to the outstanding points, and they had continued to backtrack. They said no to our biggest points, theatrical guarantee language and video packaging, but also said no to a few things like convention screenings eighteen months after release—things they had agreed to. Denise assured us that Craig Emanuel had stated emphatically that Bill Bernstein had promised a side letter guaranteeing the theatrical release, so she would call Emanuel and ask him what's up with that.

Denman said that Emanuel had called Jeff Freedman complaining that Denise was going to fire him over this deal and asked to be transferred to Bill Bernstein, who didn't take the call. Keith and I discussed whether we should pass this information on to Denise and decided it wasn't our business to do so. Best to stay out of that attorney/client relationship. Plus, let Mad Dog Emanuel do his job and try to wrestle the theatrical guarantee out of Paramount.

Denise confirmed that Emanuel told her Bernstein guaranteed a separate letter was coming that would address the theatrical guarantee. Emanuel absolutely assured Denise that this was a done deal.

Denman then said there would be no side letter. Somebody was not communicating.

Going Rogue

On March 27, Emanuel sent another letter to Bernstein. He asked for the side letter "confirming the theatrical release commitment," and also said, "I would ask that Paramount consider making a good faith payment to my clients now whilst any remaining issues are resolved. As you can appreciate, my clients are under considerable financial burden at the moment."

I felt like enough was enough. I faxed Emanuel a letter and copied Denise, Keith, and my attorney, Todd Stern, which read:

I reviewed your March 27 fax to Bill Bernstein. Nice work pulling the theatrical release commitment out of Paramount. I look forward to seeing the side agreement. Also, while I appreciate that you are working on behalf of Denise Crosby and the *Trekkies*/Paramount deal, I would also appreciate that you remain mindful of the fact you do not represent me on this matter. Please do not refer to your "clients" in any way that might imply you represent me, and do not refer to me as "under considerable financial burden." Not only untrue, this is a weak negotiating stance. I assume you have negotiated other distribution deals, and will agree that an astute seller does not advertise desperation. It is also inappropriate for you to ask for a "good faith payment" in advance of signing some kind of deal memo, without confirming that both Keith and I are open to such a concept. I can't speak for Keith or Denise, but I oppose this. I feel that accepting money in advance of completing and signing a deal would be a grave mistake, as it implies acceptance of Paramount's deal and weakens our remaining leverage; if Paramount reneges, we may still take this film to another studio.

Emanuel didn't respond.

Keith said to me, "The poor guy; I feel sorry for him."

"Why?"

"I feel sorry for anybody who gets on your shit list."

"Good point."

On April 2, a seventy-five-page revised contract came in. The most significant points of contention were still video packaging and theatrical guarantee. I suggested we insist on meeting with Denman and Bernstein to resolve the points. Otherwise, this would drag into September, and there's no way we were going to maintain "exclusive negotiations" until then.

Joel Soisson cautioned, "Push Paramount as far as you possibly can, but don't walk away from this deal."

Trying to Maintain Leverage

I called Marc Abraham to feel him out on the potential of resurrecting a Universal deal, to give us an idea of how hard we can dig in our heels with Paramount. I told him about Paramount's flip-flopping, delays, and seeming indifference, and that if he could get Universal to match the Paramount deal, we would much prefer to work with him.

Abraham said he didn't think the guys at Universal would want to get in the middle because they'd get an ugly call from Friedman and Dolgen saying, "What the hell are you doing? We won, you lost. We were in exclusive negotiations."

I said we would have to withdraw from exclusive negotiations first, and if Abraham wanted an ace in the hole, he could have it. He said he would discreetly check it out at Universal.

Emanuel told David Steinberg that Bill Bernstein had gotten a commitment to release *Trekkies* in a minimum of three cities, and it would be put in the contract proper, not a side letter after all. The lawyers set a conference call for April 14.

On Monday, April 13, Keith, Denise, and I called Rob Friedman. His assistant said he was out of the office. We asked to set up a conference call to discuss meeting with the distribution team.

The Boss Calls

Keith was out of the office when Friedman called back an hour later. I picked up, "Hi, it's Roger."

He said, "Hi, what's the topic of the call?" Friedman was right down to business.

"We just want to talk about meeting with the distribution team. Could you hold on while I get Keith and Denise on the phone?"

He said, "No. That's not necessary. We don't have a deal yet. I thought we had a deal when we walked out of that meeting."

"What we said was, we looked forward to receiving a deal memo, and you skipped that stage and sent us a long-form contract."

"I don't know anything about that. All I know is we had a deal, and now Craig Emanuel has introduced changes, and I have to leave it to the lawyers."

"Well, four months have passed, and it's frustrating for everybody. In the spirit of filmmakers working together, we wanted to set up the call so we could help get things moving."

"I can't do anything until we have a deal. Now it's up to the lawyers. I'd say the same thing to Keith and Denise."

"Lawyers are deal breakers."

"I agree."

"I believe if we could sit down together, we could resolve everything in an hour and close it. But now Alexandra Denman has to call Bill Bernstein, and he has to call you, and the delays add up."

"That's true."

"If you had gone to a deal memo, we could have avoided this."

"I don't know about that. There's nothing more I can say about that."

"Okay, I'll relay this to Keith and Denise." Which is what I did an hour later when Keith arrived at the office.

Keith's reaction was, "He's blaming the lawyers."

"Yeah," I said, "and then agreeing that the delays are because the lawyers have to report to him."

Denise said, "I am continually amazed and flabbergasted by Paramount's behavior."

Keith said, "Oh come on, Denise, you've dealt with them before—and you even warned us."

She said, "Yeah, that's right."

The lawyers' call lasted an hour and forty-five minutes. David Steinberg was optimistic afterward. They worked out terminology for the lesser points.

We found out why Rob Friedman thought we were changing the deal. Apparently, when Paramount offered to guarantee three cities, Emanuel demanded five. Keith was somewhat distressed by the direction of this point of negotiation. He felt like we were eroding our moral high ground because we never agreed to a commitment for a minimum number of cities, which was true.

On April 24, Alexandra Denman said a three-city theatrical commitment would include San Jose, Dallas, and Atlanta, with an outside date of

December 31, 1999. The fact that they were including the words "theatrical commitment" was a huge win. They said no to our video packaging language and offered instead a "reasonable allocation."

Steinberg said to Alexandra Denman, "With this, you could package *Trekkies* with the next *Star Trek* movie and allot my clients a nickel a unit." Denman couldn't deny this.

Later, another lawyer from Paramount, Anthony Mosawi, called Steinberg and said, "Is this video packaging language really a deal breaker?"

He said that he had been told that it was.

David Mamet's *The Spanish Prisoner* (1997) has a line of dialogue that had always stuck with me: "Always do business as if the person you're doing business with is trying to screw you, because he probably is. And if he's not, you can be pleasantly surprised."

The Last Point

On May 1, Steinberg sent over a list of all our remaining comments, including our one major point: video packaging.

Mosawi said, "If we eliminate all these other points and resolve the video packaging, do we have a deal?" I could almost see Mosawi nodding "yes" at us on the other side of the phone.

On May 14, the video-packaging language came in, but there was no guarantee *Trekkies* would be released on its own before being packaged with other titles. We wanted our film to have its own home-video window first because that's where the biggest money is, so we held out.

Mosawi asked if they agreed to a short window of four months, would we have a deal?

Steinberg suggested we propose six months, which is the longest a normal window would be anyway.

Paramount agreed to the six-month non-packaged window but would give no further description of the word "release." They refused to describe it as "bona fide" because there's an implied overall covenant of good faith already incorporated in a contract—which was logical. For the next month, we went back and forth on the rental-window definition.

Paramount again argued that they didn't want to set a precedent. "We don't know how we'll position the home-video release. We can't be told how to market our products, and that's why we've given you such a large advance."

Our position was: We simply wanted an unencumbered sell-through home-video release specified, a release like any other film would get.

John Ferraro revealed it was all about one guy in home video who didn't want to be told what to do. "Even if you get your guarantee, the guy's going to be angry that he was pushed, and he'll have a bad attitude that will work against your project."

Mosawi said he got a call from E. Barry Haldeman, Executive Vice President in charge of Business Affairs, who chewed him out about the home-video window thing, saying, "We're not ever going to budge on this point. Tell them, don't even think they'll take this to some other studio, or we'll sue their ass." An interesting admission on their part that they planned to close the deal no matter what. Steinberg's opinion was they would have sued us if we walked away and that we would have won, but they had the resources to grind us down. We agreed to their six-month release-window language. There was no way we were going to abandon the deal, but up to that point, we had to make Paramount (and our attorneys) believe we might. That's the only way we had leverage left to push the deal as far as we did.

Sign on the Dotted Line

On July 7, the final contracts came in. Six months and three weeks after agreeing to move forward with Rob Friedman at Paramount, we signed a contract—make that eight copies of a seventy-page contract, six hundred pages of hard-fought legalese, and forty spaces requiring our three signatures.

On July 13, we gathered at Keith's office. I signed first. Denise second. Keith said he wanted to go last "in case I change my mind."

Much later, I realized we had made one big mistake. A scheme to watch out for is when distributors charge "interest" on an advance, treating it like a loan. An advance is not a loan, but if they treat it like one, until that advance is fully recouped, that interest keeps compounding, putting you further away from breakeven.

A few days later, John Fitzgerald at the AFI Film Festival called to say they loved my next film *Suckers* and wanted to have the world premiere. I was happy to accept. World-premiering my film was something the AFI had just barely missed out on a year ago with *Trekkies*.

Keith called Cece Karz in the Paramount publicity department to express that we wanted to make an announcement about the deal.

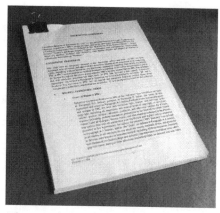

The signed distribution contract for Trekkies, licensing the film to Paramount Pictures Corporation.

Karz said that Paramount would only make an announcement once they had plans to release the film, not the acquisition. Knowing that, we decided to release the acquisition news ourselves.

Blaise Noto called Keith back the next day to reverse course. He said they would do a press release and do it quickly if that's what we wanted. He said, "I'll fax something over to Rob Friedman to look at."

Unfortunately for Noto, we had already "leaked" the story to *Variety*. Keith decided to keep his mouth shut about that. When *Variety* called Paramount to verify the story, Karz wasn't happy to hear about the leak. On August 8, 1998, *Variety* published an article.

Paramount Beams Up *Trekkies*

by Dan Cox and Andrew Hindes

Looking to keep its most lucrative franchise in the family, Paramount Pictures has paid $1.25 million for *Trekkies*, the Roger Nygard documentary about fans of the *Star Trek* series and films. No release date has been set, but according to Robert Friedman, Paramount Motion Picture Group vice chairman, the film will be distributed theatrically through Paramount Pictures—not its fledgling specialty division.

Barely a rewrite of our press release but with the addition of a quote from Rob Friedman, who went on record discussing the theatrical release.

I was invited to be on a panel at an IFP (Independent Filmmaker Project) film financing conference. At the reception, I met Jonathan Dana (film rep super-agent). He mentioned that Friedman was the first person he met in this industry. I told him about our Paramount deal and then asked, "From what you know of Rob Friedman, would you say he's a man of his word?"

Dana said through a sideways smile, "He works for Dolgen." He paused, as if that was answer enough, then elaborated, "Rob's not going to lose his job over your film." In other words, "Get your guarantee on paper."

On Thursday, October 8, 1998, the bank called and said the money from Paramount had been deposited.

Two years and two months after commencing shooting.

Eighteen months after the first distributor screening.

Nine months after shaking hands with Rob Friedman.

Nearly three months after signing the contract.

We finally got paid.

Denise was jubilant, "Let's enjoy this moment. Today, Trekkies Productions is a million-dollar company."

We were finally able to pay our crew and credit cards. It's an amazing feeling to go from debtor to creditor overnight.

CHAPTER FOURTEEN

Never Stop Creating

The end is the beginning.

There are many ways into the documentary business. Everyone has a different success story, and they all seem exceptional. Rachel Grady's perspective is: "If you're curious, fascinated by human behavior, and have a high tolerance for risk, it's a great job." Producer Jonathan Vogler said it's a good thing there's not a singular, straight path into the business. "Otherwise, there would be a long line, and few would get in." To keep working in the industry, Vogler recommended, "Be someone people like working with, who they *want* to call for help on their projects. Observe, and look at how a documentary is made. Check out the line items in a budget, and find one of those jobs that you can do, so you'll be able to work on other people's documentaries. That way, you can pay your bills while learning and making your own films."

Ken Burns avoids using the word "career," because when he was working on *Huey Long* (1985), poet and novelist Robert Penn Warren turned to him and said, "Careerism is death." And so, Burns refers to his work as his "professional life." According to Burns, "If you want to be a doctor, lawyer, or feature filmmaker, I could tell you what I thought your path to that would be. It wouldn't ensure your success. But all the documentary filmmakers I know and respect have come at it from an entirely *unique* path. They've blazed their own trails." Burns's mentor, Jerome Liebling, used to say to him, "Go, see, do, be." "Go" means get out there and start trying—failing as well as succeeding. "See" means don't presume you already know in advance. Be curious and willing to have your preconceptions obliterated. "Do" means actually go make a project. And "be" is a humanistic concept about being present in the moment.

Publicist Sylvia Desrochers and documentarian Marina Zenovich recommend that filmmakers look into labs like the ones at the Sundance Institute. The Documentary Edit and Story Lab and the Documentary Film Producers Lab are held in the summers. Desrochers said, "You're going to be in a better position by meeting people in the documentary world who can help you move forward in that career."

When Liz Garbus started in the business, she worked with a more senior filmmaker, Jonathan Stack, on *The Farm: Angola, USA* (1998). "I think that gave me a framework and the confidence to go out in the world and continue. So it could be a mentor that you find, it could be a producer, it could be an incredibly great partnership with an editor." Garbus began with vérité films. But when she started having children, the logistical needs of her life began to dictate the style of her films. It was no longer reasonable to jump on a plane with a twenty-four-hour notice. She tried to find films she could make as a working mother, something with a more structured format, which still spoke to her soul and passions. "One film in that style was *Bobby Fischer Against the World*, the kind of project where I could plan it two weeks in advance and arrange childcare."

Documentaries are a team endeavor—you are married to your partners for the duration. Are you the kind of person with whom other filmmakers want to collaborate? Freida Lee Mock suggested that a person's spirit makes a difference. "We enjoy collaborators who are positive, generous, resourceful, passionate, and ready to jump in because there's so much to do to get the project over the finish line. You're with a community of like-minded people, and that makes the hard work and the love of the art and craft of storytelling rewarding and fun, especially when the audience at the premiere gives you that burst of enthusiastic feedback!"

Davis Guggenheim's father, Charles Guggenheim, won four Academy Awards for his documentaries *Nine from Little Rock* (1964), *Robert Kennedy Remembered* (1968), *The Johnstown Flood* (1989), and *A Time for Justice* (1994). Davis Guggenheim said, "I grew up thinking I could never be as good of a filmmaker as my dad. He was like a Patrick Mahomes or a Michael Jordan." Despite being in his father's shadow, Guggenheim moved to Los Angeles after college and worked his way up the ladder until he was producing and directing in television, which helped pay for his sojourns into the documentary world. "And today, there are more and more form-breaking, adventurous, wild movies in the nonfiction space. So it's a great time to be making documentaries." Davis Guggenheim did pick up his own Academy Award for *An Inconvenient Truth* (2006).

Producer Michael Tollin's mantra is *persistence, perseverance, patience.* Once, when Tollin was pitching an idea to Barry Bonds while Bonds was in the batting cage, Tollin said, "Barry, give me thirty seconds. Hear me out, if you will. The worst you can say is no."

When Bonds came out of the cage, he looked Tollin dead on and said, "The worst I can say is no? How about fuck no?"

Tollin didn't give up. Ultimately, Tollin turned no into yes. Tollin loves math and baseball. He grew up thinking about Ted Williams's adage that baseball is a game of failure: "A man can succeed three times out of ten and go to Cooperstown [the Baseball Hall of Fame]." Tollin said, "In our business, you can fail ninety-seven out of 100 times and still go to whatever Hall of Fame will have you." Willie Mays, Roberto Clemente, and Frank Robinson outshone Hank Aaron in the 1950s and 1960s, but Aaron passed Babe Ruth and was standing in the 1970s as the home-run king. "Hank's motto, which I've applied to my career," Tollin said, "is be the tortoise, not the hare." Tollin added, "If you love what you do, just keep doing it. Ask yourself: *Am I having more fun or less?* I've been at this for forty-five years, and I'm still loving it. I'm going to keep doing it."

Burns said modestly, "There're many filmmakers with more talent than me, but I've been persistent. What I do is I work really, really hard." At around age twenty-three, when Burns began working on *Brooklyn Bridge* (1981), he kept two gigantic, three-ring binders, each filled with hundreds of rejection letters. "I kept these on my desk for two dozen years because people would look at me and say, 'This kid is trying to sell me the Brooklyn Bridge. Ha, ha, ha.' And then turn me down."

After a screening of *The Fire Within: A Requiem for Katia and Maurice Krafft* (2022), I asked Werner Herzog what advice he gives young filmmakers. Herzog began by describing how much easier it is for filmmakers today compared to when he started in the business. At that time, 35mm celluloid was expensive, clumsy, and slow. Today, a cell phone can shoot at cinema quality, and a laptop can edit. Herzog said young filmmakers are often into what he termed a culture of complaint. "I can't find any finances." Or, "The film industry doesn't understand my vision." At age sixteen, Herzog similarly felt nobody took him seriously. "My puberty was late. I was thrown out everywhere." So, he got a job working the night shift as a welder in a steel factory. It took him two and a half years to save enough money to finance his first project. Herzog's advice is, "Follow your vision. Be courageous. Be intrepid. Roll up your sleeves, earn some money, and make a film. If you are able-bodied and smart enough, you can make a feature documentary at cinema quality for under $10,000. I am a storyteller, and I have a vision that I have followed since I was nineteen years old when I made my first film, and it has carried me along."

You also have to have a plan. Herzog recalled when a young filmmaker came up to him at the Sundance Film Festival and said, "I've shot 850 hours of footage, and I've been editing for two and a half years."

Herzog said, "My heart sank. This young man did not know what he was doing, where he was going with his project. I said to him, 'Please, please, please, shoot what you really want for the screen. We are filmmakers. We are not garbage collectors.'" Editing is refining raw ore to a pure form. The editing process begins during writing, is a concern during shooting, and continues in earnest once you arrive in the editing suite.

Marina Zenovich financed her first film, *Independent's Day* (1998), on credit cards. She used that as an angle for the posters she handed out to promote screenings of the film. She recalled, "It was ridiculous. That's something you do in your twenties, if you're stupid. But in making that first film, I became a filmmaker. I found something that I wanted to do." She added this advice: "Believe the magnets! It's all the slogans you find: never, never, never give up. If you are the kind of person who gives up, it's the wrong profession for you." She added that setbacks are what made her who she is. "The years where I didn't get into Sundance made me hungrier. The hunger you get from rejection is the fuel that pushes you forward." Now that she has a solid track record as a documentarian, who can deliver strong portraits of complex individuals, job offers come to her. She recalled a breakfast meeting where a cable executive handed her a list of persons they wanted to make films about and said, "Pick one." All she had to do was point, and she had a budget.

This industry is about creativity and entertainment. If you are an engaging, curious, enthusiastic person, you and your audience will enjoy the interaction, and festivals and streamers will look forward to seeing you again

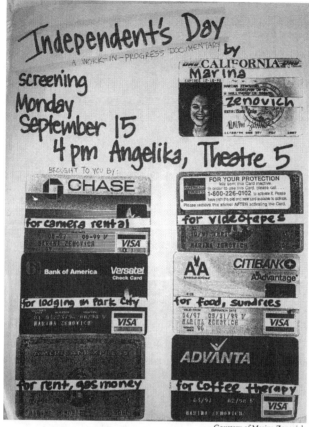

Courtesy of Marina Zenovich.

Marina Zenovich handed out this flier to publicize her first documentary, Independent's Day *(1998).*

and again. If you see a movie, TV series, or documentary and think, *I can do something as good as that,* it's not enough. You need to create something *better.* To be a part of what is arguably the most prestigious industry in the world means competing against thousands of others with the same dream. And you have to beat them. How? By working harder. At the office, be the first to arrive and the last to leave. Never have to be told to do something twice. Be organized and get everything done. The most successful people are often not the most talented; they are the most driven. Persistence gets a product over the finish line. It doesn't matter how talented you are if you don't finish. Stamina gives you an edge, and you will rise to the top.

Some may not understand how you can work so hard. Personal relationships will suffer if you don't find others who appreciate your need to compete. It's lonely spending so much time practicing your art. It's easier to put it off and party, play video games, or scroll the Internet. When I waste a day being nonproductive, I envision all the other rats pulling ahead in the race. Vacations, respect, and income must be earned. A workaholic is somebody who works too hard—*in somebody else's opinion*. Yes, of course, I'm married to my work. You are what you do. If you don't do anything, what are you?

Will you ever retire from this endeavor? What does retirement even mean? Is it reclining in a chair and watching cooking shows until you have a stroke? A favorite question we all love to dream about is: *What would I do if I won the lottery?* My answer comes easy: *If I won the lottery, I would have enough money to work until the day I died—on* my *projects.* The point is to express yourself creatively. Daily. In any way that's enjoyable and challenging. Once you make your first documentary, you are a documentarian for life. There's no leaving that group. It is an obsession that will add pain, difficulty, meaning, and purpose to your life. And with purpose comes happiness.

Remember when you wrote down your terrific idea for a theme? Work it into an engaging logline. Research your core idea. Write some killer questions. Now, start filming. Come on, let's go! You've got this!

Appendix A

Sample Interview Consent and Release Form★

For good and valuable consideration hereby received, and no further consideration will be due, the Undersigned hereby grants to _____ (Producer) its successors, assigns and licensees, the irrevocable right, license and privilege, to use, record, photograph, dub, amplify, reproduce, edit, perform, represent, exhibit, televise, transmit, stream, sell, rent, license, transfer and exploit by any and all means, and in the advertising, publicity, and exploitation thereof, the Undersigned's utterances, statements, likeness, image, recordings, voice, name, biographical information, material, artwork, photographs, drawings, music, and musical or other performances (Performance), throughout the universe, in any manner and form and by any method and process and through any media now known or hereafter known or devised, in and in connection with the project or subject or program or production presently titled or known as "_____" (Production) or any derivative works, including bonus material, other productions, websites, social media, books, posters, promotional materials, videos, outtakes, raw footage, or portions thereof or any other related material to be produced or released by Producer or by any person, individual, company, business firm, distributor, broadcast station, platform, publication or entity, its successors, assigns or licensees, to which Producer may choose to sell, license, transfer or assign the Production, or raw footage, or portions thereof. The Undersigned hereby agrees and acknowledges that Producer, its successors, assigns or licensees, is or will be the sole and exclusive owner of all copyright and other rights in and to the Production, Undersigned's appearance or Performance in the Production and the recordings thereof and the results and proceeds therefrom. The Undersigned agrees to hold Producer, its successors, assigns or licensees, or any other parties harmless against any claim, liability, loss or damage, including attorney's fees, caused by or arising from Undersigned's appearance and Performance in the Production, of any utterance made by Undersigned or

259

material furnished by Undersigned in connection with Undersigned's participation and Performance therein.

Visual description of any submitted material, artwork, photographs, or drawings (if any): _____

_____

_____.

AGREED AND ACCEPTED:

_____   _____

Signature of Undersigned   Signature of Parent or Guardian

_____   _____

Undersigned Name (Printed)   Parent or Guardian's Name (Printed)

_____   Address _____

Date   City, State Zip _____

                               Phone _____

                               Email _____

Attach photo and/or write description of Performer: _____

_____

_____

*Note to reader: Be sure to have a production attorney review this and any forms prior to use to make sure all the specific needs of your project are fully met.

Appendix B

Format Definitions

1. *Aspect ratio is the size of a frame.* It is measured by comparing width to height. Most documentaries are 16×9, sometimes reduced to 1.78:1, or expressed by the number of lines of HD resolution as 1920×1080. Another choice is the classic aspect ratio of 4×3 (1.33:1, 640×480 lines of resolution), which was a standard before the 1950s. Projects using this ratio utilize black masking on the sides, known as pillarboxing. We released *Trekkies* in its original 4×3, which is the full 16mm frame. A third choice is widescreen, utilizing a frame of 2.39:1 (rounded up to 2.40:1, 12×5). Some filmmakers have gone even wider, to 2.76:1, sometimes shooting on 70mm film. Widescreen originated after studios wanted to promote cinema as offering more than standard 4×3 television. Paramount debuted a wider 1.66:1 format with *Shane* in 1953. That same year, Twentieth Century Fox premiered CinemaScope in 2.35:1 with *The Robe* (1953), the first feature filmed with an anamorphic lens. Normal lenses are spherical, and that type of projection is called "Flat." An anamorphic lens distorts an image by compressing it, and then the image is later expanded to be viewed in a wider form called "Scope." An anamorphic indicator is when lens flares look horizontally stretched. Super Panavision is another format that shot on 65mm film with non-anamorphic lenses, stretching the ratio to 2.21:1 for *Lawrence of Arabia* (1962), and Ultra Panavision went to 2.76:1 for *It's a Mad, Mad, Mad, Mad World* (1963). Metro-Goldwyn-Mayer and Disney advocated for cropping 35mm to 1.75:1. Universal-International and Columbia Pictures backed a frame of 1.85:1 (37×20), which eventually became the most-used standard, mainly for the convenience of exhibitors, who tired of making changes for each theatrical release. Lazy projectionists sometimes miss-framed and revealed boom mics or rigging, captured in the full aperture of a 35mm frame. Some filmmakers today mask the top and bottom of the frame (letterboxing) to create this wider screen effect when viewed on a 16×9 screen.

Four aspect ratios compared: 1.78 (16×9), 1.33 (4×3), 1.85 (37×20), 2.39 (12×5).

Graphic by Gabriel Koerner.

2. **Frame rate** *is the number of images per second.* The more photos or images per second, such as thirty, fifty, or sixty, the more crisp the movie looks the more it feels "live" or like television or a sporting event. A slower frame rate, like the traditional film-camera rate of 24 fps (or European television's 25 fps) appears more "cinematic" to the eye.

3. **Resolution** *refers to the size of the frame.* Resolution quantifies the amount of visual information, specifically how many pixels make up an image. More pixels make an image look sharper (not always a benefit, such as when actors become distressed seeing too much detail, making an image unflattering). Eventually, higher and higher pixel numbers surpass differences the human eye can discern. It can make a big difference on computer screens where multiple windows are opened. High definition (HD, 1080p) has 1920×1080 lines of resolution. 1920 represents the horizontal resolution, and 1080 is the vertical resolution. The "p" in 1080p stands for "progressive scanning," which displays all the lines at once (instead of half at a time, which is what interlaced scanning does). Ultra-high-definition (UHD, 4K) has 3840×2160 lines of resolution. 8K UHD has 7680×4320 lines. 8K DCI (Digital Cinema Initiatives) is 8192×4320. The cinematography standard for DCI is a 1.9:1 aspect ratio, which can be letterboxed or cropped to 1.78:1 for 16×9 delivery. Quad

high definition (QHD or WQHD [wide quad high definition]) is a standard for 16:9 computer and television screens. QHD has a resolution of 2560×1440 pixels (sometimes called 2K or 1440p). It has quadruple the resolution of a regular HD screen's 1920×1080p.

4. ***Video bit depth*** *is the number of shades per color.* Shades are affected by the number of bits used to indicate the color of a single pixel. (A bit [binary digit] is the smallest unit of data, usually indicated by a 0 or 1, or on or off.) 8-bit video can represent a maximum of 256 different numeric values depending on how all eight of the switches are thrown, since two to the eighth power is 256 combinations. This means that each of the three color channels in an RGB (red, green, blue) system has the potential of 256 shades. Therefore, with 8-bit color, using three color channels, there are 256×256×256, which totals 16.7 million colors available. 8-bit color is common, but 10-bit allows four times as many shades per color, or 1,024 in each of the three color channels, resulting in more than a billion color shades available. 12-bit increases it sixteen times, to 68.7 billion color shades. Few people can perceive a difference between 10-bit and 12-bit signals. The advantage is that a higher bit-depth gives you more latitude in post.

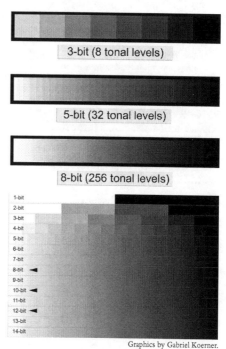

Graphics by Gabriel Koerner.

8-bit video gives 256 combinations. Three color channels (256 x 256 x 256) totals 16.7 million color shades.

10-bit allows 4 times as many shades per color, resulting in 1 billion color shades.

12-bit increases data 16 times to 68.7 billion color shades.

5. ***Chroma sampling*** *is the amount of color information per pixel.* A signal with 4:4:4 (or 444) has no compression. therefore, it delivers all information in luminance and color data.

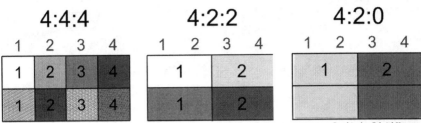

Graphics by Gabriel Koerner.

The first number is the width of the pixel, the second number is how many of the pixels in the top will have color information, the third number is how many pixels in the bottom row will have color information.

4:2:2 (or 422) is compressed and has half the color information. 4:2:0 (or 420) has one-quarter of the information.

6. ***Audio sampling*** *is the number of samples taken per second in a digital signal.* Old-style CDs were recorded at 44.1 kHz, capturing frequencies up to the 22 kHz range. 48 kHz gives a slightly higher frequency response, capturing frequencies up to 24 kHz. The difference is minuscule, but 48 kHz is a better choice. There are also 88.2 kHz, 96 kHz, and 192 kHz, sometimes used to provide greater headroom for higher frequencies and then down-sampled later to 48 kHz. 96kHz is often used for sound effects recording and ambience recordings as the higher sample rate allows more manipulation of the files later. They can be played slower and pitch transposed with greater detail. These higher sample rates generally don't come into play when recording and editing documentary sound.

7. ***Audio bit depth*** *is the number of bits available for each sample of an audio signal.* CDs have 16-bit audio, which can represent 65,536 different numeric values depending on how the sixteen switches are thrown, since two to the sixteenth power is 65,536 combinations. 24-bit audio can represent over 16.7 million distinct audio-amplitude levels. 24-bit is a good choice for recording audio. There is also an option called 32-bit float, with which a much wider range of audio values can be recorded. There is so much headroom in the 32-bit signal that you don't have to worry about distortion and level-setting. This technology can save a one-person crew who is facing unexpected audio conditions. You can add gain or "set the levels" later in the editing room. 32-bit float requires a 32-bit recorder, such as a Zoom F6 multi-track field recorder. My sound mixer, Bill Martel, always recommends a recorder that is capable

of SMPTE timecode generation (a set of standards defined by the Society of Motion Picture and Television Engineers).

8. ***Codec** (coder/decoder) is the technical processes for compressing and uncompressing video.* There are hundreds of audio and video codecs created for different uses. Video cameras have commonly used AVC (Advanced Video Coding), also referred to as H.264, MPEG-4, MPEG-4 AVC, or MPEG-4 Part 10. AVCHD (Advanced Video Coding High Definition) was developed for HD, and XAVC and XAVC-S for recording HD and 4K. HEVC (High Efficiency Video Coding, or H.265) is gaining ground for 4K content. Avid DNxHR/HD (Digital Nonlinear Extensible High Resolution) and Apple ProRes are high-quality options for shooting, but they take up more space than compressed codecs. A filmmaker's choice is limited by the camera's codec options and the storage size of the onboard SD cards. Recording to an external solid-state drive can increase options by increasing storage size.

9. ***Containers** are what codecs fit inside.* These containers deliver the whole package of files (video information, audio stream, and metadata, ready to be put together for playback). Common containers are MP4 (MPEG-4 Part 14), MOV (QuickTime), AVI (Audio Video Interleave), and MXF (Material Exchange Format).

10. ***Color space** is a technical standard specifying a range of possible colors and luminance values that can be reproduced.* Rec.709 (also known as BT.709 and ITU 709) refers to a set of image encoding and signal characteristics for HD; it covers things like frame rate, color gamut, and resolution. There is also the Rec.2020 standard for UHDTV (4K TV) and a DCI standard for 4K film. "Lossless" describes an uncompressed codec where no quality is lost—but you pay a price with a need for more hard-drive space. A "lossy" codec compresses media and stores it with some quality loss. Shooting footage with a setting on RAW (uncompressed and unprocessed image data) or Log (logarithmic footage) is lossless, capturing uncompressed data. An advantage to shooting RAW is that it gives a colorist more latitude to tweak images; otherwise, detail gets lost in shadows, and the highlights blow out. RAW looks washed out in offline editing, so a LUT (Look-Up Table, a color-grade template) is often temporarily added on top of offline footage to make it look presentable.

11. ***Video format standards*** *are NTSC, PAL, and SECAM.* They are no
    longer a concern while shooting, although you may encounter these
    older format standards in archival footage. NTSC (National Television
    Standards Committee, introduced in 1941) originated in the United
    States and has 525 interlaced lines and a frame rate of 29.97 frames per
    second. PAL (Phase Alternate Line, introduced in 1962) and SECAM
    (Sequential Color and Memory, introduced in 1967) originated in
    other countries, and they have 625 interlaced lines and a frame rate
    of 25 frames per second. HD standards have removed the problem of
    varying resolution, but frame-rate differences can reduce visual qual-
    ity if a television broadcast in a different region converts a 24fps or
    29.97fps signal to the local frame rate. And a partridge in a pear tree.

If you read Appendix B to the end, congratulations. Or my sympathies.
Whichever applies.

Notes

Chapter One

1. *Webster's New World College Dictionary, 5th Edition* (Boston: Houghton Mifflin Harcourt, 2014). https://www.yourdictionary.com/documentary.

2. Milton Bloombaum, "The Hawthorne Experiments: A Critique and Reanalysis of the First Statistical Interpretation by Franke and Kaul," *Sociological Perspectives*, vol. 26, no. 1 (January 1983), 71–88. https://doi.org/10.2307/1389160.

3. Werner Heisenberg, *Physics and Philosophy: The Revolution in Modern Science* (London: Prometheus Books, 1958), 137.

4. Richard Griffith, *The World of Robert Flaherty* (London: Victor Gollancz Ltd., January 1, 1953).

5. Walter Hines Page and Arthur Wilson Page, *The World's Work—A History of our Time*, Volume XLIV, May to October 1922 (New York: Doubleday, Page & Company, 1922), pp. 553–60.

6. New England Historical Society, "Robert Flaherty Films Inuit Life in *Nanook of the North*—and Invents the Documentary," (2022). https://www.newenglandhistoricalsociety.com/robert-flaherty-brings-nanook-north-life/.

7. Louis Menand, "Nanook and Me, *Fahrenheit 9/11* and the documentary tradition," *The New Yorker* (August 9, 2004). https://www.newyorker.com/magazine/2004/08/09/nanook-and-me.

8. Liz Ellsworth, *Frederick Wiseman: A Guide to References and Resources* (Boston: G. K. Hall & Co., 1st edition, January 1, 1979).

9. Errol Morris and Peter Bates, "Truth Not Guaranteed: An Interview with Errol Morris," *Cinéaste*, vol. 17, no. 1 (1989), 16–17. http://www.jstor.org/stable/23803048.

10. Roger Ebert, "*The Thin Blue Line*," *Chicago Sun-Times* (September 16, 1988). https://www.rogerebert.com/reviews/the-thin-blue-line-1988.

11. Bill Nichols, *Introduction to Documentary, Third Edition* (Bloomington: Indiana University Press, Kindle Edition, 2017), 54–56.

12. Ken Burns, "Agency Heads Feud, Ken Burns Takes the (Long) Road Less Traveled with 'American Buffalo,'" *The Business with Kim Masters*, Podcast (October 20, 2023), audio, 21:04. https://podcasts.apple.com/

us/podcast/agency-heads-feud-ken-burns-takes-the-long-road-less/
id73330606?i=1000632089037.

13. John Horn, "He Wants You to Be Disgusted by *Sicko*," *Los Angeles Times* (May 22, 2007). https://www.latimes.com/archives/la-xpm-2007-may-22-et-moore22-story.html.

14. Courtney Davison, "What Does 'Forks Over Knives' Mean, Anyway?" *Forks Over Knives* website (May 3, 2019). https://www.forksoverknives.com/wellness/what-does-forks-over-knives-mean/.

15. Richard Powers, *The Overstory: A Novel* (New York: W. W. Norton & Company, Kindle Edition, 2018), 336.

Chapter Three

1. Shaunak Sen, "For Director Shaunak Sen, Documentary Filmmaking is Like 'a Fever Dream,'" *The Business with Kim Masters*, Podcast (February 24, 2023), audio, 20:45. https://podcasts.apple.com/us/podcast/the-business/id73330606?i=1000601368279.

2. Errol Morris, "Play It Again, Sam (Re-enactments, Part One)," *New York Times* (April 3, 2008). https://archive.nytimes.com/opinionator.blogs.nytimes.com/2008/04/03/play-it-again-sam-re-enactments-part-one/.

3. Ibid.

Chapter Four

1. Bilge Ebiri, "Errol Morris on His Early Films, and What He Thinks of The Jinx," *Vulture* (March 27, 2015). https://www.vulture.com/2015/03/errol-morris-the-jinx-thin-blue-line.html.

Chapter Five

1. Sam Pollard, "Sam Pollard on making The League, AMPTP reopens negotiations," *The Business with Kim Masters*, Podcast (August 4, 2023), audio, 0:17. https://

podcasts.apple.com/us/podcast/sam-pollard-on-making-the-league-amptp-reopens/id73330606?i=1000623432100https://podcasts.apple.com/us/podcast/why-is-this-happening-with-chris-hayes/id1382983397?i=1000542806378.

Chapter Six

1. Lyndon Johnson, as quoted by US Army advisor James Willbanks, *The Vietnam War*, Episode Three: "The River Styx (January 1964-December 1965)," (September 19, 2017), video. https://www.pbs.org/kenburns/the-vietnam-war/episode-3.

Chapter Seven

1. Alex Gibney, "The Art of Filmmaking with Alex Gibney," *Why Is This Happening? The Chris Hayes Podcast* (November 23, 2021), audio, 20:25. https://podcasts.apple.com/us/podcast/why-is-this-happening-with-chris-hayes/id1382983397?i=1000542806378.

2. Janet Malcolm, "The Journalist and the Murderer," *The New Yorker*, March 13, 1989. https://www.newyorker.com/magazine/1989/03/13/the-journalist-and-the-murderer-i.

Chapter Eight

1. U.S. Copyright Office, Registration, Literary Works. https://www.copyright.gov/registration/literary-works/.

2. U.S. Copyright Office, Registration, Form TX. https://www.copyright.gov/forms/formtx.pdf.

3. U.S. Copyright Office, Registration, Performing Arts. https://www.copyright.gov/registration/performing-arts/.

4. U.S. Copyright Office, Registration, Form PA. https://www.copyright.gov/forms/formpa.pdf.

5. Oceanic Preservation Society website, "Since The Cove's Release in 2009." https://www.opsociety.org/our-work/films/the-cove/.

6. Carmine Gallo, "150 Years Before Twitter, Abe Lincoln Discovered How to Avoid Getting Angry on Social Media, Historian Doris Kearns Goodwin Explains Abraham Lincoln's Strategy to Keep His Cool," *Inc.* (November 6, 2018). https://www.inc.com/carmine-gallo/its-easy-to-fire-off-an-angry-tweet-or-email-take-abraham-lincolns-brilliant-advice-instead.html.

7. Maria Konnikova, "The Lost Art of the Unsent Angry Letter," *New York Times* (March 22, 2014). https://www.nytimes.com/2014/03/23/opinion/sunday/the-lost-art-of-the-unsent-angry-letter.html.

Chapter Nine

1. Box Office Mojo, by IMDbPro. https://www.boxofficemojo.com/title/tt0120915/?ref_=bo_se_r_5.

2. Box Office Mojo, by IMDbPro. https://www.boxofficemojo.com/title/tt0120370/?ref_=bo_se_r_1.

3. Keith Ochwat, "Master Fundraising & Distribution," *Show&Tell* website. https://www.showandtell.film/.

4. Roger Nygard, "On the Trekkie Trail," *Los Angeles Times* (June 20, 1999). https://www.latimes.com/archives/la-xpm-1999-jun-20-tm-48414-story.html.

5. Roger Nygard, "Conceptual Reality: It Doesn't Take Vulcan Logic to Fund Concept-Based Documentaries," *Documentary* (June 01, 2010). https://www.documentary.org/feature/conceptual-reality-it-doesnt-take-vulcan-logic-fund-concept-based-documentaries.

Bibliography

Aristotle. *Poetics*. 330 BCE.

Blow, Charles M. *The Devil You Know: A Black Power Manifesto*. New York: Harper, 2021.

Boyle, Greg. *Tattoos of the Heart: The Power of Boundless Compassion*. New York: Free Press, 2010.

Dawkins, Richard. *The Selfish Gene*. New York: Oxford University Press, 1976.

Diamond, Jared. *Guns, Germs and Steel*. New York: W. W. Norton & Company, 1997.

Ellsworth, Liz. *Frederick Wiseman: A Guide to References and Resources*. Boston: G. K. Hall & Co. 1979.

Fox, Michael J. *No Time Like the Future: An Optimist Considers Mortality*. New York: Flatiron Book, 2020.

Griffith, Richard. *The World of Robert Flaherty*. London: Victor Gollancz Ltd. 1953.

Heisenberg, Werner. *Physics and Philosophy: The Revolution in Modern Science*. London: Prometheus Books. 1958.

Nichols, Bill. *Introduction to Documentary*. Indianapolis, IN: Indiana University Press, 2001.

Norris, Frank. *The Octopus: A Story of California*. New York: Doubleday, Page, 1901.

Nygard, Roger. *Cut to the Monkey: A Hollywood Editor's Behind-the-Scenes Secrets to Making Hit Comedies*. Wayne, NJ: Applause Books, 2021.

Powers, Richard. *The Overstory: A Novel*. New York: W. W. Norton & Company, Kindle Edition, 2018.

Sinclair, Upton. *The Jungle*. New York: Doubleday, Page, 1906.

Sweeney, Julia. *God Said, 'Ha!': A Memoir*. New York: Bantam, 1997.

Filmography

4 Little Girls. 1997. USA. Spike Lee, director. Spike Lee, Sam Pollard, producers. HBO.

11th Hour, The. 2007. USA. Nadia Conners, Leila Conners Petersen, directors. Nadia Conners, Leila Conners Petersen, Leonardo DiCaprio, writers. Leila Conners, Leonardo DiCaprio, Petersen, Chuck Castleberry, Brian Gerber, producers. Warner Independent Pictures.

30 Bikes: The Story of Homestead Bicycles. 2020. USA. Brian Flint, Kevin Flint, directors. Brian Flint, Alden Olmsted, writers. Alden Olmsted, producer. Twinvision Entertainment, Drive Fast, Take Chances Productions.

30 for 30. 2009–2010; 2012–TBD. USA. Bill Simmons, Connor Schell, creators. ESPN.

Air Force One. 1997. USA. Wolfgang Petersen, director. Andrew W. Marlowe, writer. Gail Katz, Jonathan Shestack, Wolfgang Petersen, Armyan Bernstein, producers. Columbia Pictures.

All That Breathes. 2022. India, UK, USA. Shaunak Sen, director, writer. Shaunak Sen, Aman Mann, Teddy Leifer, producers. HBO Documentary Films.

American Buffalo, The. 2023. USA. Ken Burns, director. Dayton Duncan, writer. Julie Dunfey, Ken Burns, producers. Florentine Films.

American Family, An. 1973. USA. Craig Gilbert, director. Curtis W. Davis, Craig Gilbert, producers. PBS.

American Idol. 2002–TBD. USA. Simon Fuller, creator. ABC, FOX.

American Justice. 1992–2022. USA. Towers Productions, creator. Sharon Scott, Laura Fleury, Tiff Winton, producers. Towers Production, A&E.

American Revolution, The. 2025. USA. Ken Burns, director. Geoffrey C. Ward, writer. Sarah Botstein, David Schmidt, Salimah El-Amin, Ken Burns, producers. Florentine Films, PBS.

Anita: Speaking Truth to Power. 2013. USA. Freida Mock, director, writer, producer. Samuel Goldwyn Films.

Apartment, The. 1960. USA. Billy Wilder, director, producer. Billy Wilder, I. A. L. Diamond, writers. United Artists.

Armageddon. 1998. USA. Michael Bay, director. Jonathan Hensleigh, J. J. Abrams, writers. Jerry Bruckheimer, Gale Anne Hurd, Michael Bay, producers. Buena Vista Pictures.

Ascension. 2021. USA. Jessica Kingdon, director, writer. Jessica Kingdon, Kira Simon-Kennedy, Nathan Truesdell, producers. MTV Documentary Films.

At Berkeley. 2013. USA. Frederick Wiseman, director, writer, producer. Zipporah Films.

Babylon 5. 1993–1998. USA. J. Michael Straczynski, creator. Douglas Netter, J. Michael Straczynski, producers. Syndicated, PTEN, TNT.

Babysitters Club, The. 1995. USA. Melanie Mayron, director. Dalene Young, writer. Peter O. Almond, Jane Startz, producers. Columbia Pictures, Sony Pictures Releasing.

Bachelorette, The. 2003–TBD. USA. Mike Fleiss, creator. ABC.

Baseball. 1994–2010. USA. Ken Burns, Lynn Novick, directors. Ken Burns, Lynn Novick, Karen Kenton, David McMahon, producers. Florentine Films, PBS.

Beatles: Get Back, The. 2021. UK, New Zealand, USA. Peter Jackson, director, producer. Disney+.

Benjamin Franklin. 2022. USA. Ken Burns, director. Dayton Duncan, writer. Ken Burns, David Schmidt, producers. Florentine Films, PBS.

Best Years of Our Lives, The. 1946. USA. William Wyler, director. Robert E. Sherwood, writer. Samuel Goldwyn, producer. Samuel Goldwyn Productions, RKO Radio Pictures.

Big One, The. 1997. USA. Michael Moore, director, writer. Kathleen Glynn, producer. BBC Productions, Miramax.

Blues Accordin' to Lightnin' Hopkins, The. 1970. USA. Les Blank, director, writer, producer. Flower Films, Les Blank Films.

Bob Dylan: Don't Look Back. 1967. USA. D. A. Pennebaker, director, writer. John Court, Albert Grossman, producers. Leacock-Pennebaker, Inc.

Bobby Fischer Against the World. 2011. USA. Liz Garbus, director, writer. Nancy Abraham, Stanley F. Buchthal, producers. HBO.

Borat. 2006. USA, UK. Larry Charles, director. Sacha Baron Cohen, Anthony Hines, Peter Baynham, Dan Mazer, writers. Sacha Baron Cohen, Jay Roach, producers. 20th Century Fox.

Bowling for Columbine. 2002. USA. Michael Moore, director, writer. Michael Moore, Kathleen Glynn, Jim Czarnecki, Charles Bishop, Kurt Engfehr, producers. United Artists, Alliance Atlantis.

Brief History of Time, A. 1991. USA, UK, Japan. Errol Morris, director. Stephen Hawking, writer. David Hickman, producer. Amblin Entertainment, Triton Pictures.

Britney vs Spears. 2021. USA. Erin Lee Carr, director. Sloane Klevin, writer. Erin Lee Carr, Kate Barry, Sarah Gibson, producers. Story Syndicate, Netflix.

Brooklyn Bridge. 1981. USA. Ken Burns, director. Amy Stechler, writer. Ken Burns, Roger Sherman, Buddy Squires, Amy Stechler, producers. Florentine Films, PBS.

Brother's Keeper. 1992. USA. Joe Berlinger, Bruce Sinofsky, directors, writers, producers. Creative Thinking International Ltd.

Central Park Five, The. 2012. USA. Ken Burns, Sarah Burns, David McMahon, directors, writers, producers. Florentine Films, PBS.

Charm Circle. 2021. USA. Nira Burstein, director, writer. Nira Burstein, Betsy Laikin, producers. Vacancy Arts, Gigantic Pictures.

Chasing Coral. 2017. USA. Jeff Orlowsky, director. Jeff Orlowsky, Davis Coombe, Vickie Curtis, writers. Jeff Orlowsky, Larissa Rhodes, producers. Netflix.

Chasing Ice. 2012. USA. Jeff Orlowski, director. Mark Monroe, writer. Paula DuPré Pesmen, Jerry Aronson, producers. Submarine Deluxe.

Cheer. 2020–2022. USA. Greg Whiteley, Chelsea Yarnell, Arielle Kilker, directors. Arielle Kilker, Greg Whiteley, producers. Boardwalk Pictures, Netflix.

Cheers. 1982–1993. USA. Glen and Les Charles, James Burrow, creators. NBC.

Citizen Kane. 1941. USA. Orson Welles, director. Orson Welles, Herman J. Mankiewicz, writers. Orson Welles, producer. RKO Pictures, Mercury Productions, Paramount Pictures.

Civil War, The. 1990. USA. Ken Burns, director. Ric Burns, Jim Corbley, Christopher Darling, Justin Rhodes, Daniel J. White, producers. Florentine Films, PBS.

Colors Straight Up. 1997. USA. Michèle Ohayon, director, writer. Michèle Ohayon, Julia Schachter, producers. Filmakers Library.

Comedy Store, The. 2020. USA. Jonathan Vogler, producer. Mike Binder, director. Mandalay Sports Media, Showtime.

Commitments, The. 1991. Ireland, UK, USA. Alan Parker, director. Dick Clement, Ian La Frenais, Roddy Doyle, writers. Roger Randall-Cuttler, Lynda Myles, producers. 20th Century Fox, Sovereign Pictures.

Conan the Barbarian. 1982. USA. John Milius, director. John Milius, Oliver Stone, writers. Buzz Feitshans, Rafaella De Laurentiis, producers. Universal Pictures, 20th Century Fox.

Cops. 1989–TBD. USA. John Langley, Malcolm Barbour, creators. Fox.

Country Music. 2019. USA. Ken Burns, director. Ken Burns, Dayton Duncan, Julie Dunfey, producers. Florentine Films, PBS.

Cove, The. 2009. USA. Louie Psihoyos, director. Mark Monroe, writer. Paula DuPré Pesmen, Fisher Stevens, producers. Roadside Attractions, Lionsgate.

Cowspiracy: The Sustainability Secret. 2014. USA. Kip Andersen, Keegan Kuhn, directors, writers, producers. Netflix.

Crumb. 1995. USA. Terry Zwigoff, director. Terry Zwigoff, Lynn O'Donnell, producers. Sony Pictures Classics.

Da Ali G Show. 2000–2004. UK. Sacha Baron Cohen, creator. James Bobin, Dan Mazer, Steve Smith, directors. Peter Fincham, Dan Mazer, Sacha Baron Cohen, producers. Channel 4. HBO.

David Holzman's Diary. 1967. USA. James McBride, director, writer. Michael Wadleigh, producer. New Yorker Films.

Deep Impact. 1998. USA. Mimi Leder, director. Bruce Joel Rubin, Michael Tolkin, writers. David Brown, Richard D. Zanuck, producers. Paramount Pictures, DreamWorks Pictures.

Detour. 1945. USA. Edgar G. Ulmer, director. Martin Goldsmith, writer. Leon Fromkess, producer. PRC Pictures.

D.O.A. 1981. USA. Lech Kowalski, director. Lech Kowalski, Chris Salewicz, writers. Lech Kowalski, producer. Lightning Video.

Documentary Now! 2015–TBD. USA. Fred Armisen, Bill Hader, Seth Meyers, Rhys Thomas, creators. IFC.

Don't Get Me Started: The Billy Crystal Special. 1986. USA. Billy Crystal, Paul Flaherty, directors. Dick Blasucci, Billy Crystal, Paul Flaherty, writers. Billy Crystal, producer. HBO.

East of Eden. 1955. USA. Elia Kazan, director. Paul Osborn, writer. Elia Kazan, producer. Warner Bros.

Encounters at the End of the World. 2007. USA. Werner Herzog, director, writer. Henry Kaiser, Erik Nelson, Phil Fairclough, Dave Harding, Julian Hobbs, Andrea Meditch, producers. Discovery Films.

Endless Summer, The. 1966. USA. Bruce Brown, director, writer, producer. Cinema V.

Estonia Dreams of Eurovision! 2002. UK. Marina Zenovich, director, writer. Vikram Jayanti, Celia Quartermain, producers. VIXPIX Films, The Criterion Channel.

Exit Through the Gift Shop. 2010. UK. Banksy, director. Joachim Levy, writer. Jaimie D'Cruz, producer. Revolver Entertainment.

Expelled: No Intelligence Allowed. 2008. USA. Nathan Frankowski, director. Kevin Miller, Ben Stein, Walt Ruloff, writers. Logan Craft, Walt Ruloff, John Sullivan, producers. Premise Media Corporation, Rocky Mountain Pictures.

Faces of Death. 1978. USA. John Alan Schwartz, director, writer. William B. James, Herbie Lee, Rosilyn T. Scott, producers. F.O.D. Productions, Aquarius Releasing.

Fahrenheit 9/11. 2004. USA. Michael Moore, director, writer. Michael Moore, Kathleen Glynn, Jim Czarnecki, producers. Fellowship Adventure Group.

Fakin' Da Funk. 1997. USA. Timothy A. Chey, director, writer. Timothy A. Chey, Harry K. Yoo, producers. Octillion Entertainment, USA Network.

Farm: Angola, USA, The. 1998. USA. Liz Garbus, Wilbert Rideau, Jonathan Stack, directors. Bob Harris, writer. Liz Garbus, Jonathan Stack, producers. Seventh Art Releasing.

Farmer's Wife, The. 1998. USA. David Sutherland, creator, director. James Yee, David Sutherland, producers. PBS.

Fast, Cheap & Out of Control. 1997. USA. Errol Morris, director, writer, producer. Sony Pictures Classic.

Fire of Love. 2022. USA, Canada. Sara Dosa, director. Sara Dosa, Shane Boris, Erin Casper, Jocelyne Chaput, writers. Sara Dosa, Shane Boris, Ina Fichman, producers. National Geographic Documentary Films.

Fire Within: A Requiem for Katia and Maurice Krafft, The. 2022. UK, Switzerland, USA, France. Werner Herzog, director, writer. Julien Dumont, Mandy Leith, Peter Lown, Cedric Magnin, Alexandre Soullier, producers. Bonne Pioche, Brian Leith Productions, Titan Films.

First Year, The. 2001. USA. Davis Guggenheim, director. Davis Guggenheim, Julia Schachter, producers. PBS.

Fog of War: Eleven Lessons from the Life of Robert S. McNamara, The. 2003. USA. Errol Morris, director, writer. Errol Morris, Michael Williams, Julie Ahlberg, producers. Sony Pictures Classics.

Food, Inc. 2008. USA. Robert Kenner, director. Robert Kenner, Elise Pearlstein, Kim Roberts, writers. Robert Kenner, Elise Pearlstein, producers. Magnolia Pictures.

Forrest Gump. 1994. USA. Robert Zemeckis, director. Eric Roth, writer. Wendy Finerman, Steve Tisch, Steve Starkey, producers. Paramount Pictures.

Freakonomics. 2010. USA. Eugene Jarecki, Heidi Ewing, Rachel Grady, Morgan Spurlock, Alex Gibney, Seth Gordon, directors, writers. Peter Bull, Jeremy Chilnick, writers. Chad Troutwine, Chris Romano, Dan O'Meara, Craig Atkinson, producers. Chad Troutwine Films, Magnolia Pictures.

Free Solo. 2018. USA. Elizabeth Chai Vasarhelyi, Jimmy Chin, directors. Jimmy Chin, writer. Elizabeth Chai Vasarhelyi, Jimmy Chin, Shannon Dill, Evan Hayes, producers. National Geographic Documentary Films.

Frontline. 1983–TBD. USA. David Fanning, creator. PBS.

Galaxy Quest. 1999. USA. Dean Parisot, director. David Howard, Robert Gordon, writers. Mark Johnson, Charles Newirth, producers. DreamWorks Pictures.

Gates of Heaven. 1978. USA. Errol Morris, director, writer, producer. Errol Morris Films, New Yorkers Film.

G-Dog. 2012. USA. Freida Lee Mock, director, writer, producer. American Film Foundation.

Ghosts of Abu Ghraib. 2007. USA. Rory Kennedy, director. Jack Youngelson, writer. Rory Kennedy, Liz Garbus, Jack Youngelson, producers. HBO.

Gleaners and I, The. 2000. France. Agnès Varda, director, writer, producer. Cinè-tamaris.

God Said, 'Ha!' 1998. USA. Julia Sweeney, director, writer. Quentin Tarantino, producer. Miramax.

Good Night Oppy. 2022. USA. Ryan White, director. Helen Kearns, Ryan White, writers. Brandon Carroll, Justin Falvey, Darryl Frank, Matt Goldberg, Jessica Hargrave, Ryan White, producers. Amazon Studios.

Grace Jones: Bloodlight and Bami. 2017. UK,, Ireland. Sophie Fiennes, director, writer. Sophie Fiennes, Shani Hinton, Katie Holly, Beverly Jones, producers. Blinder Films, Kino Lorber.

Great Buster, The. 2018. USA. Peter Bogdanovic, director, writer. Peter Bogdanovic, Charles S. Cohen, Roee Sharon, Louise Stratten, producers. Cohen Media Group.

Grey Gardens. 1975. USA. David Maysles, Albert Maysles, directors, writers, producers. Portrait Films.

Grizzly Man. 2005. USA. Werner Herzog, director, writer. Kevin Beggs, Phil Fairclough, Andrea Meditch, Erik Nelson, Jewel Palovak, producers. Lions Gate Films.

Hank Aaron: Chasing the Dream. 1995. USA. Michael Tollin, director, writer. Fredric Golding, producer. Turner Pictures, TBS.

Harry & Meghan. 2022. USA. Liz Garbus, director. Ashley B. Carey, Mike Langer, Neha Shastry, Elyssa Hess, Giona Jefferson, producers. Netflix.

Hemingway. 2021. USA. Ken Burns, Lynn Novick, directors, writers, producers. Florentine Films, PBS.

He Named Me Malala. 2015. USA, UAE. Davis Guggenheim, director, writer. Walter Parkes, Laurie MacDonald, Davis Guggenheim, producers. Searchlight Pictures, National Geographic Channel.

High School. 1968. USA. Frederick Wiseman, director, writer, producer. Zipporah Films.

High Strung. 1991. USA. Roger Nygard, director. Robert Kuhn, Steve Oedekerk, writers. Rubin M. Mendoza, Roger Nygard, producers. Film Brigade Productions.

Hoop Dreams. 1994. USA. Steve James, director. Frederick Marx, Steve James, writers. Frederick Marx, Steve James, Peter Gilbert, producers. Fine Line Features.

Hospital. 1970. USA. Frederick Wiseman, director, writer, producer. Zipporah Films.

Hubble. 2010. USA. Tony Myers, director, producer. Tony Myers, Frank Summers, Graeme Ferguson, writers. Tony Myers, Graeme Ferguson, producers. Warner Bros, IMAX.

Huey Long. 1986. USA. Ken Burns, director. Geoffrey C. Ward, writer. Ken Burns, Richard Kilberg, producers. Florentine Films, PBS.

Ice on Fire. 2019. USA. Leila Conners, director. Leonardo DiCaprio, Mathew Schmid, producers. HBO.

Ice Storm, The. 1997. USA. Ang Lee, director. James Schamus, writer. Ang Lee, James Schamus, Ted Hope, producers. Searchlight Pictures, 20th Century Fox.

I Didn't See You There. 2022. USA. Reid Davenport, director. Keith Wilson, producer. Cinetic Media.

Inconvenient Truth, An. 2006. USA. Davis Guggenheim, director. Al Gore, writer. Laurie David, Lawrence Bender, Scott Z. Burns, producers. Paramount Classics.

Independent's Day. 1998. USA. Marina Zenovich, director, writer, producer. SundanceTV, Criterion Channel.

In the Company of Men. 1997. Canada, USA. Neil LaBute, director, writer. Mark Archer, Stephen Pevner, producers. Sony Pictures Classics.

In the Soup. 1992. USA. Alexandre Rockwell, director. Tim Kissell, Alexandre Rockwell, writers. Jim Stark, Hank Blumenthal, Chosei Funahara, producers. Triton Pictures, Fantoma, Factory 25.

Inventor: Out for Blood in Silicon Valley, The. 2019. USA. Alex Gibney, director, writer. Nick Bilton, Jessie Deeter, Erin Edeiken, Alex Gibney, producers. HBO.

It Might Get Loud. 2008. USA. Davis Guggenheim, director, writer. Thomas Tull, Davis Guggenheim, Lesley Chilcott, Peter Afterman, producers. Sony Pictures Classics.

It's a Mad, Mad, Mad, Mad World. 1963. USA. Stanley Kramer, director. William Rose, Tania Rose, writers. Stanley Kramer, producer. United Artists.

Jackass: The Movie. 2002. USA. Jeff Tremaine, director. Jeff Tremaine, Johnny Knoxville, Steve-O, Bam Margera, Jason Acuña, Chris Pontius, Spike Jonze, Dave England, Ehren McGhehey, Preston Lacy, Brandon DiCamillo, Dimitry Elyashkevich, Sean Cliver, Loomis Fall, Vernon Chatman, writers. Jeff Tremaine, Spike Jonze, Johnny Knoxville, producers. Paramount Pictures, MTV Films.

Jackie Brown. 1997. USA. Quentin Tarantino, director, writer. Lawrence Bender, producer. Miramax.

Jazz. 2001. USA. Ken Burns, director. Geoffrey Ward, writer. Ken Burns, Lynn Novick, producers. Florentine Films, PBS, BBC.

Jerry Brown: The Disrupter. 2022. USA. Marina Zenovich, director. Marina Zenovich, P.G. Morgan, Paula Michalchyshyn, producers.

Jesus Camp. 2006. USA. Heidi Ewing, Rachel Grady, directors, writer, producers. Magnolia Pictures.

Jinx: The Life and Deaths of Robert Durst, The. 2015. USA. Andrew Jarecki, director. Andrew Jarecki, Marc Smerling, producers. HBO.

Johnstown Flood, The. 1989. USA. Charles Guggenheim, director, writer, producer. Guggenheim Production.

Juice. 1992. USA. Ernest R. Dickerson, director. Gerard Brown, Ernest R. Dickerson, writers. David Heyman, Neal H. Moritz, Peter Frankfurt, producers. Paramount Pictures.

Kareem: Minority of One. 2015. USA. Aaron Cohen, director, writer. Clare Lewins, Deborah Morales, Jon Weinbach, Bentley Weiner, Ron Yasser, producers. HBO.

Kentucky Fried Movie, The. 1977. USA. John Landis, director. Jim Abrahams, David Zucker, Jerry Zucker, writers. Robert K. Weiss, producer. United Film Distribution Company.

Kid Stays in the Picture, The. 2002. USA. Nanette Burstein, Brett Morgen, directors. Brett Morgen, writer. Nanette Burstein, Graydon Carter, Brett Morgen, Christine Peters, producers. USA Films. Focus Features.

King of Kong: A Fistful of Quarters, The. 2007. USA. Seth Gordon, director, writer. Ed Cunningham, producer. Picturehouse.

Koyaanisqatsi. 1982. USA. Godfrey Reggio, director. Ron Fricke, Michael Hoenig, Godfrey Reggio, Alton Walpole, writers. Godfrey Reggio, producer. Island Alive, New Cinema.

Lance. 2020. USA. Marina Zenovich, director. Marina Zenovich, P.G. Morgan, producers. Disney+, ESPN Films.

Lassie. 1994. USA. Daniel Petrie, director. Matthew Jacobs, Gary Ross, Elizabeth Anderson, writers. Lorne Michaels, producer. Paramount Pictures.

Last Chance U. 2016–2020. USA. Greg Whiteley, creator. Netflix.

Last Dance, The. 2020. USA. Jason Hehir, director. ESPN, Netflix.

Last Waltz, The. 1978. USA. Martin Scorsese, director. Mardik Martin, writer. Robbie Robertson, producer. United Artists.

Lawrence of Arabia. 1962. UK. David Lean, director. Robert Bolt, Michael Wilson, writers. Sam Spiegel, producer. Columbia Pictures.

League, The. 2023. USA. Sam Pollard, director. Bob Motley, Byron Motley, writers. Robin Espinola, Nickson Fong, Jen Isaacson, Dave Sirulnick, producers. Magnolia Pictures.

Lemmy. 2010. USA, UK. Greg Olliver, Wes Orshoski, directors, writers, producers. Damage Case Films & Distribution, VMI Worldwide.

Liar Liar. 1997. USA. Tom Shadyac, director. Paul Guay, Stephen Mazur, writers. Brian Grazer, producer. Universal Pictures.

Life in a Day. 2011. UK, USA. Kevin Macdonald, Loressa Clisby, Tegan Bukowski, directors. Liza Marshall, producer. National Geographic Films.

Little Dieter Needs to Fly. 1997. Germany, UK, France. Werner Herzog, director, writer. Lucki Stipetić, producer. Werner Herzog Filmproduktion, Anchor Bay Entertainment.

Louis Theroux's Weird Weekends. 1998–2000. UK. Louis Theroux, creator. IFC.

Lowndes County and The Road to Black Power. 2022. USA. Geeta Gandbhir, Sam Pollard, directors. Vann R. Newkirk II, Dema Paxton Fofang, writers. Jessica Devaney, Dema Paxton Fofang, Anya Rous, producers. Greenwich Entertainment.

Making a Murderer. 2015–2018. USA. Laura Ricciardi, Moira Demos, directors. Julie Ahlberg, Producer. Netflix.

Man on Wire. 2008. UK, USA. James Marsh, director. Philippe Petit, writer. Simon Chinn, producer. Discovery Films, Magnolia Pictures.

Man With a Movie Camera. 1929. Soviet Union. Dziga Vertov, director, writer. VUFKU, Amkino Corporation.

Marcel the Shell with Shoes On. 2021. USA. Dean Fleischer Camp, director. Dean Fleischer Camp, Jenny Slate, Nick Paley, screenplay. Elisabeth Holm, Andrew Goldman, Caroline Kaplan, Paul Mezey, Dean Fleischer Camp, Jenny Slate, Terry Leonard, producers. Cinereach, A24.

March of the Penguins. 2005. France. Luc Jacquet, director. Luc Jacquet, Jordan Roberts, writers. Yves Darondeau, Christophe Lioud, Immanuel Priou, producers. National Geographic Films.

Maya Lin: A Strong Clear Vision. 1994. USA. Freida Lee Mock director, writer. Freida Lee Mock, Terry Sanders, producers. Asian Crush, Digital Media Rights.

Maynard. 2017. USA. Sam Pollard, director. Wendy Eley Jackson, Sam Pollard, writers. Autumn Bailey, Karl Carter, Donald Jarmond, Jason Orr, Winsome Sinclair, Dolly R. Turner, producers. PBS.

Metamorphosis: Man Into Woman. 1990. USA. Lisa Leeman, director, writer. Claudia Hoover, producer. PBS.

Michael Jackson's This Is It. 2009. USA. Kenny Ortega, director. Kenny Ortega, Michael Jackson, writers. Randy Phillips, Kenny Ortega, Paul Gongaware, producers. Columbia Pictures, Sony Pictures Entertainment.

Microcosmos. 1996. France, Switzerland, Italy, United Kingdom. Claude Nuridsany, Marie Pérennou, directors, writers. Christophe Barratier, Yvette Mallet, Jacques Perrin, producers. BAC Films, Miramax.

MLK/FBI. 2020. USA. Sam Pollard, director. Benjamin Hedin, Laura Tomaselli, writers. Benjamin Hedin, producer. IFC Films.

Mo' Better Blues. 1990. USA. Spike Lee, director, writer, producer. Universal Pictures.

Model. 1981. USA. Frederick Wiseman, director, writer, producer. Zipporah Films, PBS.

Mondo Elvis. 1984. USA. Tom Corboy, director, writer, producer. Facets Multimedia Distribution.

Moon Over Broadway. 1997. USA. Chris Hegedus, D. A. Pennebaker, directors. Wendy Ettinger, Frazer Pennebaker, producers. Bravo Cable, Pennebaker Hegedus Films, Artistic License.

Mr. Smith Goes to Washington. 1939. USA. Frank Capra, director. Sidney Buchman, Lewis S. Foster, writers. Frank Capra, producer. Columbia Pictures.

My Sister Liv. 2022. USA, Australia. Alan Hicks, director. Alan Hicks, Paula DuPré Pesmen, Andrew McAllister, Jordan Swioklo, writers. Paula DuPré Pesmen, Camilla Mazzaferro, producers. Submarine Entertainment.

Nanook of the North. 1922. USA. Robert J. Flaherty, director, writer, producer. Pathé Exchange, United Artists.

Nature of Existence, The. 2010. USA. Roger Nygard, director. Roger Nygard, Paul Tarantino, producers. Blink, Inc.

Navalny. 2022. USA. Daniel Roher, director. Diane Becker, Shane Boris, Melanie Miller, Odessa Rae, producers. CNN Films, HBO Max.

Nine from Little Rock. 1964. USA. Charles Guggenheim, director. Charles Guggenheim, Shelby Storck, writers. Shelby Storck, producer. Guggenheim Production.

Nobody's Business. 1996. USA. Alan Berliner, director, writer, producer. ITVS International, Milestone Film & Video.

Off the Menu: The Last Days of Chasen's. 1997. USA. Shari Springer Berman, Robert Pulcini, directors. Julia Strohm, producer. Northern Arts Entertainment.

Olympia Part One: Festival of the Nations. 1938. Germany. Leni Riefenstahl, director, writer, producer. Olympia Film GmbH, Excelsior Pictures Corp.

One of Us. 2017. USA. Heidi Ewing, Rachel Grady, directors, writers, producers. Loki Films, Netflix.

Osbournes, The. 2002–2005. USA. Greg Johnston, Jeff Stilson, Sharon Osbourne, Lois Curren, producers. MTV.

Out of the Past. 1947. USA. Jacques Tourneur, director. Daniel Mainwaring, James M. Cain, Frank Fenton, writers. Warren Duff, producer. RKO Radio Pictures.

Overnight. 2003. USA. Tony Montana, Mark Brian Smith, directors, writers, producers. Ronnoco Productions, Cinetic Media.

Paradise Lost: The Child Murders at Robin Hood Hills. 1996. USA. Joe Berlinger, Bruce Sinofsky, directors, writers, producers. Creative Thinking International Ltd., HBO.

Pelé. 2021. UK. Ben Nicholas, David Tryhorn, directors, writers, producers. Netflix.

Planet Earth. 2006. UK. Alastair Fothergill, creator. Alastair Fothergill, Mark Linfield, directors. Discovery Channel.

Prophecy II, The. 1998. USA. Greg Spence, director. Gregory Widen, Matt Greenberg, Greg Spence, writers. Joel Soisson, W.K. Border, producers. Dimension Films.

Racetrack. 1985. USA. Frederick Wiseman, director, writer, producer. Zipporah Films.

Rashomon. 1950. Japan. Akira Kurosawa, director. Akira Kurosawa, Shinobu Hashimoto, writers. Minoru Jingo, producer. Daiei Film, RKO Radio Pictures.

Real World, The. 1992–2019. USA. Mary-Ellis Bunim, Jonathan Murray, creators. MTV.

Return with Honor. 1999. USA. Freida Lee Mock, Terry Sanders, directors. Freida Lee Mock, Terry Sanders, Christine Z. Wiser, writers, producers. American Film Foundation, Sanders & Mock Productions.

Road to Wellville, The. 1994. USA. Alan Parker, director, writer. Alan Parker, Armyan Bernstein, Robert F. Colesberry, producers. Columbia Pictures.

Robe, The. 1953. USA. Henry Koster, director. Gina Kaus, Albert Maltz, Philip Dunne, writers. Frank Ross, producer. 20th Century Fox.

Robert Kennedy Remembered. 1968. USA. Charles Guggenheim, director. Charles Guggenheim, L. T. Iglehart, writers. Charles Guggenheim, producer. Guggenheim Productions.

Robin Williams: Come Inside My Mind. 2018. USA. Marina Zenovich, director, writer. Alex Gibney, Shirel Kozak, Nancy Abraham, producers. HBO Documentary Films.

Roger and Me. 1989. USA. Michael Moore, director, writer, producer. Warner Bros.

Roman Polanski: Odd Man Out. 2012. USA. Marina Zenovich, director. P.G. Morgan, Chris A. Peterson, Marina Zenovich, writers. Lila Yacoub, Marina Zenovich, producers. HBO.

Roman Polanski: Wanted and Desired. 2008. USA, UK. Marina Zenovich, director. Joe Bini, P.G. Morgan, Marina Zenovich, writers. Marina Zenovich, Jeffrey Levy-Hinte, Lila Yacoub, producers. Submarine Entertainment, HBO.

Roosevelts: An Intimate History, The. 2014. USA. Ken Burns, director. Ken Burns, Geoffrey C. Ward, writers. Paul Barnes, Pam Tubridy Baucom, Jim Corbley, Erik Ewers, Katie Wilson, producers. Florentine Films, PBS.

RUTH: Justice Ginsburg in Her Own Words. 2019. USA. Freida Lee Mock, director, producer. Freida Lee Mock, M. A. Gollan, writers. Sanders & Mock Productions, American Film Foundation, Kino Lorber.

Salesman. 1969. USA. Albert Maysles, David Maysles, Charlotte Zwerin, directors. Albert Maysles, David Maysles, writers, producers. Maysles Films.

Sammy Davis, Jr.: I've Gotta Be Me. 2017. USA. Sam Pollard, director. Laurence Maslon, writer. Sally Rosenthal, producer. PBS.

Searching for Sugar Man. 2012. Sweden, UK, Finland. Malik Bendjelloul, director, writer. Malik Bendjelloul, Simon Chinn, producers. Red Box Films, Sony Pictures Classics.

Shakers: Hands to Work, Hearts to God, The. 1984. USA. Ken Burns, Amy Stechler, directors, producers. Tom Lewis, Amy Stechler, Wendy Tilghman, writers. Florentine Films, PBS.

Shane. 1953. USA. George Stevens, director. A. B. Guthrie Jr., Jack Sher, writers. George Stevens, producer. Paramount Pictures.

Sherman's March. 1985. USA. Ross McElwee, director, writer, producer. First Run Features, PBS.

Sicko. 2007. USA. Michael Moore, director, writer. Michael Moore, Megan O'Hara, Susannah Price, producers. Lionsgate.

Six Days in Roswell. 1999. USA. Timothy B. Johnson, director. Roger Nygard, producer. Blink, Inc., Synapse Films.

Slavery By Another Name. 2012. USA. Sam Pollard, director. Sheila Curran Bernard, writer. Daphne McWilliams, producer. PBS.

Sling Blade. 1996. USA. Billy Bob Thornton, director, writer. Larry Meistrich, David L. Bushell, Brandon Rosser, producers. Miramax.

Social Dilemma, The. 2020. USA. Jeff Orlowski, director. Jeff Orlowski, Davis Coombe, Vickie Curtis, writers. Larissa Rhodes, producer. Exposure Labs, Netflix.

Some Kind of Heaven. 2021. USA. Lance Oppenheim, director, writer. Lance Oppenheim, Melissa Oppenheim, Darren Aronofsky, Jeffrey Soros, Simon Horsman, Kathleen Lingo, Pacho Velez, producers. Magnolia Pictures.

Spanish Prisoner, The. 1997. USA. David Mamet, director, writer. Jean Doumanian, producer. Sony Pictures Classics.

Sparkler. 1997. USA. Darren Stein, director. Darren Stein, Catherine Eads, writers. Jennifer Amerine, Kimberly Jacobs, producers. Dream Entertainment, Columbia TriStar Home Video.

Speed Cubers, The. 2020. USA. Sue Kim, director. Tanzir Islam Britto, writer. Sue Kim, Evan Krauss, Chris Romano, producers. Romano Films. Netflix.

"Squire of Gothos, The." 1967. USA. Gene Roddenberry, creator. Don McDougall, director. Gene Roddenberry, Gene L. Coon, producers. Desilu Productions, NBC.

Star Trek. 1966–1969. USA. Gene Roddenberry, creator. Gene Roddenberry, Gene L. Coon, John Meredyth Lucas, Fred Freiberger, producers. Desilu Productions, NBC.

Star Trek: The Next Generation. 1987–1994. USA. Gene Roddenberry, creator. Gene Roddenberry, Maurice Hurley, Rick Berman, Michael Piller, Jeri Taylor, producers. Paramount, Syndicated, CBS.

Star Wars: Episode I—The Phantom Menace. 1999. USA. George Lucas, director, writer. Rick McCallum, producer. Walt Disney Studios, 20th Century Fox.

Still: A Michael J. Fox Movie. USA. 2023. Davis Guggenheim, director. Davis Guggenheim, Annetta Marion, Jonathan King, Will Cohen, producers. Concordia Studio, Apple Original Films.

Streetwise. 1984. USA. Martin Bell, director. Cheryl McCall, writer, producer. Angelika Films.

Suckers. 2001. USA. Roger Nygard, director. Roger Nygard, Joe Yannetty, writers. W.K. Border, producer. HBO, Blink, Inc., Synapse Films.

Super Size Me. 2004. USA. Morgan Spurlock, director, writer, producer. Samuel Goldwyn Films, Roadside Attractions.

Survivor. 2000–TBD. USA. Charlie Parsons, creator. CBS.

There's Something Wrong with Aunt Diane. 2011. USA. Liz Garbus, director. Julie Gaither, Liz Garbus, producers. Moxie Firecracker Films, HBO.

Thin Blue Line, The. 1988. USA. Errol Morris, director, writer. Mark Lipson, producer. Miramax, PBS.

This Is Elvis. 1981. USA. Malcolm Leo, Andrew Solt, directors, writers, producers. Warner Bros.

Three Identical Strangers. 2018. USA, UK. Tim Wardle, director. Tim Wardle, Grace Hughes-Hallett, writers. Becky Read, Grace Hughes-Hallett, producers. Neon, CNN Films.

This is Spinal Tap. 1984. USA. Rob Reiner, director. Christopher Guest, Michael McKean, Harry Shearer, Rob Reiner, writers. Karen Murphy, producer. Embassy Pictures.

Time for Justice, A. 1994. USA. Charles Guggenheim, director, writer, producer. Guggenheim Productions.

Titicut Follies. 1967. USA. Frederick Wiseman, director, writer, producer. Zipporah Films.

Training Day. 2001. Antoine Fuqua, director. David Ayer, writer. Bobby Newmyer, Jeffrey Silver, producers. Warner Bros.

Treasure of the Sierra Madre, The. 1948. USA. John Huston, director, writer. Henry Blanke, producer. Warner Bros.

Trekkies. 1997. USA. Roger Nygard, director. W.K. Border, producer. Neo Art & Logic, Paramount Classics.

Trekkies 2. 2004. USA. Roger Nygard, director. Michael Leahy, producer. Neo Art & Logic, Paramount Pictures.

Truth About Marriage, The. 2020. USA. Roger Nygard, director, writer, producer. Blink, Inc., Gravitas Ventures.

Truth or Dare. 2018. USA. Jeff Wadlow, director. Michael Reisz, Jillian Jacobs, Christopher Roach, Jeff Wadlow, writers. Jason Blum, producer. Universal Pictures.

Up [series of documentaries]. 1964–2019. UK. Michael Apted, Paul Almond, directors. Claire Lewis, producer. ITV (Granada Television), BBC One.

Vernon, Florida. 1981. USA. Errol Morris, director, writer, producer. Now Yorker Films.

Vice. 2013–2021. USA. Shane Smith, creator. HBO, Showtime.

"Vice Sports: John and the Dons." 2016. USA. Jonathan Vogler, director. Michael Tollin, Mason Gordon, Jonathan Vogler, Catlin Callaway, producers. Mandalay Sports Media, Vice Media.

Vietnam War, The. 2017. USA. Ken Burns, Lynn Novick, directors. Sarah Botstein, Lynn Novick, Ken Burns, producers. Florentine Films, PBS, ARTE.

Waco: The Rules of Engagement. 1997. USA. William Gazecki, director. William Gazecki, Dan Gifford, Michael McNulty, Ron Nelson, writers. William Gazecki, Michael McNulty, producers. Myriad Pictures.

Waiting for Guffman. 1996. USA. Christopher Guest, director. Christopher Guest, Eugene Levy, writers. Karen Murphy, producer. Castle Rock Entertainment, Sony Pictures Classics.

Waiting for Superman. 2010. USA. Davis Guggenheim, director. Davis Guggenheim, Billy Kimball, writers. Michael Birtel, Lesley Chilcott, producers. Paramount Pictures.

War. 2007. USA. Philip G. Atwell, director. Lee Anthony Smith, Gregory J. Bradley, writers. Steve Chasman, Christopher Petzel, Jim Thompson, producers. Lionsgate.

War on Democracy, The. 2007. UK, Australia. Chris Martin, John Pilger, directors. John Pilger, writer. Chris Martin, Wayne Young, producers. Granada Productions.

War Room, The. 1993. USA, Canada. Chris Hegedus, D. A. Pennebaker, directors. R. J. Cutler, producer. Cyclone Films.

Way Down, The. 2021–2022. USA. Marina Zenovich, director. Cecilia Salguero, Ann Finnegan, Gina Scarlata, producers. HBO Max.

Weiner. 2016. USA. Josh Kriegman, Elyse Steinberg, directors. Josh Kriegman, Elyse Steinberg, Elie B. Despres, writers. Josh Kriegman, Elyse Steinberg, producers. Sundance Selects. Showtime.

Welfare. 1975. USA. Frederick Wiseman, director, writer, producer. Zipporah Films.

What Happened, Miss Simone? 2015. USA. Liz Garbus, director, writer. Liz Garbus, Amy Hobby, Justin Wilkes, Jayson Jackson, producers. Moxie Firecracker Films, RadicalMedia, Netflix.

What We Leave Behind. 2022. USA, Mexico. Iliana Sosa, director. Iliana Sosa, Isidore Bethel, writers. Emma D. Miller, Iliana Sosa, producers. Marcona Media.

When the Cat's Away. 1996. France. Cédric Klapisch, director, writer. Aïssa Djabri, Farid Lahouassa, Manuel Munz, producers. Sony Pictures Classics.

When We Were Kings. 1996. USA. Leon Gast, director, writer. Leon Gast, Taylor Hackford, producers. Gramercy Pictures.

Who is America? 2018. USA. Sacha Baron Cohen, creator. Tim Allsop, Melanie J. Elin, Nicholas Hatton, Daniel Gray Longino, Andrew Newman, Dan Swimer, producers. Showtime.

Who is Bernard Tapie? 2001. France, USA. Marina Zenovich, director. Marina Zenovich, Vikram Jayanti, Frédéric Forestier, producers. The Criterion Channel.

Why We Fight. 1942–1945. USA. Frank Capra, Anatole Litvak, directors. Julius J. Epstein, Philip G. Epstein, Anthony Veiller, writers. Frank Capra, producer. United States Office of War Information, War Activities Committee of the Motion Picture Industry.

Wild Wild Country. 2018. USA. Maclain Way, Chapman Way, directors. Juliana Lembi, Chapman Way, Maclain Way, producers. Netflix.

Woodstock. 1970. USA. Michael Wadleigh, director, writer. Bob Maurice, producer. Warner Bros.

Working in Rural New England. 1975. USA. Ken Burns, director, writer, producer. Hampshire College TV.

Index

Page references for figures are *italicized*.

About the Author

Photograph by Daniel Lightfoot.

Roger Nygard is perhaps best known for his acclaimed documentary *Trekkies*, about the most obsessive fans in the universe. Nygard's other documentary work includes *Six Days in Roswell*, a profile of UFO fanatics, *The Nature of Existence*, which investigates the world's philosophies, religions, and belief systems, *The Truth About Marriage*, covering an even more challenging subject than existence itself, and *The Comedy Store*, a docuseries about the world-famous Los Angeles comedy club. Nygard has also directed television series such as *The Office* and *The Bernie Mac Show*. His work as a film editor includes *Grey's Anatomy*, *The League*, and Emmy-nominated episodes of *Who Is America?*, *Veep*, and *Curb Your Enthusiasm*. Nygard's previous books are *Cut to the Monkey: A Hollywood Editor's Behind-the-Scenes Secrets to Making Hit Comedies* and *The Truth About Marriage: How to Find Love, Stay Together, and Keep the Passion Alive*.